Teaching Woodwinds

Teaching Woodwinds

H. Gene Griswold
Professor Emeritus
Towson University

Routledge
Taylor & Francis Group

LONDON AND NEW YORK

First published 2008, 2005 by Pearson Education, Inc.

Published 2016 by Routledge
2 Park Square, Milton Park, Abingdon, Oxon OX14 4RN
711 Third Avenue, New York, NY 10017, USA

Routledge is an imprint of the Taylor & Francis Group, an informa business

ISBN: 9780131577121 (pbk)

Cover Design: *Bruce Kenselaar*

Library of Congress Cataloging-in-Publication Data
Griswold, H. Gene.
     Teaching woodwinds / H. Gene Griswold.
          p.   cm.
Includes bibliographical references and index.
     ISBN 0-13-157712-3
     1. Woodwind instruments—Instruction and study.   2. Woodwind instruments.   I. Title.
     MT339.5.G75 2008
     788.2'19071—dc22   2007009249

Contents

Preface

This book is the result of having taught woodwind methods courses at Towson University in Baltimore for the past thirty-five years. The book was developed as a *workbook* for the hundreds of students who passed through my classes and who went on to teach instrumental music in Maryland and other Mid-Atlantic states. I dedicate this book to those students.

Over the years I discovered the value of having quickly accessed solutions to specific performance problems that arise in class. This was brought home to me early in my teaching career when a former member of the class was interviewed about his student teaching experience. He related how his supervisory teacher informed him that his first assignment was to rehearse a B♭ major scale with the woodwind section of a junior high band. In order to prepare for this assignment, the student teacher described how he spent many hours reviewing relevant pedagogy by looking up information in his woodwind textbook for each of the five woodwind instruments located in five separate prose-written chapters.

As a result of this discussion, I started reorganizing my course *workbooks* by integrating pedagogical materials for all five woodwind instruments under specific teaching topics rather than dividing the materials into separate sections for each instrument. For example, the aforementioned student teacher could simply have accessed a list of teaching points such as "Hand and Finger Position," "Articulation," and "Intonation" for information on all five woodwind instruments, rather than looking up each of these three topics in five separate chapters. To further assist future student teachers, I began to use outline/checklist formats in order to provide more efficient access to information that could be applied directly to the teaching tasks at hand—see Chapters 1 and 2. I also included procedures for teaching specific scales to an *entire* woodwind section—see pages 136–185.

The *Hands-on Overview* (see Chapters 3, 4, and 5) was initially developed for a two-week refresher course offered during the summer months for instrumental teachers who were seeking a review of the techniques and fingerings on all five woodwinds. Instruments and reeds were made available so that students could work through these assigned materials on each of the five instruments. Since time was so limited, I tried to develop a more comparative and systematic approach to teaching fingerings and techniques so that the members of the class could more easily compare and make pedagogical connections between the five instruments. For this teaching task I developed fingering charts for all five woodwind instruments based on six circles representing the three middle fingers of each hand—see page xiii. Using these six-note patterns as points of departure, I discovered that one could introduce fingerings within specific categories such as octave/register mechanisms, break crossings, registers, throat tones, thumb keys, pinky key clusters, forefinger clusters, and twig keys. I also discovered that it was more helpful for these teachers to have an *overview* of the techniques and fingerings for all five instruments on the same page rather than dividing the pedagogy into five separate sections for each instrument. It should be noted that these exercises are not ensembles, but are to be performed and practiced individually.

Another challenge I encountered with undergraduate students was how to avoid teaching procedures which isolated students in the class into their individual parts. In their *workbooks* I wanted students to have a *visual* as well as *aural* reference to problems and accomplishments of classmates performing on other instruments. After much experimentation, I decided on an opposite-page format used in the *Technique/Tunes: Twenty-five Class Lessons* that allowed students to experience an ensemble director's overview of the pedagogical approaches to all five woodwind instruments simultaneously. Relevant pedagogical notes and fingerings are inserted directly into the scores and students are encouraged to add their own notes and comments during class performances and instruction— see page 137. These *Class Lessons* are linked directly to specific *Student/Teacher Duets*—see pages 187–214.

Perhaps the most important outcome and challenge of a woodwind pedagogy class is the student's development of solid tonal and expressive concepts on each of the five woodwind instruments. This can be especially difficult when students have diverse musical and academic backgrounds, (i.e. percussion, string, and brass majors sitting next to woodwind majors as well as freshmen sitting next to seniors who are planning to fulfill student teaching requirements the following semester).

Although live performances, demonstrations, and suggested lists of recordings are helpful in developing a student's *aural* concept of articulation, tone quality, and so on, I have concluded nothing works as effectively in this regard as the actual playing of an assigned duet with one's teacher or an advanced player. For this reason I decided to revive a set of time-proven (nineteenth century) pedagogical *Student/Teacher Duets*—see pages 187–214. The goal here is to provide a *live and immediate aural reference* to which a student can strive within an ensemble setting with the woodwind teacher, advanced players in the class, and/or with woodwind majors in and out of class. The availability of verbal exchange as well as tonal exchange between teacher and student makes for the perfect teaching combination. This was true over a hundred years ago when these duets were written and is still true today.

Note: Over the years, I have come to recommend certain brands, vendors, and Web sites to my students. While I cannot guarantee service nor do I endorse any specific brand or vendor, some readers may find this information useful. Therefore, I decided to include this information.

H. Gene Griswold

Acknowledgments

At the top of my list of acknowledgments are the students who went through several generations of workbooks and handouts in my woodwind methods courses at Towson University.

Others who contributed their time and talent to this project include: Amy Betten and Ron Santana, colleagues at Towson University's Center for Instructional Advancement and Technology (CIAT) who assisted me with the fingering designs and photos respectively; my former students, Dr. Richard Spittel and Dr. Christopher Schaub, as well as my colleague, Dr. Michael Mark who provided proof readings and guidance; for the photos my present and former students, Eddie Sanders, Allison Yacoub, Denis Karp, Jane Marsilio, Sabrina McLaughlin, and Andrew Delclos; and finally my music department colleagues Dr. Terry Ewell (bassoon and chair of the department), Sara Nichols (flute), Marguerite Baker (clarinet), Leslie Starr (oboe), and Michael Bayes (saxophone) for their support and advice.

I owe a debt of gratitude to the reviewers of this book: Wendy Herbener (Ithaca College); Jon Beebe (Appalachian State University); and Dr. Joanne M. Britz (Pittsburg State University). Their constructive and informative comments on selected chapters enabled me to expand this project into a complete book.

I would also like to thank the people at Prentice Hall with whom I worked in order to make this publication possible. These include Richard Carlin, Executive Editor; Sarah Kiefer, Editorial Assistant; Mary Rottino, Senior Managing Editor; Lisa Iarkowski, Assistant Director of Project Management; Jean Lapidus, Production Liaison; Ang'john Ferreri, Image Permission Coordinator; and Sasha Anderson-Smith, Associate Marketing Manager.

I would especially like to thank three individuals who provided their constant support and professional expertise throughout the entire publication process. These include Frank Weihenig, Production Editor, Debra Nichols, Copy Editor, and Carrie Crompton.

Above all, I would thank my wonderful wife, Sylvia, for her unwavering support and assistance throughout this project as well as throughout my teaching and performance career.

Introduction

The primary goal of this workbook is for students, as future teachers, to analyze and apply the woodwind pedagogy required for performing/teaching music at the beginning, intermediate, and advanced levels.

This book is a workbook to be used on the music stand in the practice room, methods class, or on the teaching job. Rather than separating information about each of the five woodwind instruments into five prose-written chapters, an opposite-page format allows the user to experience an ensemble director's overview of pedagogical approaches for all five woodwinds simultaneously.

A comparative approach to the five woodwind instruments is emphasized throughout. In the sections *Fundamentals* and *Teaching Guides and Checklists*, aspects of teaching/playing the woodwinds have been integrated into readily accessed outlines and checklists.

Performance materials are found in the following sections: (1) *Hands-on Overviews—Parts I, II, and III;* (2) *Twenty-five Class Lessons* based on tunes and scales found in band method books; (3) *Student/Teacher Duets*; and (4) *Alternate Fingerings*.

1. The *Hands-on Overviews—Parts I, II, and III,* serve as a systematic introduction to the basic fingerings and techniques of the five woodwind instruments—see pages 55–106. The exercises in the *Overviews* are intended to be performed by individual students as warm-ups and, at the same time, offer the class a comparative (as well as pedagogical) study of the fingering systems and acoustical behavior of all five woodwind instruments.

2. Since pedagogical analysis of scores is an important task for future teachers, the *Technique/Tunes: Twenty-five Class Lessons* feature a hands-on approach for twenty-five tunes commonly found in band method books—see pages 133–186. Each tune and its pedagogical analysis is presented in score form so that users are offered a visual reference to pedagogical problems (and solutions) being experienced by other members of the class.

3. The *Student/Teacher Duets* are linked directly to the *Technique/Tunes: Twenty-five Class Lessons,* enabling students to actually participate in live performances with the teacher or with advanced players in and out of class. The duets are in score form so that any number of students can participate at one time—see pages 187–214. The duets offer opportunities for the more advanced students to "practice teach" beginning students in and out of class. It should be noted, however, that many of the "teacher" parts are technically within reach of nonwoodwind majors.

4. *Alternate Fingerings* are presented so they can be comparatively studied. The exercises utilizing alternate fingerings may be performed individually as well as in an ensemble setting. A woodwind quintet written at an advanced high school level is also offered for analysis.

The final section of this workbook is devoted to *self-testing devices*—see pages 239–314. These include exercises in preparing scores for rehearsals, study questions regarding the pedagogy for each instrument, and a list of relevant terminology. Also included are bibliographies of books, magazines, and Web sites as well as blank fingering charts for reviewing and testing of fingerings.

Abbreviations Used in This Book

ALT—alternate fingering (all woodwinds)

BC—break crossing (all woodwinds)

F—forked fingering (oboe)

FLK—flick key (bassoon)

LH—left hand

MP—mouthpiece

OK—octave key (saxophone)

PK—palm keys (saxophone)

RH—right hand

RHD—right hand down (clarinet)

RK—register key (clarinet)

SOK—side octave key (oboe)

TK—twig key—(all woodwinds)

TOK—thumb octave key (oboe)

TTT—touch-tone-teaching (all woodwinds, except flute)

WK—whisper key (bassoon)

$\frac{1}{2}$ **H** (half-hole fingering on oboe, bassoon, clarinet)

Fingering Diagrams Used in This Book

The circles in the fingering diagrams below represent the three middle fingers of each hand. The five woodwind instruments require the use of these six fingers to perform a six-note basic scale used as a basis for teaching all other fingerings. See pages 60–61.

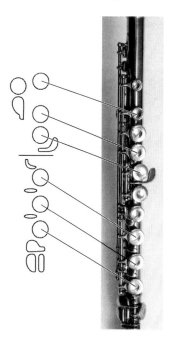

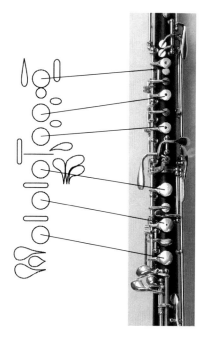

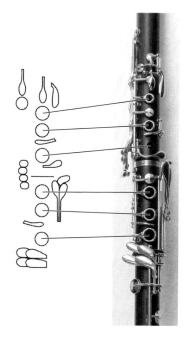

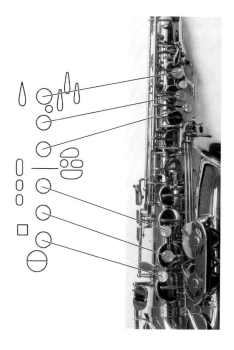

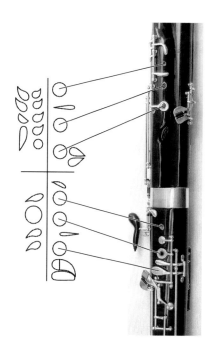

Teaching Woodwinds

1 *Fundamentals*

Daily Care—General

- USE CORK GREASE ON ALL TENON JOINTS (CLARINET AND OBOE) AS NEEDED. Use a light application of cork grease on oboe reed corks, saxophone necks, and bassoon bocals. Thoroughly rub grease into pores of cork and wipe off the excess grease. Wipe grease from fingers before handling the instrument.

- DO NOT USE LUBRICANT ON THE SLIDING JOINTS OF THE FLUTE AND SAXOPHONE. If these joints fit too tightly when being assembled, vigorously rub the contact points with a clean cotton cloth in order to remove tarnish/dirt buildup.

- MOST BASSOON TENONS ARE WRAPPED WITH THREAD RATHER THAN CORK. Therefore remove or add soft cotton thread or waxed dental floss for a snug (not tight) fit and rub with cooking paraffin (not cork grease).

- STORE DOUBLE REEDS IN VENTILATED CASES AND SINGLE REEDS IN HOLDERS AFTER USE. Do not soak reeds in the mouth (saliva deteriorates the cane). Keep small plastic containers or clear film containers filled with water in instrument cases for reed soaking. Before playing, avoid candy and soft drinks (these deteriorate the reeds). Fox double reed cases and Vandoren reed holders are reasonably priced, hold reeds securely, and allow air to circulate around the reeds.

- CHECK FOR MOISTURE UNDER PADS. Remove water by blowing under the pad of the clogged tone hole and/or by sliding cigarette paper under the affected pad and pressing the key in order to blot the moisture.

- SILK SWABS ARE RECOMMENDED, SINCE THEY ARE LINT FREE.

- USE A SMALL SOFT PAINT BRUSH TO REMOVE DUST UNDER KEYS. Be careful not to unhook springs.

- PREVENT GRENADILLA WOOD (OBOES AND CLARINETS) FROM CRACKING. Avoid rapid and extreme changes in humidity and temperature. Bassoons made of maple wood tolerate more expansion and contraction. Nonwood bassoons need more time to warm up; the keys may bind on a cold instrument due to contraction.

Assembly—General

- DAMAGE TO STUDENT INSTRUMENTS. Generally occurs during assembly/disassembly and transport, not while performing on the instruments. Gently shake case to see if parts fit snugly.

- AVOID UNDUE FORCE WHEN ASSEMBLING. Keep tenon corks lubricated for ease in assembly (see above). Avoid excessive hand pressure on key clusters and key rods when assembling. Be extremely careful with connecting levers (bridge keys). Keep connecting levers raised until properly aligned and avoid forcing/bending keys during assembling.

- DISASSEMBLE ALL INSTRUMENTS IN REVERSE ORDER. Memorize the configuration of the case so that each part fits properly back into the case.

Assembly—Flute

General

- Avoid force when assembling. To avoid hand pressure on keys when assembling, hands should hold the joints where there are no keys (see photos).

- If joints seem to be too tight when assembling, take a clean cotton cloth and rub the tarnish and residue from both the outside and inside of the joints. Do not use lubricant on sliding joints.

- There are no bridge keys or connecting levers on the flute.

Assembly* (two steps)

1. Place the foot joint on the middle section. To avoid pressure on the keys, grip middle section at upper end and the foot joint at lower end where there are no keys. Turn foot joint to accommodate length of right pinky—in general, key rod of foot should align with the middle of keys on the middle joint.

2. Place the head joint on the middle joint. Align so that the center of the embouchure hole is in line with the center of the keys. (Some flutists align the far side of the embouchure hole with the center of the keys.) Head joint alignment affects holding position and embouchure formation—see http://www.jennifercluff.com/lineup.htm.

Daily Care

- After playing, swab the bore using a dry cotton cloth threaded onto the cleaning rod and wrapped over the end of the rod.

- Wipe off fingerprints with a cotton cloth.

- If there is moisture under pads or if pads are sticking, insert absorbent cloth between key and tone hole and gently close key.

* For all instruments, disassemble in reverse order.

Assembly—Oboe

General

• Dip the reed in water up to the thread binding, remove, and place on music stand. Reed will continue to soak during assembly.

• **Handle with extreme care.** Oboes are more susceptible to damage than any other woodwind instrument.

   1. Keep corks lightly greased for ease in assembly (including the reed cork).

   2. Avoid force when assembling, and avoid pressure on the key clusters.

   3. There are Four Bridge Keys (Connecting Levers) on Oboes: three between the upper and lower joints and one between bell and lower joint (not found on some student oboes).

Soaking reed

Assembly

1. Place the bell on the lower joint. Hold the lower joint with thumb rest in palm of right hand and fingers curved around on the keys. With the left hand, hold down the B♭ connecting lever and gently twist on bell (some student oboes do not have this key).

2. Put the upper joint on the lower joint. Hold upper joint so bridge keys stay open. Hold the lower joint near the bell where there are no keys. Align the three bridge keys with minimal twisting.

3. Insert the reed (all the way) into the upper joint—thumb and forefinger should grip the reed at the top of cork, not on the reed binding. Use a small amount of cork grease on the reed cork, if necessary. If the reed is difficult to remove, try rocking it from side to side while pulling with the thumb and forefinger.

Daily Care

• After playing, place the reed in a ventilated reed case.

• Swab the oboe after each playing session (use caution here). Oboes have conical bores and swabs may easily become stuck. If this happens, take the instrument to a repair person. The safest oboe swabs are the silk swabs that have a "safety cord" on the back end and will clean the entire instrument while fully assembled—see http://www.hodgeproductsinc.com/. To remove moisture from under pads or if pads are sticking, insert cigarette paper between the key and the tone hole and gently close the key.

Assembly—Clarinet

General

Place the reed in water during assembly—dip both ends in water container so the entire reed is soaked, not just the tip. If the tip of the reed is wavy, continue soaking it until wrinkles disappear. Grease corks if necessary.

Soaking reed

Assembly

1. Hold lower joint near the bottom where there are no keys—with the other hand twist the bell onto the lower joint.

Bell onto lower joint

2. With the right hand, grasp lower joint near the bottom where there are no keys—hold upper joint with left palm against the body on underside and press key rings of upper joint with finger tips to raise bridge key. Push the two joints together with slight rotary motion—keep eyes on raised bridge key to align.

Lower joint onto upper joint

3. Twist larger end of barrel unto the upper joint.
4. Insert the mouthpiece into small end of barrel—align the flat of the mouthpiece with the thumb hole and register key.
5. Place the soaked reed on the flat part of the mouthpiece. Center the reed so that the tip is slightly below the tip of the mouthpiece leaving a "hairline" of the mouthpiece visible (see below).
6. Put ligature in place with loosened screw(s) and gently tighten screw(s). If there are two ligature screws, the lower one should be slightly tighter than the upper screw. Screws should always be on the player's right side and tightened with player's right hand.

Hairline

- Place tip of reed so "hairline" of MP is visible.
- If reed is too hard, increase the hairline area.
- If reed is too soft, decrease the hairline area.

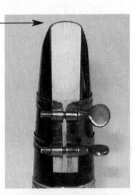

Daily Care

- After each playing session, remove and store the reed in a reed holder.
- Swab clarinet after each playing session.
- Do not swab the mouthpiece—clean it with a soft cotton cloth.

Reed hairline

Assembly—Saxophone

General

Place reed in water while assembling—dip both ends in water container so the entire reed is soaked, not just the tip of reed (see clarinet assembly). If the tip of the reed is wavy, continue soaking until wrinkles disappear.

Assembly

1. After putting the neck strap around neck, remove saxophone by grasping the bell with the right hand and the bottom of the saxophone with the left hand (see photo). Remove the end plug end fasten the neck strap to the saxophone with the left hand.

2. Loosen tension screw near the top of saxophone with right hand. Pick up neck by placing fingers on the *sides* of the neck (see photo) not on the top where the octave key is located. When inserting neck into body of saxophone, avoid putting hand pressure on the octave key. If the neck is resistive, clean connecting joint by vigorously rubbing the sliding surfaces of the neck and saxophone with a dry cotton cloth. Line up connecting lever so that *octave key on top of neck is closed*—gently tighten screw (see photo).

3. Push mouthpiece onto neck and align so that the flat part of the mouthpiece faces downwards in line with the saxophone. Mouthpiece should cover one-half or more of the cork. Rub grease into the cork if needed. After a few weeks of intonation adjustment, mark the cork with a sharp felt pen so that the student twists the MP up to the same mark each time.

4. Reed/Mouthpiece Assembly—see Steps 5 and 6 under Clarinet Assembly.

Daily Care

- After each playing session, remove and store the reed in a reed guard.
- Remove the mouthpiece and swab the neck after each playing session.
- Clean mouthpiece with a soft cotton cloth.
- Wipe saxophone with a clean cloth—no need to polish.
- Some teachers recommend pad savers (devices left in the bore to absorb moisture).

Assembly—Bassoon

General

- Dip both ends of the reed in water container so the entire reed is soaked, not just the tip of reed. Remove from water—the reed will continue to soak.
- Make certain tenons and corks are well lubricated.
- Place seat strap toward front of chair or if using a neck strap, put neck strap around neck.

Reed soaking

Seat strap
on chair

Assembly

1. Place wing joint into boot (avoid finger pressure on keys)

2. Align bridge key between wing and boot

3. Hold the large end of the long joint and insert it into the boot. Avoid hand pressure on keys and use minimal twisting. The metal tab under keys on long joint should be about 1/8 inch from the wood of the wing joint. If bassoon has a locking mechanism near the top of the wing, make certain it is aligned and locked.

Locking
mechanism

Metal tab

Long joint
into boot

Assembly—Bassoon

4. Close the key pad on the bell and gently push bell unto long joint. Align bridge key.

5. Insert the bocal into the wing joint. CAUTION: Bocals are expensive, made of very thin metal and are easily damaged. Apply cork grease if necessary. Hold bocal near the cork. Align small bocal hole to the whisper key pad. Make certain key pad is not damaged. Both the whisper key and the pancake key (see p. 13) should close the bocal hole.

6. Attach hand rest. Students with small hands may not be able to use a hand rest; see hand position, on page 15.

7. Take reed from water, remove excess water, and place on bocal using a slight twisting motion. Make certain reed is parallel to the floor.

Inserting Bocal

Daily Care

- After playing, place the reed in a ventilated reed case.

- Blow out the bocal after each playing session.

- Swab the bocal every week with a bocal swab (available from http://www.hodgeproductsinc.com/).

- Bassoons should be equipped with two swabs: a wing swab and a boot swab (available from http://www.foxproducts.com/).

- CAUTION: Make certain that there are no knots or wrinkles in the swabs before using. Unlike the cylindrical bores of the flute and clarinet, the bores of the bassoon, oboe, and saxophone are conical. Swabs become stuck more easily when being pulled through conical bores. If this happens, take to a repair person.

- Drop the weight of the wing swab through the large end of the wing and pull through slowly. Use caution.

- Swab the boot—use the boot swab only. Insert the boot swab into the larger bore, shake so that the swab makes a "U" turn at the bottom of the boot. Then pull the swab slowly through *both* bores.

- Tenons are wrapped with thread rather than cork since bassoons are made of porous maple wood and tend to expand and contract with the seasons. Therefore, remove or add thread for a snug (not tight) fit and rub with cooking paraffin (not cork grease).

Body Position

Flute

- Head up
- Bring flute to mouth
- Flute should be parallel to lips
- Flute may be parallel with floor (or slightly tilted downward)
- Chest up (lift rib cage off abdominal muscles)
- In sitting position, right elbow should not hook over back of chair

Good posture with flute

Oboe

- Head straight and level
- Bring oboe to mouth
- Oboe held at 40-degree angle (slightly higher than the clarinet)
- Chest up (lift rib cage off abdominal muscles)

Good posture with oboe

Clarinet

- Chest up (lift rib cage off abdominal muscles)
- Clarinet held at a 30- to 40-degree angle
- Experiment: raise or lower clarinet in order to find the best tone quality
- Angle accommodates relationship of upper and lower teeth (occlusion)
- Two primary points of contact involved in holding the clarinet:

    (1) upper teeth and (2) right thumb
- Right thumb pushes upward so that mouthpiece is firm against upper teeth

Good posture with clarinet

Body Position

Saxophone

- Hold the instrument directly in front of body. Younger students may have to hold the instrument to the side of the body resting the saxophone on right leg
- Do not rest instrument on chair
- Adjust length of neck strap so the end of the MP touches center of lower lip
- Head erect, chin up, eyes straight ahead, shoulders up but relaxed
- Weight of saxophone is supported by neck strap only, not hands or chair. Saxophone is balanced by right and left thumbs creating fulcrum with a neck strap
- Feet flat on floor—shoulders and back do not touch back of chair
- Tenor/baritone saxophones—held to the right side of the body
- Soprano sax—held more in a straight line like the oboe

Good posture with saxophone

Bassoon

- The seat strap is used more widely than the neck strap—use a neck strap when standing
- Sit on seat strap placed toward front of chair (see p. 8) and attach seat strap to bassoon
- Sit straight, head straight and level—chest up
- Bassoon rests against right leg
- Long joint rests against index finger of left hand
- Bassoon is balanced between left index finger and right hand (on hand rest)
- Adjust seat strap—do not adjust your body to the bassoon
- Bocal slants downward slightly—head should tilt down slightly
- Adjust height of bassoon by moving the seat strap
- IMPORTANT: student looks over the right side of the bassoon at the music stand
- For younger students having trouble stabilizing the bassoon, try a BG bassoon leather seat strap with adjustable Velcro cup. (see http://www.millermarketingco.com/bg/index.htm)

Good posture with bassoon

Hand/Finger Position

General

Hand/finger position may be checked by playing "open tones" that require minimal finger contact with the instrument. Keep fingers close to keys and tone holes. Use the fleshy part of fingers on tone holes and keys, not the tips of fingers. The fulcrum on the flute and saxophone refers to the pivotal point for two opposing forces (i.e., a "see-saw" effect). Compare these guidelines with the photos on pages 14–15.

Flute (head joint alignment affects holding position—see p. 4)

OPEN TONE: C♯

POINTS OF CONTACT: (1) lower lip, (2) base of left forefinger, (3) right hand thumb

WEIGHT BEARING: Shelf created by base of left forefinger

FULCRUM: Left forefinger (right thumb pushes embouchure plate against chin)

LEFT HAND:
  Wrist bends
  Flute rests on shelf of *sharply curved* forefinger—see page 14
  Thumb over B key
  Pinky over G♯ key

RIGHT HAND:
  Thumb directly under first and second fingers
  Thumb does not extend past body of flute
  Thumb pushes forward for fulcrum with left forefinger
  Flute should rest on the firm flesh close to the thumbnail,
    not on the flat, fleshy part of the thumb
  Pinky presses E♭ key

Oboe

OPEN TONE: C

POINTS OF CONTACT:
  1. Left hand thumb anchored at 2 o'clock angle just below thumb octave key (TOK)
  2. Right thumb, between tip and first knuckle placed on thumb rest

WEIGHT BEARING: Right thumb

FULCRUM: None

LEFT HAND:
  Fingers slanted toward keys so that index finger is in
    position to press SOK (side octave key)
  Thumb anchored at 2 o'clock angle just below TOK
  Pinky over G♯ key
  Fingers curved, but left hand ring finger is less curved

RIGHT HAND:
  Do not push thumb too far past thumb rest
  Pinky over low C key

GENERAL:
  Depending on their length, fingers slant slightly upwards
  Note that finger span on oboe is larger than on clarinet—see page 14

Clarinet

OPEN TONE: G

POINTS OF CONTACT:
  1. Right thumb, midway between tip and first knuckle, placed under thumb rest
  2. Upper teeth placed on mouthpiece approximately $\frac{1}{2}$ inch from tip

WEIGHT BEARING: Right thumb (pushes MP toward upper teeth)

Hand/Finger Position

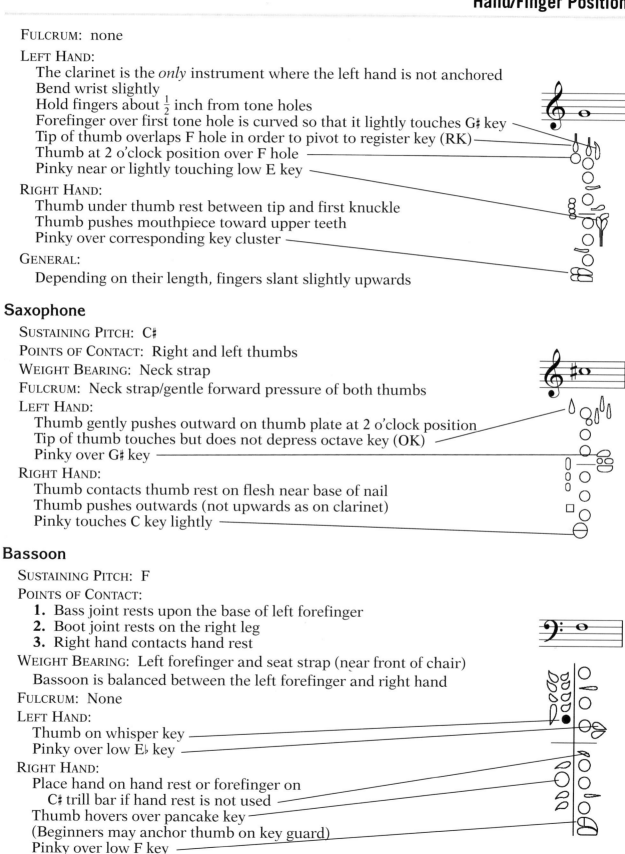

FULCRUM: none

LEFT HAND:

The clarinet is the *only* instrument where the left hand is not anchored
Bend wrist slightly
Hold fingers about $\frac{1}{2}$ inch from tone holes
Forefinger over first tone hole is curved so that it lightly touches G♯ key
Tip of thumb overlaps F hole in order to pivot to register key (RK)
Thumb at 2 o'clock position over F hole
Pinky near or lightly touching low E key

RIGHT HAND:

Thumb under thumb rest between tip and first knuckle
Thumb pushes mouthpiece toward upper teeth
Pinky over corresponding key cluster

GENERAL:

Depending on their length, fingers slant slightly upwards

Saxophone

SUSTAINING PITCH: C♯

POINTS OF CONTACT: Right and left thumbs

WEIGHT BEARING: Neck strap

FULCRUM: Neck strap/gentle forward pressure of both thumbs

LEFT HAND:

Thumb gently pushes outward on thumb plate at 2 o'clock position
Tip of thumb touches but does not depress octave key (OK)
Pinky over G♯ key

RIGHT HAND:

Thumb contacts thumb rest on flesh near base of nail
Thumb pushes outwards (not upwards as on clarinet)
Pinky touches C key lightly

Bassoon

SUSTAINING PITCH: F

POINTS OF CONTACT:

1. Bass joint rests upon the base of left forefinger
2. Boot joint rests on the right leg
3. Right hand contacts hand rest

WEIGHT BEARING: Left forefinger and seat strap (near front of chair)

Bassoon is balanced between the left forefinger and right hand

FULCRUM: None

LEFT HAND:

Thumb on whisper key
Pinky over low E♭ key

RIGHT HAND:

Place hand on hand rest or forefinger on
    C♯ trill bar if hand rest is not used
Thumb hovers over pancake key
(Beginners may anchor thumb on key guard)
Pinky over low F key

Hand/Finger Position

Left Hand	Right Hand

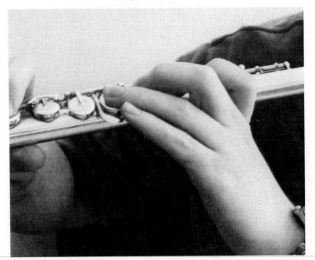 

Flute

Oboe

Clarinet

Hand/Finger Position

Left Hand	Right Hand

Saxophone

Bassoon (front view)

Bassoon (showing thumb keys)

Embouchure—Generalities

Visual versus Aural Analysis

Although the *visual analysis* of embouchure appearance is an important teaching element, *aural analysis* of the resulting tone quality, intonation, articulation, and expression is even more important. Students and teachers should use a mirror often in order to point out visible attributes and problems of the embouchure. But from the earliest stages of development, students also need to be taught the desired attributes of a "good tone." Performing the student/teacher duets on page 187–213 will help one acquire a concept of good tone as well as concepts of good articulation and intonation.

Facial Musculature

A rounded facial musculature is desirable for forming the embouchures on all five woodwind instruments.

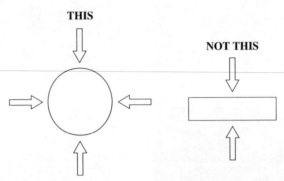

This mental image is not only applicable to the rounded lip cushioning used on double reeds, but also on single reeds where the goal is to allow the lower lip to flex by keeping the lower teeth from biting upwards and to keep mouth and throat open even though the upper teeth are contacting mouthpieces.

Although the actual aperture on the flute is elliptical (about the size of a bassoon reed tip opening), the muscles controlling the inner and outer parts of the lips must focus from all directions in order to create the desired lip aperture and, at the same time, an open throat.

Throat Openings and Tongue Positions

Syllable selection influences throat openings—experiment with the following:

"tee," "teh," "tuh," "tah," "toll" (as if cooling mouth from hot food)

Throat opening increases ——————————→
Tongue position lowers ——————————→

Throat openings will have an influence on tone quality and pitch especially on tones with open fingerings (throat tones)—see pages 62–63.

Apertures and Air Speeds

In general, smaller apertures create faster air speeds and larger apertures create slower air speeds.

The speed of the air stream used on flute is controlled by the size and shape of the lip aperture. A smaller lip aperture is required for softer/higher tones while larger lip apertures are required for louder/lower tones. The flute is the only woodwind instrument requiring absolute control of the *direction* of the air stream (controlled by the lower lip and jaw). The air stream used on oboe and bassoon is controlled by the size of reed apertures (regulated by circular lip cushioning). Smaller reed apertures (tip openings) are required for softer/higher tones while larger reed apertures (tip openings) are required for louder/lower tones.

Embouchure—Generalities

The apertures created by single reeds and their mouthpieces are more stationary during performance and the required air speed is more constant. Aperture size on single reeds is determined by reed strength and the opening between the reed and mouthpiece as well as the lower-lip pad.

Adjusting the air speed to the desired tone quality, volume, and pitch is an important pedagogical element on all five woodwind instruments. However, the ideal air speed on any wind instrument is the speed initiated by an impulse to sing the note through the instrument. Developing a natural "singing impulse" is important for an instrumentalist and plays a role in the aural development of the student. The only woodwind instrument that is totally dependent on the speed of the air stream without aperture movement and/or manipulation is the recorder. Practicing long tones on a recorder allows students to focus solely on the air stream since the aperture on recorder is stationary and cannot be regulated or manipulated by the embouchure.

Distance

Distance is an important factor on all woodwind embouchures. Adjustments of air speed and aperture size are directly related to distance. On the flute, the distance between the lower lip and the outer edge of the embouchure hole is critical; the amount of lower lip covering the embouchure hole is greater for higher and softer tones and less for lower and/or louder notes—see the next page.

On double reeds, the distance that the reed is inserted into the mouth is crucial to tone quality, volume, pitch, and register. More double reed inserted into the mouth produces a louder volume, a sharper pitch, and higher register. Less reed in the mouth produces a softer tone quality, softer volume, a flatter pitch, and lower registers. On the oboe, reed insertion into the mouth is generally minimal and only the tip of the reed protrudes into the mouth. The distance that the bassoon reed protrudes into the mouth beyond the lips varies among players and is determined by the size and shape of the mouth cavity and throat opening of each individual.

On single reeds, the distance of upper teeth placement on the mouthpiece, determined by the student's occlusion and the angle at which the instrument is held, is an important factor in determining tone quality. Also important on single reeds is the distance factor regarding lower-lip placement on the reed. That distance is best determined by carefully sliding a business card between the reed and mouthpiece until it stops and marking that point with a light pencil mark in order to find the ideal control point for lower-lip contact (see p. 20).

Mouthpiece/Reed Pitches

The above generalities may be checked and measured on all the woodwind instruments by using the chart on mouthpiece/reed pitches located on page 24. It is important to make the student aware of not only the pitches to be achieved, but also the desired tone quality and articulation required for these exercises.

Developing Flute Embouchures

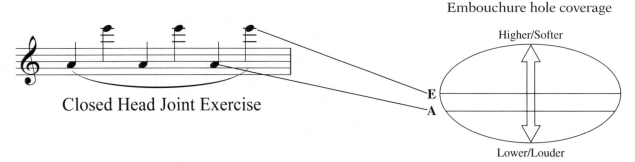

Closed Head Joint Exercise

Embouchure hole coverage

Higher/Softer

E
A

Lower/Louder

Goal: match volume and tone quality of both upper and lower tones

- Hold head joint with left hand—cover open end with the palm of the right hand
- Head joint should be parallel with the line of the lips
- Outer rim of hole should be slightly higher than inner rim
- Start with approximately $\frac{1}{4}$ of the embouchure hole covered by the lower lip
- Higher notes will be louder at first—instead of overblowing, extend the lower lip forward
- Size and direction of the air stream is formed by inner surface of lips
- Turn lower lip outward so that the air passes over the inner lip tissue
- For high notes, pucker slightly (increases coverage and raises air stream)
- For lower notes—lower lip covers less of the embouchure hole
- Lower notes will project better if the tone is "buzzy" or "edgy" (created by smaller lip apertures and a well-aimed air stream)

Five Primary Factors

1. Air speed
   - Faster for high and loud tones
   - Slower for low and soft tones

2. Aperture size
   - Smaller apertures increase air speed
   - Larger apertures decrease air speed

Flute embouchure

3. Coverage (see diagram above)
   - For high/soft tones: cover **more** of the embouchure hole with lower lip
   - For low/loud tones: cover **less** of the embouchure hole with the lower lip

4. Aperture shape
   - Aperture shape resembles the opening of a bassoon reed
   - Be aware of the aperture shape of both inner and outer surfaces of the lips

5. Direction of air stream (see soda straw exercise on the next page)
   - High/soft tones: aim the air stream higher—lower jaw pushes outward slightly
   - Lower/louder tones: aim the air stream lower—lower jaw recedes slightly

Developing Flute Embochures

Paper Aperture Exercise

- Helps student understand embouchure principles
- Use a business card: fold the card lengthwise into thirds in order to create a flattened windway; seal with plastic tape—the paper aperture should be approximately 2 cm wide and 1.5 mm high
- Put end of flattened card into mouth—hold card with left hand, hold flute with right hand

Paper aperture exercise

The paper aperture exercise demonstrates four embouchure principles:

1. Air speed
   - With the left hand, place end of card so that it covers $\frac{1}{4}$ of tone hole
   - Blow slow/fast/slow/fast to produce octaves
2. Coverage and distance
   - With the left hand place end of card so that it covers one-fourth of tone hole
   - While blowing a gentle air stream, slide card forward and back in order to produce octaves
3. Size
   - Squeeze aperture of card so that it opens 3 mm or more
   - Note the "airy" tone quality (versus centered)
4. Direction (aiming the air at the outer edge of the tone hole)
   - With left hand, place end of card so that it covers one-fourth of tone hole
   - While blowing, keep card in place and turn flute slightly inward in order to produce octaves

Soda Straw Exercise

This exercise helps the student understand the role of the jaw in controlling the *direction* of the air stream. Take an ordinary soda straw or a small cocktail straw and place the end in mouth—while blowing, push out and recede lower lip in order to raise and lower straw.

Condensation Exercise

This exercise helps the student understand the size and shape of the aperture. Using a mirror, observe condensation spot caused by warm air passing over the cold embouchure plate. Observe size and shape of this spot while playing. Have students observe each other.

Whisper Tones (sometimes referred to as "whistle tones")

These are very soft harmonics often used on the flute to relax the embouchure and to help achieve control of very slow air streams. Play middle D and make a diminuendo into total silence. Just before the silence one can detect faint whistling. Next, blow very gently and try to start the whistle tone without the diminuendo. Experiment with this technique.

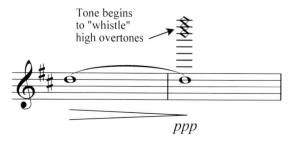

Tone begins to "whistle" high overtones

ppp

Harmonics

See p. 217.

Developing Single Reed Embouchures

To determine the placement of the lower lip on the reed:

1. Insert a business card between reed and mouthpiece
2. Place small pencil mark on reed surface where the paper stops
3. Bottom lip should contact reed at the pencil mark for optimum control

Marking reed

Clarinet—Practice the embouchure steps below with MP + barrel/neck:

1. B♭ Clarinet: MP + barrel = F♯
2. Alto Clarinet in E♭: MP + neck = G♯
3. Bass Clarinet in B♭: MP + neck = C♯

MP + barrel/neck

Saxophone—Check the embouchure steps below with MP + neck:

1. Alto Saxophone in E♭: MP + neck = G♯
2. Tenor Saxophone in B♭: MP + neck = E
3. Baritone Saxophone in E♭: MP + neck = G♯

MP + neck

Saxophone embouchure

Clarinet embouchure

General

- Upper teeth placed on MP about $\frac{1}{2}$ to $\frac{3}{4}$ inch from the tip
- Too much MP in mouth causes squeaks and a tone that is too loud and flat
- Too little MP in mouth creates thin-sounding tone that is too soft and sharp
- Mouthpieces of the larger saxophones and clarinets should be inserted further into mouth

Developing Single Reed Embouchures

- Lower lip is placed at the pencil mark where the MP meets the reed (see p. 20)

- Lower lip turned back slightly over teeth—half of the red of the lower lip should be showing and half of the red is turned over teeth

- In order to seal lips around MP, pronounce the syllable "emm"

- Think circular, a rounded facial musculature is desirable—see p. 16

- Keep the chin flat, stretched and pointed downwards providing a firm and flexed surface on which the reed can vibrate

- The embouchure *allows* the air to do the work—*do not force* the reed to work

- DO NOT BITE—lower teeth simply support lower lip and allow the lip to flex

- Upward pressure on the reed should be from lower lip muscles, not the jaw or teeth

- Taking a breath: keep upper teeth on MP and breathe through corners of mouth

- Starting tones: tongue placed just under the tip of the reed

- Tonguing: (1) inhale AIR, (2) suspend AIR, (3) release AIR—(see pp. 28–30)

- Unlike the flute and double reeds, the single reed embouchures are more firm and static

Clarinet

- Angle of instrument is 30 to 40 degrees depending on student's occlusion

- Air is directed across the MP while instrument is held at down angle

- Right thumb pushes upward so that upper teeth contact MP about $\frac{1}{2}$ inch from the tip

- If student continues to choke the tone by biting upwards with lower teeth, teacher can place thumb and forefinger on the barrel and gently pull MP upward while student plays

- Causes of squeaks: dry reed, cracked reed, reed not centered on MP, unbalanced reed, excessive jaw or teeth pressure, embouchure too tight, too much MP in mouth, poor finger coverage of tone holes; incorrect air speed, poor MP

Saxophone

- Unlike clarinet, MP enters the mouth at approximately a 90-degree angle

- Air is directed straight into MP

- Experiment with the amount of MP in mouth

- Right thumb pushes MP into mouth

- Left thumb pushes MP out of mouth

Developing Double Reed Embouchures

General

Three-step embouchure formation:
1. Place tip of reed on lower lip
2. Roll lower lip in slightly
3. Cushion, encircling reed with the lips (visible red part of the lip varies depending on lip thickness)

Three factors that regulate pitch and volume:
1. Cushion
   - Firmer cushion for higher and softer tones—decreases reed aperture
   - Softer cushion for lower and louder tones—increases reed aperture

2. Distance (amount of reed that is in mouth)
   - More reed in mouth for higher and louder tones
   - Less reed in mouth for lower and softer tones
   - NOTE: reed does not actually slide on lip surface, but moves in and out with lip

3. Speed
   - Slower air speed for lower and softer tones
   - Faster air speed for higher and louder tones

Oboe

Experiment with these two exercises:
1. Oboe Reed Buzz
   - Do not confuse "reed buzz" with the "reed crow" (see p. 24)

2. D Octave Exercise
   - At first, control the pitches with the air speed only
   - Concentrate only on fingering changes
   - Next, work to balance cushion, distance, and speed to control dynamics

1) Oboe reed buzz

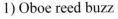

2) D octave exercise

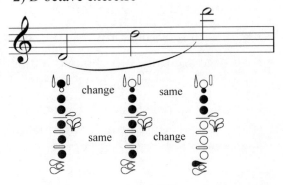

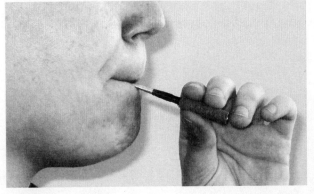

Reed Buzz

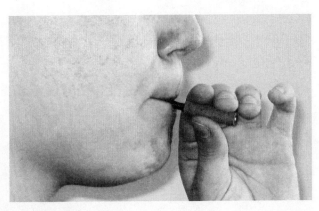

Reed Crow

Developing Double Reed Embouchures

Bassoon

Experiment with these three exercises:

1. Reed Buzz—Do not confuse "reed buzz" with the "reed crow" (see p. 24)

2. Bocal Buzz

3. G Octave Exercise
   - At first, control the pitches with the air speed only
   - Concentrate only on fingering changes
   - Next, work to control dynamics by balancing cushion, distance, and speed

Compared to oboe, clarinet, and saxophone, the bassoon embouchure is the most unrestrained.

1) Bassoon reed buzz

2) Bocal buzz

3) G octave exercise

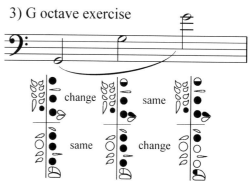

Reed Buzz

Bocal Buzz

Reed Buzz

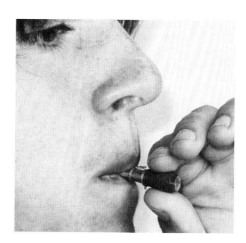

Reed Crow

Mouthpiece/Reed Pitches

FLUTE: CLOSED HEAD JOINT

Start with approximately one-fourth of the embouchure hole covered with the lower lip
First, produce the high E by simply using a faster air stream
Then try using a slower air stream and extending the lower lip forward for the top note
GOAL: to play both tones with the same volume (see p. 18 for more details)

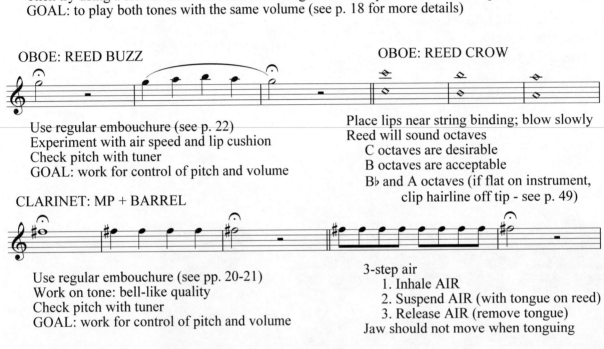

OBOE: REED BUZZ

Use regular embouchure (see p. 22)
Experiment with air speed and lip cushion
Check pitch with tuner
GOAL: work for control of pitch and volume

OBOE: REED CROW

Place lips near string binding; blow slowly
Reed will sound octaves
  C octaves are desirable
  B octaves are acceptable
  B♭ and A octaves (if flat on instrument,
    clip hairline off tip - see p. 49)

CLARINET: MP + BARREL

Use regular embouchure (see pp. 20-21)
Work on tone: bell-like quality
Check pitch with tuner
GOAL: work for control of pitch and volume

3-step air
  1. Inhale AIR
  2. Suspend AIR (with tongue on reed)
  3. Release AIR (remove tongue)
Jaw should not move when tonguing

ALTO SAXOPHONE: MP + NECK

Use regular embouchure (see pp. 20-21)
Work on tone: bell-like quality
Check pitch with tuner
GOAL: work for control of pitch and volume

3-step air
  1. Inhale AIR
  2. Suspend AIR (with tongue on reed)
  3. Release AIR (remove tongue)
Jaw should not move when tonguing

BASSOON: REED BUZZ

Use regular embouchure (see p. 23)
Experiment with air speed and lip cushion
Check pitch with tuner
GOAL: work for control of pitch and volume

BASSOON: REED CROW

Place lips near first wire; blow slowly
Reed will sound octaves
  F octaves are desirable
  E and E♭ octaves are acceptable
  D octaves (if flat on instrument, clip
    hairline off tip - see p. 49)

Pop Tests

Air leakage near the vibrating source on woodwind instruments can be extremely detrimental to tone production. Pop tests are a means of checking the air leakage between single reeds and mouthpieces, air leakage within double reeds themselves, and air leakage within the flute head joint. Do not oversaturate reeds. Reeds can be dipped, removed from the water, and will continue to soak as one assembles the rest of the instrument

- Check for leakage in the head joint of the flute by covering the open end with the right hand. Then, create an air vacuum by placing lips on the lip plate and sucking out air creating an air vacuum inside the head joint. Pull right hand away quickly in order to create an air pop. If it does not pop, the head cork is leaking and it should be sent to a repair person.

Head joint "pop" test

- For single reeds, place hand over barrel or neck to create a vacuum pop. Reeds must be thoroughly soaked to create a pop. Single reeds should be totally submerged in water and then removed. On clarinet and saxophone, leakage may occur between the mouthpiece and reed. This will cause squeaks and poor tonal response in all registers. Make certain the reed is soaked and that it has been centered on the mouthpiece with ligature screws properly tightened—see pp. 6–7.

Clarinet "pop" test

Saxophone "pop" test

- Oboe reeds should be dipped into water (up to the string binding) and removed. Bassoon reeds should be totally submerged in water and then removed. If the reeds do not pop, more soaking is required or there is a leak in the reed. Double reeds with severe leaks are poorly constructed and should be discarded.

Oboe "pop" test

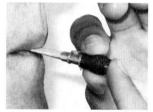
Bassoon "pop" test

- Clear plastic film containers (available at camera stores) make good water containers. They are waterproof and can be placed in students' cases, which saves trips to the water fountain. Change the water frequently.

- Dry reeds contract and warp, causing poor response and tone. Wet reeds expand and produce optimum vibration.

- Reeds must ventilate when stored. Do not use airtight reed cases. A ventilated reed case, with moderate humidity to prevent reeds from warping, is recommended.

Touch-Tone-Teaching

By simply using one finger, an instrumental teacher can demonstrate valuable insights to students regarding their embouchure and air speed. The following exercises compare the air speed adjustments required on each of the five woodwind instruments.

Flute

Since the flute does not have octave keys, touch-tone-teaching does not apply. However, the head joint exercise is highly recommended in order to introduce students to *air speed* versus *air direction* on the flute.

Head joint exercise:

• Sustain: Using the head joint only, cover the open end and sustain second space A.

• Overblow: While sustaining A, deliberately overblow the twelfth above (high E).

• Desirable: Instead of overblowing, extend the lower lip forward, raising the direction of air stream in order to achieve the upper note and keep the same dynamics throughout.

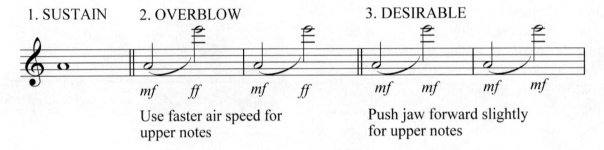

Use faster air speed for upper notes   Push jaw forward slightly for upper notes

Oboe

• Teach the student the correct air speed by introducing the **TOK** (thumb octave key) and **SOK** (side octave key).

• Have the student play the lower note.

• Then the teacher presses the designated octave key for the second note.

• Notice that the upper notes will be flat and that a faster air stream is required for the upper notes.

• The student then practices the exercise with pitch adjustments using increased air speed and/or a firmer lip cushion.

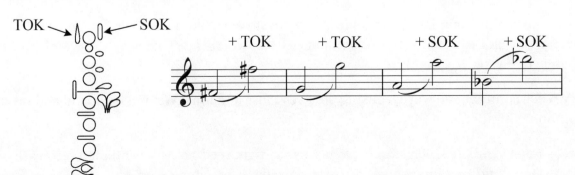

Touch-Tone-Teaching

Clarinet

- Have the student play these low notes with a full tone.
- Then the teacher reaches around the clarinet and presses the RK (register key)—see photo on p. 29.
- The teaching point here is that if the student is achieving a fully supported tone for the lower note, the upper note should sound reasonably in tune without embouchure adjustment.

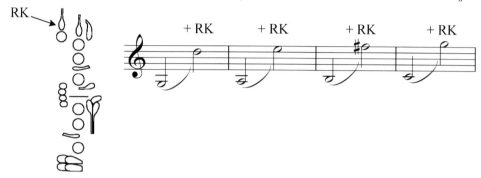

Saxophone

- Have the student play the lower notes of the following exercise with a full tone.
- Then the teacher reaches around the saxophone and presses the OK (octave key) for the second note.
- The teaching point here is that if the student is achieving a fully supported tone for the lower note, the upper note should sound reasonably in tune without embouchure adjustment.

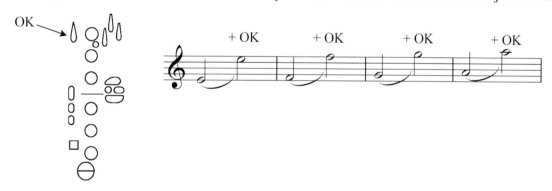

Bassoon

- Teach the student the correct air speed by introducing the "flick" or "speaker" keys.
- Have the student play the lower note with the WK (whisper key) down.
- Then the teacher taps or presses the designated flick key for the second note.
- Note that the upper notes will be flat—a faster air stream is required for the upper notes.
- The student then practices moving his/her thumb from the WK to "tap" the indicated flick key.

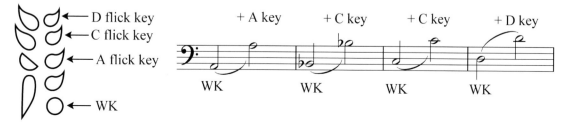

Breathing

Teaching Points For All Woodwind Instruments
- Sing/play concepts: start with short notes (phrases) and gradually expand the length
- One's musical performance begins with inhalation through the mouth, not articulation
- Fill lungs from bottom to top—keep chest expanded for tonal resonance when exhaling
- Avoid: rib cage restriction due to bad posture
- See throat openings and tongue positions on page 16
- THREE-STEP AIR METHOD for reed instruments (does not apply to flute)
  1. Inhale AIR
  2. Suspend AIR (with tongue on reed)
  3. Release AIR (removing tongue)
- FOUR-STEP TONGUE/RELEASE METHOD (all instruments)
  1. Practice STARTING notes with the TONGUE: "too"
  2. Practice STARTING notes with the AIR: "hoo" (helps focus the air stream)
  3. Practice RELEASING notes with the AIR: "too"
  4. Practice RELEASING notes with the TONGUE: "toot"

Extending Phrase Length
Besides inhalation, being able to prolong an air stream is dependent on the speed of the air stream: *small* apertures create *faster* air streams—*larger* apertures create *slower* air streams. Measure student's progress in sustaining an air stream. Use metronome set at 60 and count beats for students and/or ensembles. Create contests: "who can play (sing) the longest tone?"
- Slowly exhale making a prolonged "hissing sound" through the teeth
- Sing a prolonged "oh" or "ah"
- Blow a prolonged air stream through straws: try small cocktail straws first, then move to larger soda straws
- Use numbers to create *intensity drives*—use for long tone practice for individuals and ensembles:

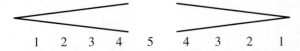

    1   2   3   4   5   4   3   2   1

  - Soft = a smaller lip/reed aperture and a slower air stream
  - Loud = a larger lip/reed aperture and a faster air stream
  - Faster air speed on flute, oboe, saxophone and bassoon raises the pitch
- Faster air speed on clarinet tends to lower the pitch

For Flutists: Aiming The Air Stream
The flute is the only woodwind which requires absolute control of the *DIRECTION* of the air stream. Have the students make a pencil dot on the palm of their hands:
- Have students blow a narrow and prolonged air stream on the pencil dot
- Raise and lower the air stream against the hand
- Note the role of the lower jaw (lip) in aiming the air stream

Breathing

For Oboists

Backed-up air pressure is often a problem with oboe students. The tiny reed aperture requires the student to release air in the lungs before inhaling new air. One procedure for addressing this issue is to teach "half-breaths." Stevens Hewitt, in his *Method for Oboe*, offers an effective exercise of practicing half-breaths with a metronome set at 60: "To breathe quickly should become second nature. One should never seem to breathe hurriedly or spasmodically. . . . Practice half-breaths. Push out an 'accented' breath, fast ('out'), then push in an 'accented' breath, ('in') on the next rest."

HALF-BREATHS:

For Single Reeds

A more constant air support is required for single-reed instruments—see touch tone teaching on pp. 26–27. To demonstrate this principle, have the student play a full and sustained tone in the chalumeau register and the teacher (or another student) touches the RK.

Another effective exercise is for the teacher to finger the instrument while the student provides the air stream. (Make certain the student holds the barrel with the right hand.) This can be a very revealing exercise to the student especially when the teacher fingers a passage or scale encompassing all three registers on one student breath.

Touching register key

Checking air stream

For Oboe and Bassoon

Unlike the single reeds, the air speed used on the oboe and bassoon (as well as flute) must *fluctuate* according to register and volume. The teacher can demonstrate this principle using simply one finger—see touch-tone-teaching on pp. 26–27.

Articulation

Three step sequence for teaching basic articulation on all woodwind instruments:
1. Slurring
2. Legato tonguing
3. Staccato tonguing

Three basic steps:
1. Inhale AIR
2. Suspend AIR
3. Release AIR

Mouthpiece/reed exercises:
1. Jaw should not move during articulation
2. Use syllable "duh"; tongue "floats" on air stream and stays close to contact point
3. Mirror practice is highly recommended
4. Keep embouchure and lip cushioning circular

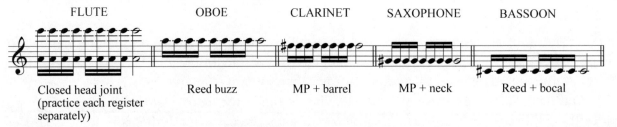

FLUTE — Closed head joint (practice each register separately)

OBOE — Reed buzz

CLARINET — MP + barrel

SAXOPHONE — MP + neck

BASSOON — Reed + bocal

Flute

• Practice with closed head joint alone before moving to flute

• Legato tonguing should be mastered before staccato

• Arch tongue slightly

• Strike back of teeth at point where the gums begin

• To find the best location try using different syllables; "dah," "duh," "deh," "dee"

• Keep the tongue forward

• Introduce double tonguing to second-year students: "duh-guh duh-guh"

• Slur first in order to check accurate finger movement, then apply articulation

Using Articulation To Improve Tone On Flute

• Try "tongueless" attacks use: "hee," "huh," "heh, " "peh, " "poo, " "purr"
  (activates diaphragmatic "push" for each note)

• Have student spit as if to remove crumb from tip of tongue

• Have student spit rice seeds:
  ○ low register—spit a few feet away
  ○ middle register—a little farther away
  ○ upper register—spit across the room

• As the student spits the seed farther, air speed increases

Articulation

Reed Instruments

- In general, tip of tongue touches the tip of the reed (or slightly below the tip)—this may vary somewhat according to the instrument and individual

- Legato tonguing should be mastered before staccato tonguing

- Motion of the tongue should be up and down, not back and forth

- Have student vocalize syllables "duh duh duh duh" all on one air stream—then play same pattern on instrument

- Always keep air flowing—alternate sustained tones with tonguing patterns

- Tongue "floats" on the air stream and stays close to its contact point

- Jaw should not move during articulation

- Releasing the tone
  - Most of the time, release tone by stopping air stream: "duh"
  - Tongue is used to stop tone only in very short staccato: "tut"
  - Practice attacks and releases without use of tongue ("huh")
    (activates diaphragmatic "push" for each note)

- Fast tongued passages: slur first then tongue the same passage in order to develop accurately coordinated fingers

- Practice various degrees of attack: from most legato to extreme sforzando

- Practice various degrees of release: from morendo release to accented release

- Normally tone must not surge after the attack

- For low notes on double reeds and saxophone: jaw pulled down; lips protrude slightly

- For beginners, avoid "slap tonguing" (sometimes used on saxophone for a special effect especially on low notes)

- For beginners, avoid "anchor tonguing": locking the tip of tongue behind lower teeth and pushing forward with back of tongue striking the reed further back on the tongue (sometimes used by jazz trumpeters and saxophonists)

Intonation

General

Performing the student/teacher duets on pages 187–213 with an advanced player or a woodwind major will be helpful in establishing references to intonation and tone quality.

PITCH RAISED	PITCH LOWERED
Flute	
Less coverage with lower lip	More coverage with lower lip
Flute rolled outward	Flute rolled inward
Head raised	Head lowered
Direction of air higher	Direction of air lower
Faster air speed	Slower air speed
Head joint pushed in	Head joint pulled out

To allow for small pitch adjustments up or down, flute manufacturers usually tune the flute somewhat sharp expecting that the player will keep the head joint pulled out slightly (about $\frac{1}{8}$ inch). The tuning stopper (head cork) is also set by the manufacturer so that, when the handle of the cleaning rod is inserted into the head joint, the mark on the end of the rod should appear at the center of the embouchure hole. *Slow octave practice is recommended for checking intonation.* Find a lower-lip placement to prevent excessive sharpness on the C and C♯ in and above the staff. Lower-lip placement and air adjustment are directly related to the head joint exercise described on p. 18.

Oboe	
Faster air stream	Slower air stream
More reed in mouth	Less reed in mouth
Firmer lip cushion	Softer lip cushion
Harder reeds	Softer reeds
Shorter reeds	Longer reeds (69–70 mm = normal)
Closed tip	Open tip (.05 mm = normal)

Make certain that the reed cork is fully inserted into the oboe. One may manually open (flatten) or close (sharpen) the reed tip opening by applying pressure with the thumb and forefinger—see p. 48. Maintain a firm air stream and circular lip cushion in order to keep the pitch stable. Check the oboe reed buzz and oboe reed crow on p. 24 as well as the 3-D octave exercise—see p. 22.

Clarinet	
Slower air stream	Faster air stream
Firmer embouchure	Softer embouchure
Stronger reed	Softer reed
More mouthpiece in mouth	Less mouthpiece in mouth

First: Tune MP + barrel pitches—B♭ Clarinet: MP + barrel = F♯

MP + barrel/neck

Alto Clarinet in E♭: MP + neck = G♯; Bass Clarinet in B♭: MP + neck = C♯

Second: Tune written G on clarinet by pulling/pushing barrel

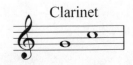

Clarinet

Third: Tune written C on clarinet by pulling/pushing middle joint

Intonation

PITCH RAISED	PITCH LOWERED
Saxophone	
Push mouthpiece farther on neck	Pull mouthpiece
Firmer embouchure	Looser embouchure
Stronger reed	Softer reed
More mouthpiece in mouth	Less mouthpiece in mouth
Faster air stream	Slower air stream
Firmer lip pressure	Looser lip pressure

MP + neck

Saxophone

First: Tune MP + neck pitches—Alto Saxophone in E♭: MP + neck = G♯; Tenor Saxophone in B♭: MP + neck = E; Baritone Saxophone in E♭: MP + neck = G♯

Second: Tune written G on saxophone by pulling/pushing MP

Third: Tune written C on saxophone by pulling/pushing MP

Adjust mouthpiece on neck for ideal spot on cork—mark with a ballpoint pen so the mouthpiece is put on the same place each time—see p. 7.

Bassoon	
#1 Bocal	#2 Bocal (standard) or try #3
Closed reed tip	Open reed tip (1 mm = normal)
Faster air stream	Slower air stream
Firmer lip cushion	Softer lip cushion
More reed in mouth	Less reed in mouth
Harder reeds	Softer reeds
Shorter reeds	Longer reeds (55 mm = normal)

One may manually open (flatten) or close (sharpen) the reed tip opening by applying pressure with the thumb and forefinger—see p. 48. Maintain a firm air stream and circular lip cushion in order to keep pitch stable. Check bassoon reed buzz and bassoon reed crow on p. 24 as well as the 3-G octave exercise on p. 23.

General Tuning Procedures

Use a tuner that can sound pitches. Play slow arpeggios while reference pitch is sounding—eliminate beats. Check the intonation of tones involved in primary break crossings—see page 67.

General Intonation Tendencies

Extreme high registers tend to be sharp

Throat (open) tones tend to be unstable

Cold instruments play flatter

Warmer instruments play sharper

Vibrato

As on string instruments, vibrato warms and enhances the tone of woodwind instruments. The mechanics of producing vibrato are discussed below. However, as with singers, vibrato eventually becomes a personalized and intuitive enhancement of the instrumentalist's expression and tone. Vibrato studies on wind instruments usually do not occur until students have mastered consistent tone production and intonation.

Vibrato is a rather elusive technique and in woodwind pedagogy there is much debate as to whether the pulsating mechanism comes from the throat or diaphragm. In teaching the mechanics of vibrato, teachers often start with slow diaphragmatic pulses, and then move to throat pulses, which eventually end up in the vocal mechanism (larynx). The vibrato used on saxophone is probably more related to string vibrato in that the lower jaw (lip) simply *pulsates directly on a vibrating reed* as the string player's finger *pulsates directly on a vibrating string*. Vibrato is rarely used on the clarinet.

Exercises to Develop Vibrato

One of the best descriptions found on vibrato development is the six steps given in Stevens Hewitt's fine book, *Method for Oboe* under "To Develop the Muscles for Vibrato" (p. 48). (The six steps are quoted here with the permission of the author):

1. Whistle "Yankee Doodle."
2. Whistle on one note.
3. Whistle with no sound. Discover the muscles that you are using.
4. Find, and use, those muscles to play your vibrato with a long tone, so that it "knocks," (sound-silence-sound-silence).
5. Find the tempo of your natural equilibrium on the metronome. (Four pulses to 76?)
6. Level off the peaks and valleys so that the vibrato does not knock, into a perfect sine curve.

Another well-known exercise used to activate the desired breathing and pulsating mechanisms is to have flutists, oboists, and bassoonists sing the syllable "heh" while touching the pulsating mechanism in the throat with the thumb and forefinger. Saxophonists (and clarinetists) use the syllable "yeh":

heh heh heh heh heh
yeh yeh yeh yeh yeh

heh heh heh heh heh
yeh yeh yeh yeh yeh

heh heh heh heh heh
yeh yeh yeh yeh yeh

After singing the complete scale a few times, students play the same exercise on their instruments verbalizing the same syllables into their instruments, gradually moving from eighth-note pulses to triplets and sixteenth notes:

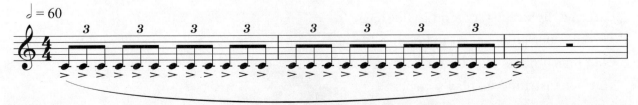

Vibrato

Once the vibrato mechanism has been activated, the next step is to work for control. Teach the student to turn it on and off, as well as to vary the vibrato speeds within a phrase. This is an important transition between the mechanical and artistic applications of vibrato. For example, a teacher might allude to "temperatures of specific notes" by suggesting that the student "warm" (slow vibrato) his/her tone on a particular part of the phrase, or that one tone in the phrase should be "searing hot" (fast vibrato) while the others are cool and cold (straight tone).

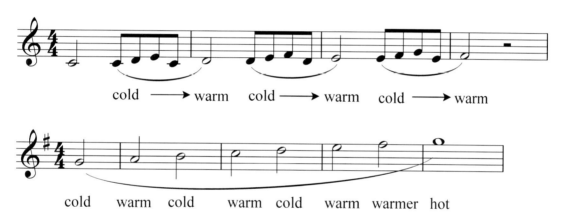

Other key words that are effective in teaching variance of vibrato and tonal intensity are "notes of becoming" and "notes of being."

These tonal illusions can of course be applied to one single tone. Keep in mind that one usually has to teach extreme contrasts at first before moving to more nuanced applications. Also an instrumentalist has to approach tonal contrasts much like an actor—the size and acoustics of the performance space is a definite factor in projecting contrasts and nuance in one's vibrato.

Clarinetists, for the most part, do not apply these vibrato concepts. However, the clarinet has the widest dynamic range of all the woodwind instruments and the effective tapering of clarinet tones into nothingness is a trademark of the instrument that is simply not achievable on the other woodwind instruments.

2 Additional Teaching Guides and Checklists

Selecting Students

In general, flute, clarinet, saxophone, and recorder are more accessible as starting instruments. Oboe and bassoon may require more private instruction especially in the beginning stages of development.

Selecting Flute Students

- Sufficient student interest is important
- Have prospective student try closed head joint exercise (see p. 18)
- Student should be in at least the fourth grade
- Arms long enough (too short—tend to make embouchure lopsided)
- Hands big enough for student to reach G♯ key with left pinky
- Orthodontic problems—retainer plates usually cause difficulty in tonguing, but may not need to be worn while playing
- Above-average breath capacity
- Piccolo is not a starting instrument, it should be played by those who are accomplished flutists
- Sufficient motor skills and coordination
- Even teeth
- Avoid uneven lip lines ("Cupid's Bow")
- Avoid excessive under- or overbites
- Smooth lip surface is an asset

Selecting Oboe Students

- Sixth or seventh grade is best for starting
- Responsible student—*oboe is the most fragile of woodwind instruments*
- Can student study privately? (providing a reed source)
- Good tonal and pitch discrimination—choral experience is helpful
- Rather large finger span—larger than for clarinet
- Prior instrument is helpful: flute, saxophone, voice, piano
- Sufficient student interest is important
- Does student show drive, perseverance, and reed-making ability?
- Protruding lower jaw (occlusion) may hinder embouchure formation
- Even front teeth

Selecting Clarinet Students

- Students can be started in elementary school
- Finger span large enough to hold instrument
- Normal lips, teeth, and chin formation
- Tooth structure—slight overbite is preferred
- Can student produce a good tone on F♯ with the barrel and mouthpiece?
- Sufficient student interest is important

Selecting Students

Selecting Saxophone Students

- Sufficient student interest is important
- Alto and tenor saxophones best for starting
- Soprano, baritone, and bass saxophones should be left to advanced students
- Physically large enough to hold instrument—prospective student should be able to reach the three right-hand keys with curved fingers and reach the low-pinky C key without pulling the hand out of position
- Left hand—prospective student should be able to reach G♯ and C♯ keys with pinky while maintaining the left-hand guide position
- Normal lips, chin, and teeth

Selecting Bassoon Students

- Sufficient student interest is important
- Can student study privately? (providing a reed source)
- Large enough hands—the bassoon requires the largest finger span of all the woodwinds
- Prospective student must have perseverance
- Potential for reed making
- Good tonal and pitch discrimination is important
- Transfer: saxophone makes a good pre-bassoon instrument, as does clarinet
- Flute, piano, and voice also make good transfer instruments
- Seventh or eighth grade best for transfer
- A short upper lip may hinder embouchure formation
- Protruding jaw may adversely affect embouchure formation

Recorder as a Pre-Woodwind Instrument

Similar Techniques
- Edge-tone (flute)
- Subtle variance of air speed is crucial
- Tonguing
- Half-hole fingerings
- Break crossings
- Vibrato application
- All major scales and chromatic scales
- Cross fingerings
- Finger positioning
- Smooth articulation and note connection
- Large amount of literature—historical

Similar Fingerings
- Soprano recorder similar to flute, oboe, saxophone, and clarion register of clarinet
- Alto recorder similar to bassoon and chalumeau register of clarinet

Differences
- Releases (must use tongue on releases)
- Absence of keys
- No octave-key mechanisms (except thumb half holes)

Common Problems

From James Thornton's *Woodwind Handbook* (1963) with copyright permission from Southern Music Company, San Antonio, Texas.

Flute
___ arm position
___ right-hand thumb position
___ finger position
___ aperture too large
___ air directed poorly
___ not enough breath support
___ E♭ key left off
___ incorrect F♯ fingering
___ E–F♯ connection sloppy
___ use of thumb B♭ in sharp keys
___ incorrect high-note fingerings
___ C and C♯ in second and third octave are often sharp
___ blowing sharp in upper octave
___ poor legato playing
___ tonguing between teeth
___ leaving first finger of the left hand down on D and D♯ fourth line

Oboe
___ head dropped too low
___ right-hand thumb position
___ finger position
___ lips too far over teeth
___ biting
___ bottom lip too far under
___ teeth too close together
___ lips set too far apart
___ reed too dry
___ not enough support
___ half-hole technique incorrect
___ changes of octave keys incorrect
___ incorrect use of F keys
___ sloppy legato using forked F
___ incorrect high note fingerings
___ inaccurate pitch in upper register
___ poor note connection and articulation
___ bad pitch and color on second C
___ no knowledge of reed adjustment

Clarinet
___ not enough mouthpiece in mouth
___ reed too soft—reed too dry
___ reed not placed on mouthpiece correctly
___ ligature not tight enough
___ poor left-hand position—third finger in each hand pulling
___ poor posture
___ too much bite on mouthpiece—biting to get high register

Common Problems

___ chin bunched up toward reed
___ too much bottom lip turned under
___ finger too far on a key
___ left forefinger jumping from E hole to A key

Saxophone

___ holding sax incorrectly
___ failure to grease cork on neck
___ bent or out-of-line connecting lever (most vulnerable key)
___ bent keys or rods as a result of improper assembly
___ reed improperly placed on mouthpiece
___ head inclined downward—restricts air flow
___ slouched body—affects breathing
___ reed too dry
___ not maintaining good fulcrum in holding position
___ no knowledge of useful alternate fingerings
___ not enough mouthpiece in mouth
___ dirty mouthpiccc and reed
___ too much bite
___ poor hand position
___ faulty pitch due to lack of control of air and embouchure
___ incorrect chromatic fingerings on B♭ and F♯

Bassoon

___ not enough reed in mouth
___ lips over teeth too far
___ too much grip
___ chin bunched up
___ lips not separated
___ jaw not pulled down
___ air used incorrectly
___ bent bocal
___ dirty bocal
___ bad position
___ reed too dry
___ tip too open
___ loose wires or string (on reed)
___ reed too heavy
___ no knowledge of alternate fingerings
___ lack of support for upper register
___ biting upper register tones
___ no knowledge of reed adjustment
___ incorrect use of whisper key
___ incorrect use of half-hole fingerings
___ lacking knowledge of flick keys

Selecting Instruments

NOTE:

All new instruments can be obtained on a trial period. Take new or used instrument to an advanced student or professional in order to try the instrument before the final purchase is made by the student.

Selecting a Flute

Beginning students: closed-hole models recommended
- Selmer—USA
- Gemeinhardt—Model 2SP
- Yamaha—Model YFL 225S II
- Armstrong—Model 104SP

Advanced students: open-hole model flutes have a more open and flexible sound
- Same brands as beginners but different models
- Haynes
- Powell
- Miramatsu
- Miyazawa

If buying a **USED FLUTE** check the following:
- Check action of keys—keys should not be sluggish
- Make certain tuning cork and crown in head joint are not loose
- Check intonation with a tuner
- Avoid plastic pads—they will stick

Selecting an Oboe

Beginning students
- Fox Renard Model 330 (plastic resin)

Advanced students
- Fox Model 300
- Lorée
- Covey

Specifications
- Full plateaux; conservatory system
- Left-hand F key (eliminates the need to use forked F)
- F resonance key
- Low B♭ key
- Cork pads
- Do not buy fully automatic octave key mechanism
- Silk swabs preferred
- Low C ring (B to C♯ trill)

Selecting Instruments

Selecting a Clarinet

Beginning Students

Plastic clarinets

- Buffet B10
- Selmer USA
- Plastic alto and bass clarinets are recommended (Selmer, Yamaha)

Wooden clarinets (for better sound and student progress)

- Normandy
- Buffet E-11

Advanced Students

- Buffet R-13
- Selmer
- Leblanc
- Yamaha

Selecting a Saxophone

Beginning Students

- Selmer USA
- Yamaha YAS52

Advanced Students

- Selmer—Super Action 80
- Selmer 62 Series
- Selmer Reference 54
- Yamaha 62II Series, Mark II

Selecting a Bassoon

Beginning Students

- Fox Model IV (plastic resin)

Advanced Students

- Fox Renard 222 Standard
- Fox Renard 240 Short Bore

Specifications

- High D key
- Whisper key lock
- Water tubes in bore
- CVX bocals #2 and #3

Single Reed Mouthpiece Selection

Mouthpiece Trials

Do not buy mouthpieces outright. Most companies and music stores allow for a deposit and trial period. For example:

Order up to four different mouthpieces for trial from:
Woodwind and Brasswind
http://www.wwbw.com/

You pay for shipping plus deposit equivalent to the most expensive mouthpiece.
You have 30 days to try them—all mouthpieces are returnable and refundable.
Use self-adhesive mouthpiece pads to avoid tooth marks.

Recommended Brands

Beginning Students

• Premiere by Hite (reasonably priced)—a good step-up MP for both clarinet and saxophone

Advanced Students

• Clarinet: Vandoren M13 or M15
• Saxophone: Selmer S-80 (Standard facings: C* and C**); Selmer C S-90
• Jazz alto and tenor saxophone: Meyer 7 or 8* (small chamber)
• Jazz Tenor Saxophone: Meyer 6 to 8*
• Jazz Tenor Saxophone: Otto Link 6* to 8*

Mouthpiece/Reed Selection—Three Factors

1. Facing (resistance curve)—see p. 45
   • LONG FACING requires a hard reed
   • SHORT FACING requires a soft reed

2. Tip Opening (provides resistance to breath)—see p. 45
   • CLOSED TIP OPENING requires hard reed (more resistance to air stream)
   • WIDE TIP OPENING requires a soft reed (less resistance to air stream) and requires stronger embouchure
   • A MEDIUM OPENING is recommended in most cases

3. Materials
   • HARD RUBBER is recommended
   • Avoid PLASTIC (breaks easily)

Recommended Ligatures for Students at All Levels

• Clarinet: Rovner or Bonade
• Saxophone: Rovner or Bonade (normal or inverted) or Selmer two screw
• Jazz saxophone: Otto Link with Otto Link MP
• Rovner Eddie Daniels with Meyer MP

Single Reed Mouthpiece Selection

Mouthpiece/Reed Selection

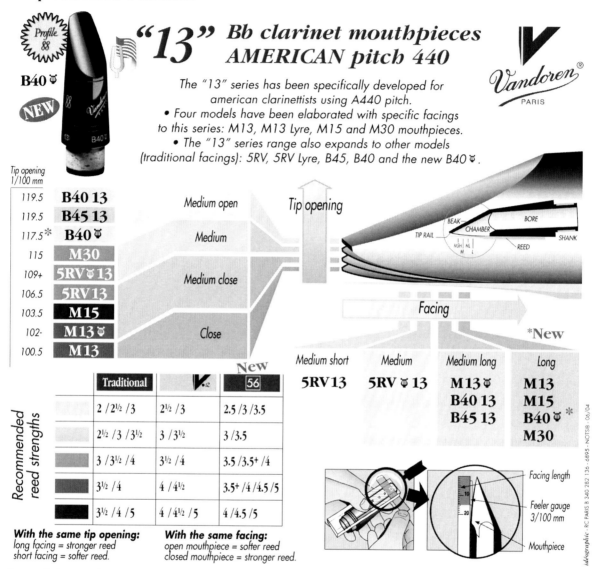

Facing and tip opening

Vandoren Copyright—Used with Permission

Single Reed Selection

Reed Selection

Mouthpiece Tip Openings
- Mouthpieces with SMALLER tip openings require HARDER reeds
- Mouthpieces with LARGER tip openings require SOFTER reeds

Mouthpiece Facings
- Mouthpieces with LONGER facings require STRONGER reeds
- Mouthpieces with SHORTER facings require SOFTER reeds

Reeds that do not work on one student's mouthpiece may work well on another student's mouthpiece. Therefore, rather than students purchasing one or two reeds at a time, teachers may want to buy reeds by the box in order to "custom fit" reeds to various student mouthpieces.

Visual Criteria For Selecting Reeds

- Avoid cane with a greenish tint—look for reed bark with a golden color
- Desirable: fine, even grain; evenly spaced grain lines
- Light test—hold up to light with blade pointing downwards
  - Look for balanced taper and silhouette
  - Reed tips should look balanced
- Thumbnail Test: make an indentation mark on the bark of the reed with thumbnail—the deeper the mark, the softer the cane; if there is no mark, the cane is hard

Aural Criteria for Selecting Reeds

- Responds freely and easily over the entire range
- All octaves/registers play well in tune without undue adjustment in embouchure and air speed
- May be controlled throughout the full dynamic range in all ranges
- Produces comfortable resistance to wind pressure
- Allows complete scope of articulations

Reed Storage

- Vito reed guard (with rubber band holder and evaporation grooves)
- Vandoren—closed case reed holders
- Selmer reed case

Recommended Brands

Beginning students (with Hite Premiere mouthpieces)
- Clarinet: Mitchell Lurie $2\frac{1}{2}$
- Saxophone: La Voz, medium

Advanced students

Clarinet
- Mitchell Lurie 3 (Intermediate)
- Vandoren 3, $3\frac{1}{2}$, 4 (Advanced)

Saxophone
- Vandoren $2\frac{1}{2}$, 3, or $3\frac{1}{2}$ (depending on mouthpiece opening)
- Jazz: Vandoren (Java or Vandoren V-16)

Single Reed Adjustment

Reed Sealing

Sealing the reed prevents warping and improves sound of the reed.

Sealing top of reed

- Lay the soaked reed on a flat surface
- Rub your thumb along the lay toward the tip
- Apply pressure to seal the pores in the cane
- Rub back surface of reed on *back* of sandpaper
- Repeat the process for three or four days

Breaking In Reeds

After soaking and sealing, play on several reeds for a few minutes each day. Repeat this process for five days. Gradually expand range upwards.

Sealing back of reed

Warping

Like any piece of porous wood, cane will swell when wet and shrink when dry. Shrinkage causes the cane to warp. Therefore, *humidity control* is important (see reed storage, p. 46).

- **Checking** for warping: Lay reed on flat surface and rock side to side. If it rocks, the reed is warped and will not vibrate freely.
- **Eliminating** warping: Place 400- or 500-grit wet/or/dry sandpaper on flat surface and rub back of reed on sandpaper until flat.
- **Preventing** warping: The flat side of reed should always rest against a flat surface. Use a reed guard or holder for storage.

Sanding back of reed

Check for Reed Leakage

Occasionally check MP and reed assembly with the pop test (see p. 25).

Extending the Life of the Reed

Avoid using only one reed—students should rotate three or more reeds.

Adjusting Reed Strengths

If the reed is too soft creating a tone quality that is too bright and sounds thin:

- Move reed up on the mouthpiece
- Clip reed with reed trimmer
- Try a higher strength reed

Clipping reed

If the reed is too hard creating a tone quality that is too dark and breathy:

- Move reed farther down on the mouthpiece
- Place 400- or 500-grit wet/or/dry sandpaper on flat surface and rub back of reed OR balance reed with careful scraping using a reed knife (advanced)
- Try a softer-strength reed

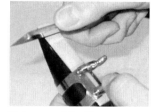

Using reed knife

Double Reed Selection and Adjustment

Reeds from private teachers are usually better than commercial reeds because a teacher is able to custom-make the reed for the individual student's embouchure, instrument, and so forth. Another alternative is to find a local teacher who will sell reeds to your students.

- **Soaking**: Double reeds soaked (or dipped) in water will respond better. Use clear (not black) film containers (free from photo shops) to carry water in instrument cases.

- **Do not soak reed in mouth**: Acids in saliva will deteriorate the reed quickly. Before playing, avoid candy and soft drinks (which deteriorate reeds).

When an oboe reed wears out, save the cork tube (staple) for future reed making and keep the cork greased to preserve the tubes. Use a ventilated reed case for storing reeds.

Three Tests

1. Check for leaks: close cork end and use the "pop" test (see p. 25).
    - Stop end of tube with finger
    - Suck air out of reed and pull reed from mouth
    - Listen for "pop"—if no "pop," reed requires more soaking

2. Check crow by placing all of the blade in the mouth up to the wrap or wire and blow very gently.
    - Listen for two pitches: high and low in octaves (see p. 24)
    - A good oboe crow will sound octaves on B or C
    - A good bassoon crow will sound octaves on E♭, E, or F

3. Check reed buzz (see p. 24)

Generally, soft reeds tend to play flat and hard reeds tend to play sharp.

Finger Molding Tip Openings

Double reed tip openings can be somewhat molded with the fingers. The average size tip openings are: Oboe—$\frac{1}{2}$ mm; bassoon—1 mm

- **If aperture is too open** (plays flat with too much resistance—may be caused by oversoaking) Gently press the *top and bottom blades* of the wet reed between the thumb and forefinger for a few seconds.

- **If aperture is too closed** (plays sharp with insufficient resistance—sounds "reedy")
  Place thumb and forefinger on the sides of the reed at the wire or binding and *gently* squeeze the reed opening of the tip. Be careful, keep your eyes on the tip opening while squeezing.

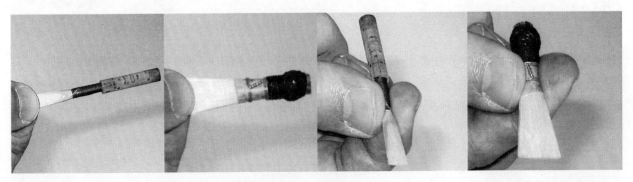

Closing oboe aperture   Closing bassoon aperture   Opening oboe aperture   Opening bassoon aperture

Double Reed Selection and Adjustment

Reed Must Be Dry for the Following

If bassoon reeds do not fit on the bocal or if there is an air leak between the bocal and reed, wait until the reed is totally dry and gently ream the tube of the reed. Reamers are available from Forrest's Double Reed Specialists at http://www.forrestsmusic.com/knivesandcutters.htm

Reaming bassoon reed

Reed Must Be Soaked for the Following

IF REED IS FLAT—Check the tip opening (see previous page), check reed buzz (p. 24), crow pitch (p. 24), and basic scales—low and high (p. 60, 68).

> Clip a "hairline" off the tip of the reed with jeweler's nippers (available from Forrest's Double Reed Specialists—see above).
>
> After clipping, the reed will have a slightly higher reed buzz and crow and will be *more resistive to the air stream*.

Clipping bassoon reed   Clipping oboe reed

IF REED IS SHARP—Check the tip opening (see p. 48), check reed buzz (p. 24), crow pitch (p. 24), and basic scales—low and high (p. 60, 68).

Double Reeds

Rub the tip of the reed at an angle over 400-grit wet and dry sandpaper as shown. Go slow—just a couple of short rubs of the reed tip on the sandpaper will alter the reed considerably. Then check the reed buzz and crow. After sanding, reeds will have a slightly lower reed buzz and crow and will be *less resistive to the airstream*.

Sanding bassoon reed tip   Sanding oboe reed tip

Other Tools Used to Adjust Double Reeds

Three of the most common tools used to adjust double reeds are: (1) the reed knife, (2) the mandrel for holding the reed, and (3) the plaque for inserting between the blades. These are shown below along with their proper holding position:

Double reed tools   Scraping oboe reed   Scraping bassoon reed

Double Reed Selection and Adjustment

Bassoon Wire Adjustments

If wires are loose, tighten with pliers by pulling slightly as you twist.

Four basic wire adjustments with needle-nose pliers

1. *Squeeze first wire* (wire closest to tip) from *sides*
   - RESULT: wider tip opening, darker, more resistant
   - CAUTION: may flatten throat tones (E and F)

2. *Squeeze first wire* from *top to bottom*
   - RESULT: smaller tip opening, generally brighter tone and less resistance

3. *Squeeze second wire* from *sides*
   - RESULT: smaller tip opening, centers sound, high register speaks better
   - Low register will not respond as well

4. *Squeeze second wire from top and bottom*
   - RESULT: larger tip opening, low register will respond more easily

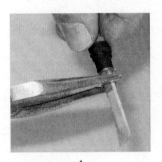 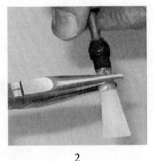  

1	2	3	4

Recommended Reed Sources:
www.reedmaker.com
http://www.hodgeproductsinc.com/

Bassoon Reed Making and Adjustment:
http://www.steesbassoon.com/select.html
http://www.2reed.net

Oboe Reed Making and Adjustment:
http://www.wfg.woodwind.org/

Oboe Reed Blanks:
Bill Roscoe Double Reeds (1-888-417-2202) http://www.doublereeds.com/index.html
Ask for: profiled oboe cane—no. 6 (medium soft to medium). You will also need to order oboe tubes (staples)—brass, natural cork, (47 mm)

Oboe Reed Making:
Have your oboe students take a couple of lessons on tying the Roscoe reed blanks to staples and/or study the procedure and video located at Michael Erickson's Web site at Western Illinois University: http://www.wiu.edu/oboe/Site/TutorialTitle.html

For Double Reed Beginners:
Fox or Selmer Fibercane reeds may be a temporary last resort solution, but as soon as the student learns the fundamentals of playing he/she should move to cane reeds.

International Double Reed Society:
A wealth of information on double reeds may be found at: http://idrs.colorado.edu. Also see:
http://www.doublereed.org/IDRSBBS/index.php

Emergency Repairs

Removing Water from Underneath Pads
1. Raise key and blow water from under the pad
2. Raise key, insert absorbent paper or cloth, blot moisture

If Pads Stick
1. Place a clean handkerchief or a new dollar bill between the pad and tone hole
2. Close tone hole and slowly withdraw the handkerchief/bill
3. Denatured alcohol on a cloth will clean excessively sticky pads

Checking Pads For Leaks
1. **Test each joint with air pressure:** close keys, stop end with hand, blow air into joint, and listen for leaks.
2. **Test each joint with vacuum test:** close keys with normal finger pressure, stop end with hand or large cork, and suck air out of bore. A vacuum indicates no leaks. Little or no vacuum indicates leaks. A vacuum may be created in the bassoon boot by closing all keys and pressing the large bore opening against one's cheek while simultaneously sucking air out of the small bore.
3. **Test by using a "feeler gauge"—a triangle cut from thin paper:** insert point of triangle between pad and tone hole—see below. Gently depress the key that controls pad and pull paper from beneath the pad. Try at various points around the suspected pad. If paper slips easily between pad and tone hole, a leak is present and pad needs to be reset by a repair person. If paper resists, pad is closing effectively and leaks are not present.

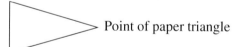 Point of paper triangle

4. **Test larger pads (saxophone and bassoon) using a "leak light:"**
   see http://www. musicmedic.com/catalog/products/tool-lt100.html

Split or Leaking Pad (emergency repair)
1. Cut piece of transparent mending tape to size of pad
2. Place tape over the tone hole with sticky side up
3. Press key and hold down for a few minutes

If Pads Come Loose or Drop Out (emergency repair)
1. Place pad in key cup—try to place in the exact original position
2. Heat key cup—use a butane cigarette lighter (matches will discolor key cup)
3. Depress key cup and hold over a flame for a few seconds in order to melt the glue
   IMPORTANT: AVOID FLAME TOUCHING BODY OF INSTRUMENT
4. When key is hot, put a cloth over hot key cap and press—hold for two minutes while glue sets

Flute adjustment screws   Oboe adjustment screws

Adjustment Screws
These control pad/key heights and are found predominantly on flutes and oboes (see photos). For sources for adjustment—see Sprenkle and Phelan in bibliography.

Lower Single Reed Instruments

Bass Clarinet

Equipment:

- Swab regularly after playing
- Apply cork grease regularly
- Do not swab mouthpieces—wash weekly with mild detergent and dry with cotton cloth
- Reeds—use 2 to $2\frac{1}{2}$ (La Voz, Rico Royal, Vandoren)
- Tenor sax reeds will work on bass clarinet, but do not work as well as bass clarinet reeds
- Do not leave reeds on mouthpieces—they will warp (use reed guard)

Pedagogy:

- Start or transfer students from clarinet or saxophone
- Finger span is greater
- Fingerings are the same as for clarinet
- Half-hole fingerings are used on high notes above C
- Sounds a major ninth lower than written—see the transposition chart
- Angle of MP is closer to saxophone (90 degrees) than to clarinet
- As on clarinet, use constant air speed
- Lower lip is not as flexed as on clarinet
- Think circular—see page 16
- Push downward on MP with upper teeth to avoid biting
- More reed and MP in mouth—insert a business card and mark the contact point (see p. 20)
- Lower jaw relaxed, throat open
- Work for a rich homogeneous tone throughout the range
  - Lower notes will come easily
  - Higher register needs time to develop

Lower Saxophones

Equipment:

- Do not swab mouthpieces—wash weekly with mild detergent and dry with cotton cloth
- Reeds—use 2 to $2\frac{1}{2}$ (La Voz, Rico Royal, Vandoren)
- Larger reeds warp more easily—use a reed guard
- Do not leave reeds on mouthpieces

Pedagogy:

- Transfer students from alto saxophone after a year of study
- Lower saxophones are heavy and require a larger finger span
- Fingerings are the same for all saxophones
- Tenor sounds a major 9th lower; baritone sounds a major 13th lower—see transposition chart
- More reed and MP in mouth—insert business card and mark contact point (p. 20)
- Lower lip not as flexed as on alto
- Push downward on MP with upper teeth to avoid biting—think circular
- Lower jaw relaxed, throat open

Transposition Chart

RULE:

If a transposing instrument plays a written C, it will sound its "name"

Flutes

Piccolo—Treble Clef
Sounds an octave higher than written

Flute—Treble Clef
Sounds as written

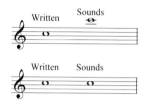

Clarinets

E♭ Clarinet—Treble Clef
Sounds a minor 3rd higher than written

B♭ Clarinet—Treble Clef
Sounds a major 2nd lower than written

E♭ Alto Clarinet—Treble Clef
Sounds a major 6th lower than written

B♭ Bass Clarinet—Treble Clef
Sounds a major 9th lower than written

Saxophones

B♭ Soprano Saxophone—Treble Clef
Sounds a major 2nd lower than written

E♭ Alto Saxophone—Treble Clef
Sounds a major 6th lower than written

B♭ Tenor Saxophone—Treble Clef
Sounds a major 9th lower than written

E♭ Baritone Saxophone—Treble Clef
Sounds a major 13th lower than written

Double Reeds

Oboe—Treble Clef
Sounds as written

English Horn—Treble Clef
Sounds a perfect 5th lower than written

Bassoon—Bass or Tenor Clef
Sounds as written

Contrabassoon—Bass or Tenor Clef
Sounds one octave lower than written

3 Hands-on Overview: Part I

Practice Tips

The definition of practice = ACCURATE REPETITION.

Develop your teaching skills while practicing: *Observe, Analyze* and *Critique* your performance.

1. Visual analysis—use a mirror often and check:
   • embouchure appearance
   • hand position/guide position (keep fingers close to the keys)
   • body position (practice standing and sitting)

2. Aural analysis—listen carefully and check:
   • tone quality
   • articulation (attack and release)
   • intonation (use a tuner for aural reference)
   • expression

N O T E :

Practicing the Student/Teacher Duets (see pp. 187–213) with an advanced player will assist in the development of one's skills in aural analysis.

Practice slowly and accurately. *Avoid practicing mistakes.* Mistakes destroy the development of accurate finger and body reflex.

Fragmenting passages and repeating them accurately develops accurate finger and body reflex.

As musical events increase concentrate on keeping hands and arms relaxed.

Isolate Techniques

• Practice the **mouthpiece pitches** (refer to p. 24).

• Practice the **basic scales** (refer to pp. 60–61).

• Practice **break crossings** (refer to pp. 67 and 71).

• Practice blowing long tones without finger movement.

• Practice finger movement without blowing—look directly at the fingers (refer to pp. 12–15).

• Practice finger movement while singing all passages.

• Practice tonguing patterns on one note (refer to pp. 30–31).

• Practice slurring first then add tonguing (refer to pp. 30–31).

Above All, Maintain a Singing Impulse

Sing/Play; Sing/Play; Sing/Play

Introduction

- As can be seen on the opposite page, all woodwind instruments have three basic registers.

- The registers of the flute, saxophone, oboe, and bassoon are based on *octaves*, whereas the clarinet is based on the *interval of a twelfth* causing it to have more "throat tones" between the registers than the other four instruments.

- The terms "chalumeau," "clarion," and "altissimo" are often used to indicate the low, middle, and high registers of the clarinet respectively.

- Except for the flute, the middle registers of the four other woodwind instruments are achieved by adding octave/register mechanisms to the fingerings of the lower register.

- The oboe and bassoon have three octave/register mechanisms while the clarinet and saxophone have only *one*.

- The pads are *opened* when octave/register keys are pressed on the oboe, clarinet, and saxophone. On bassoon, the bocal pad is *closed* when the whisper key is pressed.

- The palm keys (PK) on the saxophone are cumulative and are not octave keys—they simply extend the middle register upwards.

- The fingerings in the third and highest register of all five woodwind instruments are less systematic and less related to the lower two registers.

- The seven octave/register mechanisms on woodwind instruments are:

1. RK—register key (clarinet)

2. OK—octave key (saxophone)

3. TOK—thumb octave key (oboe)

4. SOK—side octave key (oboe)

5. $\frac{1}{2}$ H—half hole (oboe and bassoon)

6. WK—whisper key (bassoon)

7. FLK—flick or speaker keys (bassoon)

Introduction

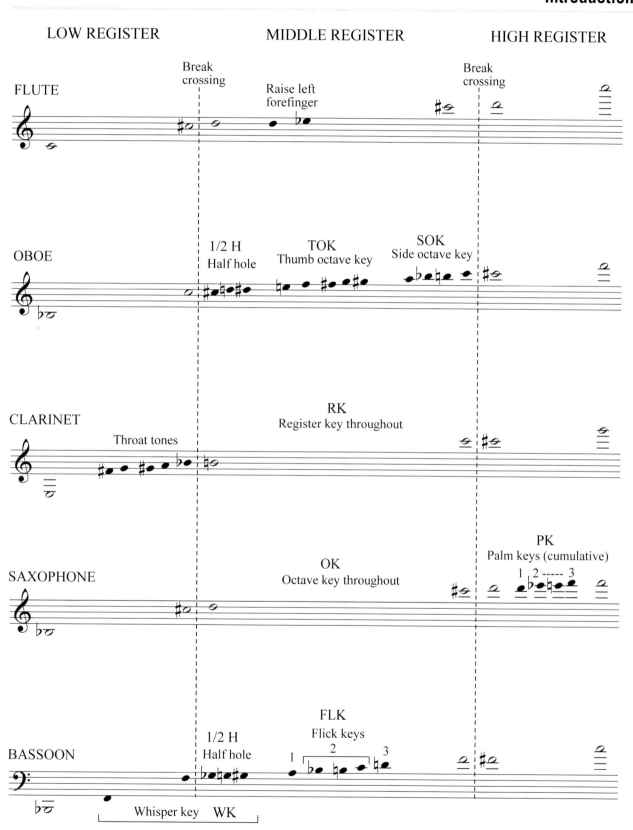

Basic Scales

All woodwind instruments require the use of the three middle fingers of each hand to perform a descending six-note basic scale:

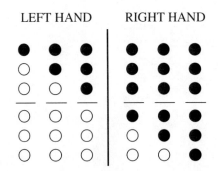

These basic fingerings are easily memorized and can provide the teacher with a fingering vocabulary of thirty fingerings for teaching the five woodwind instruments.

- Note that the interval between the left and right hands on the flute, saxophone, and clarinet is a whole step while on the bassoon and oboe, the interval is a half step (see brackets on opposite page).

- Besides the six circles (above) representing the three middle fingers of each hand, the four additional keys/tone holes involved in the basic scale exercise (see opposite page) are:

  1. B key—flute

  2. E♭ resonator key—flute

  3. Thumb hole—clarinet

  4. Whisper key—bassoon

- The basic scales are intended to be performed by individual students as warm-ups, not as an ensemble.

- Always slur and play with a full tone.

- Improvisation on these six notes is encouraged.

Memorize and practice these basic scales in front of a mirror. It is also recommended that students experiment and perform these scales while reading the following pages applicable to the instrument in hand:

- Body position (refer to pp. 10–11)

- Hand position and finger coverage (refer to pp. 12–15)

- Embouchure (refer to pp. 16–23)

- Breath support and tone quality (refer to pp. 28–29)

- Intonation (refer to pp. 32–33)

Basic Scales

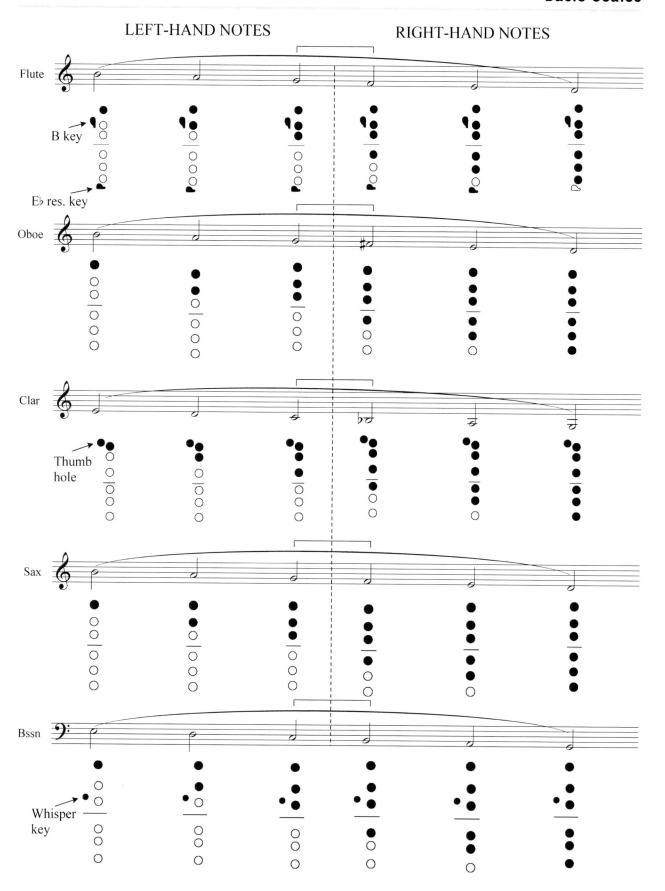

Hand/Finger Positioning

By simply adding one note to the basic scales, one may teach/learn valuable lessons about hand position and tone quality. The added notes here are *throat tones* that, for acoustical reasons, tend to have a thinner tone quality and less stable intonation compared to the "longer" fingerings.

General
- Practice each hand separately.
- Keep fingers close to the corresponding keys and tone holes.
- Repeat each exercise for each hand until memorized.
- Practice slowly and accurately to develop reliable finger reflex without thought.
- Observe the slurs—breathe after half notes only.
- When memorized, perform while checking embouchure/holding position with a mirror.
- Review information on hand position (pp. 12–15) and embouchure (pp. 16–23).

Flute
- Note that C♯ is the highest note of the lowest register of the flute. See p. 59.
- C♯ tends to be sharp—see p. 32 for adjusting pitch.
- C♯ tends to be unfocused and "airy"—see p. 18 for adjusting tone quality and intonation.
- Note that the right pinky presses the E♭ key for all notes except the final D.

Oboe
- C is the highest note of the lowest register of the oboe. See p. 59.
- C tends to be unstable—see p. 32 for adjusting the pitch.
- The tip opening (aperture) of the reed may have to be adjusted for the C. See p. 48.
- If necessary, make a crescendo to the final note in order to make the final note speak.

Clarinet
- The clarinet has more throat tones than any other woodwind instrument. See p. 59.
- Open G tends to be unstable—see p. 32 for adjusting the pitch.
- *The clarinet is the only woodwind instrument on which the left hand is not constantly anchored to the instrument.* See p. 80.
- Keep fingers close to the tone holes. On "open G" the left hand must "float." The left pinky may lightly touch (but not press) the low E key. See pp. 13 and 81.

Saxophone
- C♯ is the highest tone in the lowest register of the saxophone. See p. 59.
- C♯ tends to be unstable—see p. 33 for adjusting the pitch.
- Make certain that the reed is well soaked and that the MP is far enough in the mouth.
- If necessary, make a crescendo to the final note in order to make the final note speak.

Bassoon
- The throat tone F is the highest tone in the lowest register. See p. 59.
- F tends to be unstable—see p. 33 for adjusting the pitch.
- The tip opening (aperture) of the reed may have to be adjusted for the F. See p. 48.
- The bassoon has the largest finger spread of all the woodwind instruments.

Hand/Finger Positioning

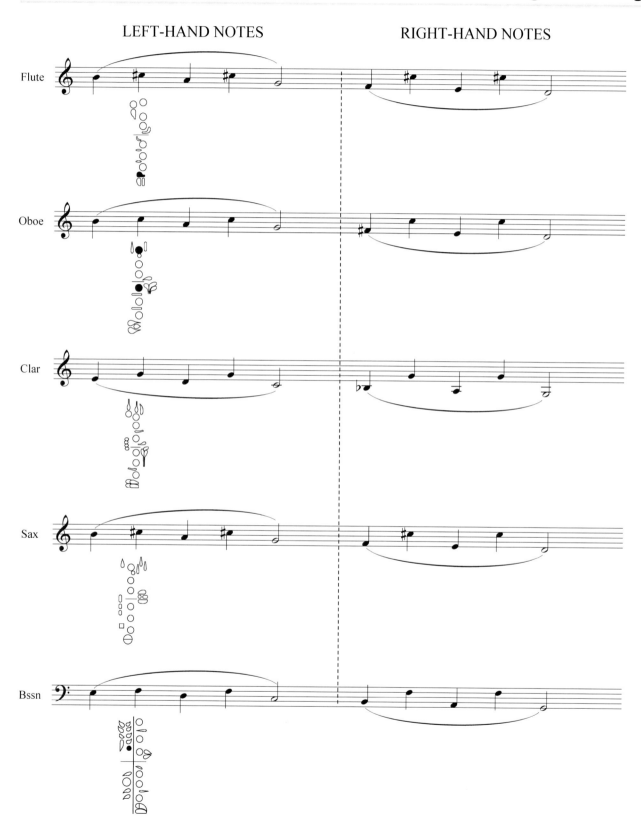

Octave/Register Mechanisms

All five woodwind instruments have octave/register mechanisms that may be introduced as melodic extensions of the descending six-note basic scale.

Flute

- Unlike the other woodwind instruments, the flute does not have octave keys. Instead, flutists rely on embouchure/air manipulation: (1) coverage, (2) aperture size, (3) air speed, and (4) air direction. These techniques are described on pp.18–19 (flute embouchure).

Oboe

- Introduce the half-hole technique ($\frac{1}{2}$ H) to your students by simply rolling the left forefinger downward onto "the tear drop" of the key (see the fingering diagram on the opposite page).

Clarinet

- Hold the left thumb at a 2 o'clock angle with the clarinet when covering the F hole. The left thumb should overlap the top of the F hole so that it can activate the RK with a simple pivot motion. A consistent and steady air speed is required for this exercise.

- Unlike the other woodwind instruments, it is not necessary to make embouchure adjustments for wide upward leaps on the clarinet. This can be demonstrated by having the student play this exercise and hold the lowest note while another student (or teacher) reaches over and depresses the RK. See photo on p. 29.

- Another demonstration is to turn the barrel around so that the reed is in line with the finger holes. Have the student hold the barrel with the right hand and blow a constant air stream while the teacher or a clarinet major fingers this exercise. See photo on p. 29.

Saxophone

- As with clarinet, hold the left thumb at a two o'clock angle and overlap the OK (octave key) so that the thumb can activate the OK with a simple pivoting motion (see touch-tone-teaching p. 27). Keep the air stream steady and fully supported throughout this exercise.

Bassoon

- As with the oboe, introduce the half-hole technique by rolling (not sliding) the left forefinger downward. On the oboe, the forefinger is rolled downward onto another part of the *plateau* key while on the bassoon the forefinger is rolled downward in order to uncover a small portion of the actual tone hole.

- For intonation correction on the upper G, add the low E♭ key.

Octave/Register Mechanisms

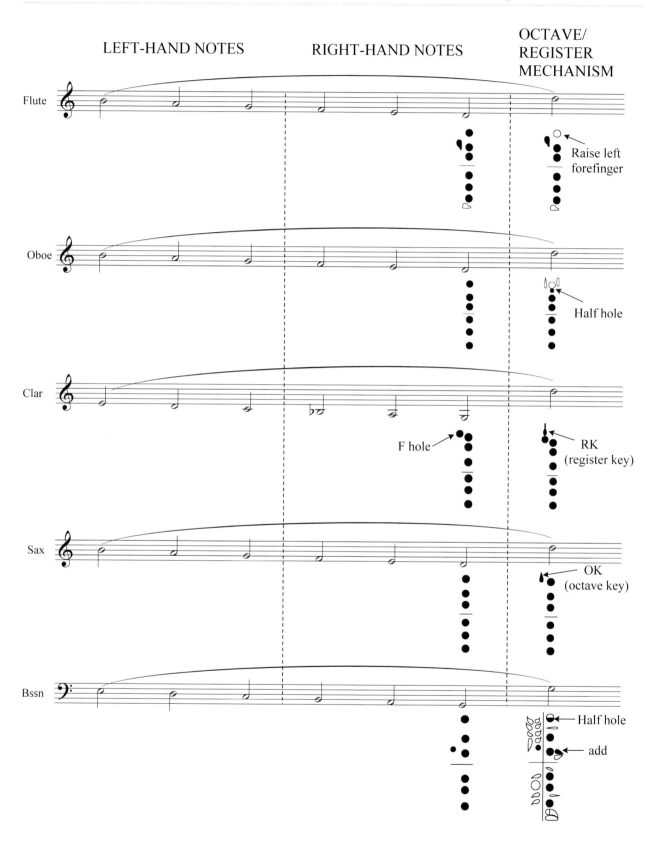

LEFT-HAND NOTES   RIGHT-HAND NOTES   OCTAVE/ REGISTER MECHANISM

Flute

Raise left forefinger

Oboe

Half hole

Clar

F hole   RK (register key)

Sax

OK (octave key)

Bssn

Half hole

add

Primary Break Crossings

A constant goal for players of woodwind instruments is to match timbre and intonation *between* registers.

- Students may be made aware of this common goal by extending the basic scale exercises to include these primary break crossings between the middle and lower registers.

- When executing break crossings, control of timbre and intonation is dependent on air speeds, throat openings, and embouchure control—see pp. 16–17.

- When introducing break crossings, check the following:

  1. Keep fingers close to the corresponding tone holes and keys.

  2. Concentrate on maintaining guide position in both hands.

  3. Avoid movement of the instrument when crossing the break:
     a. Beginning flutists often experience problems with holding the instrument steady when crossing the break. The left thumb *should not support* the flute. Check the three fulcrum elements: (1) chin (just below lower lip), (2) base of the curved left forefinger, and (3) right thumb (pushed forward slightly).
     b. Beginning clarinetists may also experience instability in holding position during break crossings. This can be helped by introducing RHD (right-hand-down) fingerings: keep the right hand in place (as shown) and move only the left hand.

  NOTE:

  Right-hand-down fingerings appear in gray and are not part of the normal fingerings, but are a pedagogical device to help students with break crossings.

Ear Training

- Match the tone qualities of the last two notes in the exercise on p. 67. The last note, being a throat tone tends to sound thin and airy when compared to "long" fingerings. Developing a *singing impulse* is helpful—have the student sing the last two notes of the exercise, then play them. Repeat several times. Experiment with throat openings and tongue positions—see p. 16.

- Check the intonation of the last note of the example—throat tones tend to be unstable—see p. 32–33.

Primary Break Crossings

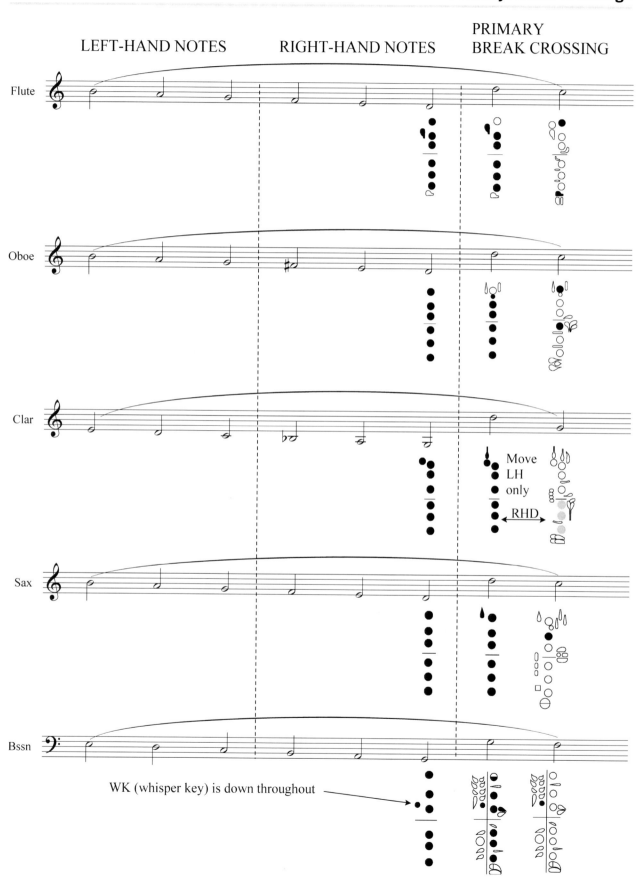

LEFT-HAND NOTES   RIGHT-HAND NOTES   PRIMARY
BREAK CROSSING

Flute

Oboe

Clar

Move
LH
only

RHD

Sax

Bssn

WK (whisper key) is down throughout

Middle Registers

The middle registers on all five woodwind instruments may be introduced and explored in the same manner as the low register: by using the basic scale concept (as shown here).

These thirty additional fingerings are easily memorized and when combined with the fingerings of the lower basic scale (see pp. 60–61), the woodwind teacher may easily acquire a basic woodwind fingering vocabulary of sixty fingerings.

RIGHT HAND   LEFT HAND

The middle-register fingering patterns for all five instruments are identical to their low register except for the addition of the following octave/register mechanisms indicated on the opposite page:

- Flute: raised left forefinger (on D only)
- Oboe: half hole ($\frac{1}{2}$ H); thumb octave key (TOK); side octave key (SOK)
- Clarinet: register key (RK)
- Saxophone: octave key (OK)
- Bassoon: whisper key (WK); half hole ($\frac{1}{2}$ H)

N O T E :

Regarding the use of TOK and SOK on the oboe—since most oboes have a semi-automatic octave key system, some oboists simply add the SOK to the TOK as indicated on the opposite page. However, other oboists go from G to A by "rocking" the wrist, automatically lifting the left ring finger and sliding the thumb off of the TOK.

N O T E :

The last note of the bassoon part deviates from the basic scale fingering pattern shown above. Although the one-finger E is an alternate fingering, use (teach) the standard "long" fingering shown on the opposite page.

While Practicing the Exercise on page 69

- FLUTE: Note that the E♭ key is down for all notes except D.
- FLUTE, OBOE, BASSOON: While ascending, slightly increase the air speeds and support while simultaneously diminishing lip and reed apertures.
- OBOE, BASSOON: If necessary, take slightly more reed into mouth for higher notes.
- SINGLE REEDS: Avoid biting upwards; lower teeth should allow lower lip to flex; push MP toward upper teeth; keep airstream constant. This exercise may require harder reeds.
- ALL INSTRUMENTS: check embouchure control and air speeds with the following:

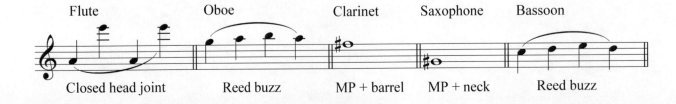

Flute   Oboe   Clarinet   Saxophone   Bassoon

Closed head joint   Reed buzz   MP + barrel   MP + neck   Reed buzz

Middle Registers

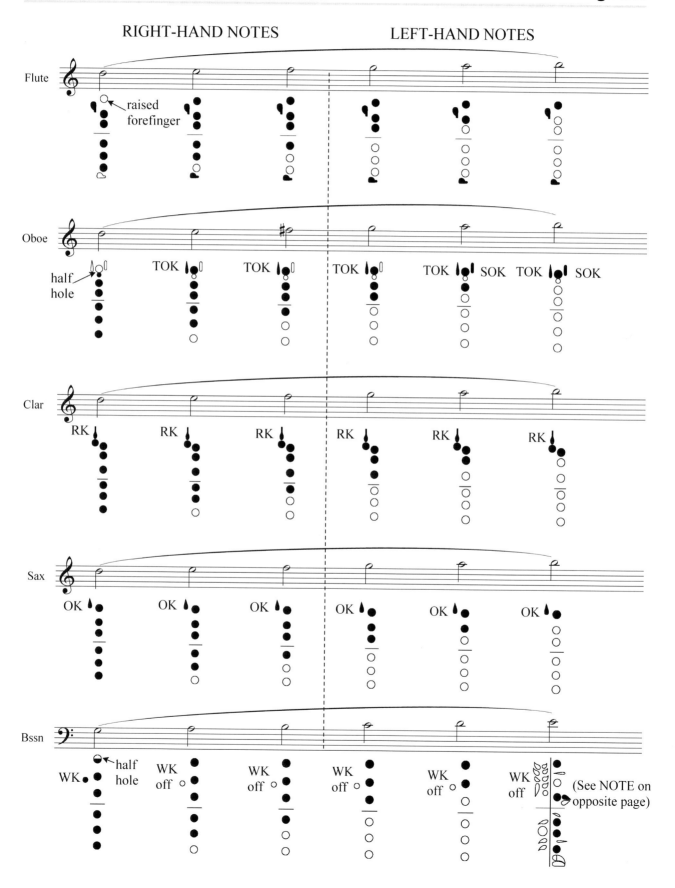

More on Break Crossings

General

- Sing first, then play.
- Keep fingers close: maintain guide position in both hands.
- Avoid movement of the instrument when crossing the break.
- Check intonation on the third note of this exercise (open throat tones tend to be unstable).
- Mirror practice is recommended.

Flute

- Do not allow the flute to move when crossing the break.
- Teach *balanced* holding position—check holding fulcrum in this order: (1) jaw, (2) left forefinger, (3) right thumb and pinky.
- Check student's use of the left forefinger—raise on D, down on C and E.
- Eb resonator key is down on E and C, not on D.
- Check the tone quality and intonation of third-space C (which tends to be sharp).

Oboe

- Use half hole on D and TOK on E.
- Roll, do not slide, to half hole.
- Check holding position on pp. 12 and 14.

Clarinet

- THIS IS A LEFT-HAND EXERCISE—the right hand remains stationary (RHD) throughout.
- Maintain the left-hand guide position by having the left pinky touch the low E key while the left forefinger *rolls* upward from the F# hole to touch the A key.
- Isolate this important forefinger movement by practicing this exercise:

Left pinky should touch this key cluster while playing the above pattern

Saxophone

- The left thumb assumes a 2 o'clock position with the line of the instrument.
- Use minimal left-thumb movement when activating the OK—pivot, do not slide.
- Check the holding position. Maintain the fulcrum between the two thumbs and the neck strap. See p. 13.

Bassoon

- Half hole on G—*roll*, (do not *slide*) to the half hole. See pp. 64–65.
- The WK (whisper key) is down on F and G.
- The WK is off on A♮ and above.

More on Break Crossings

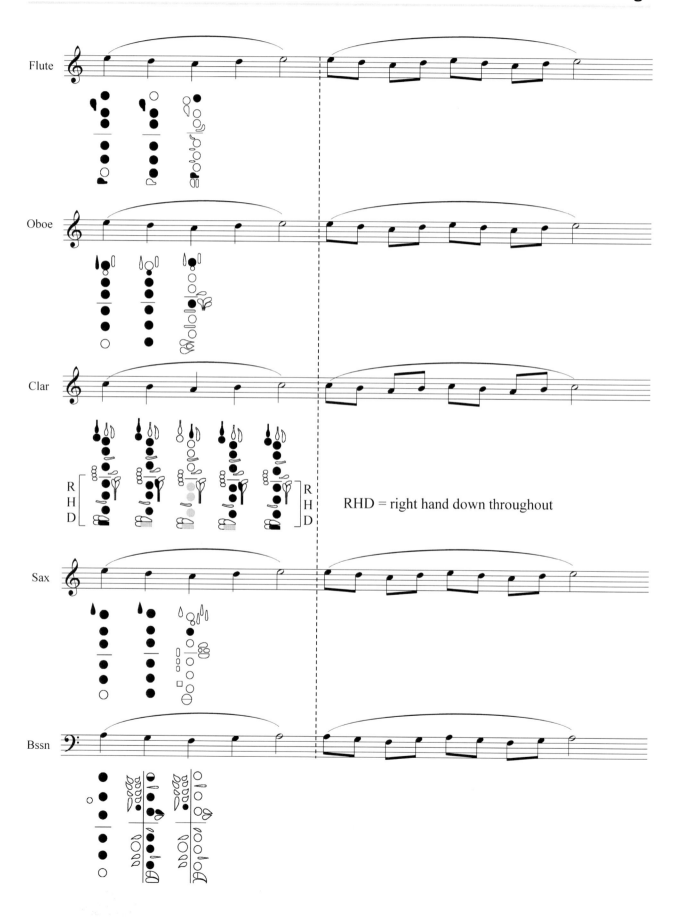

RHD = right hand down throughout

More Octave/Register Mechanisms

This exercise combines lower and middle registers allowing the student to further investigate and practice octave/register mechanisms. (refer to p. 58).

Note the similarity of the basic fingerings for all five woodwind instruments.

Flute

Octave exercises are recommended for flute students of all levels, because the playing of octaves leads to the control of:

1. air *direction* (higher for high notes)
2. lip *coverage* of embouchure hole (more for higher tones)
3. aperture *size* (smaller for higher tones)
4. air *speed* (faster for higher tones)

Oboe

The oboe student employs three octave mechanisms:

1. $\frac{1}{2}$ H—half hole on 3 Ds (D♭, D♮, D♯)
2. TOK—thumb octave key used on E to G♯
3. SOK—side octave key used on A and above (see pp. 58–59)

The teacher may employ the "touch-tone-teaching" concept here (refer to p. 26)

Clarinet and Saxophone

The simplest mechanisms are on the clarinet and saxophone where the same keys are used throughout. The teacher may employ the "touch-tone-teaching" concept here (refer to p. 27)

Bassoon

The bassoon student employs three octave mechanisms:

1. $\frac{1}{2}$ H—half hole on 3 Gs (G♭, G♮, G♯)
2. WK—whisper key is off on A and above
3. FLK—flick key directions:
   - Start the lower note with the whisper key (WK) down.
   - On the second beat, raise the thumb toward the flick key.
   - On the third beat, "flick" (tap) the designated key and increase the air speed.

The teacher may employ the "touch-tone-teaching" concept here (refer to p. 27)

More Octave/Register Mechanisms

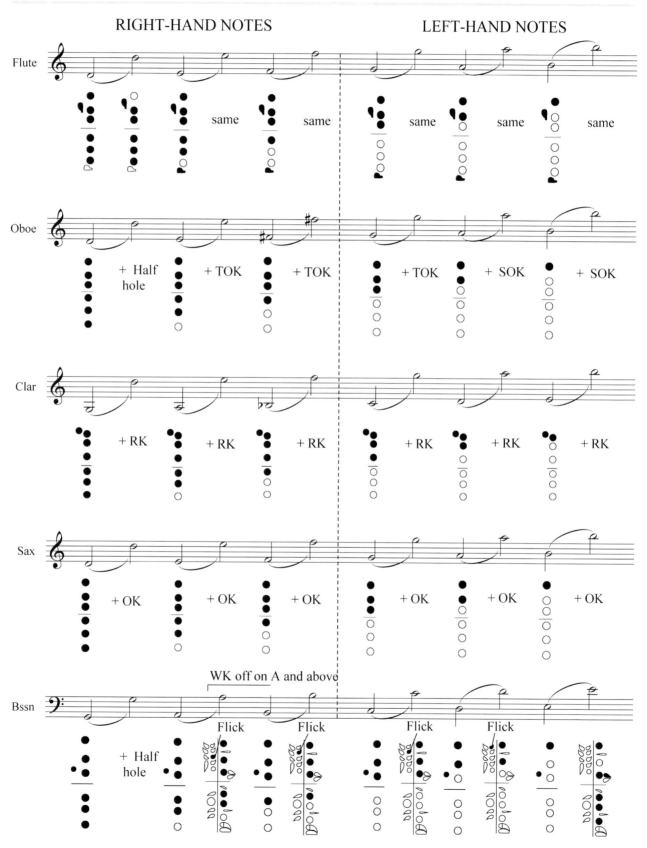

4 Hands-on Overview: Part II

Basic Scale: Chromatic—Low Registers

The basic scale exercise can be applied to the learning and teaching of chromatic scales on all five woodwind instruments. *Note that fingerings are not given for basic scale notes.*

General

- Practice each hand separately.
- Repeat each exercise for each hand until memorized.
- Practice slowly and accurately to develop *reliable finger reflex without thought*.
- Observe the slurs—breathe after half notes only.
- When memorized, check embouchure and holding position using a mirror.
- Develop a singing impulse with the instrument: sing first, then play.

Flute

- For lower notes: cover less of the embouchure hole with the lower lip. See p. 18.
- Low notes will sound weak at first.
- Reduce aperture size and lip coverage in order to produce more "edge" and an open tone in the lower notes.

Oboe

- Use the three-step embouchure formation: (1) place, (2) roll, and (3) cushion. See p. 22.
- Use "circular" lip cushioning.
- For low notes to speak readily, play on the tip of the reed.
- Use a slow, but well-supported airstream—relax the throat.

Clarinet

- Keep the air speed constant.
- The regular fingerings will create *cross fingerings* (two adjacent fingers moving in opposite directions). Therefore, use alternate fingerings for these chromatic passages.
- Work for a well-focused tone. Avoid hollow sounding *sub-tones* caused by insufficient breath support.

Saxophone

- Note the similarity between the clarinet and saxophone fingerings.
- Keep the air speed constant.
- The regular fingerings here create *cross fingerings* (two adjacent fingers moving in opposite directions). Therefore, use alternate fingerings for these chromatic passages.

Bassoon

- Watch intonation on the first two notes—if the reed is too soft, E will be flat. See pp. 48–49
- Use a slow, but well-supported air stream—relax the throat.
- Use "circular" lip cushioning. See pp. 22–23.

Basic Scale: Chromatic—Low Registers

LEFT-HAND NOTES   RIGHT-HAND NOTES

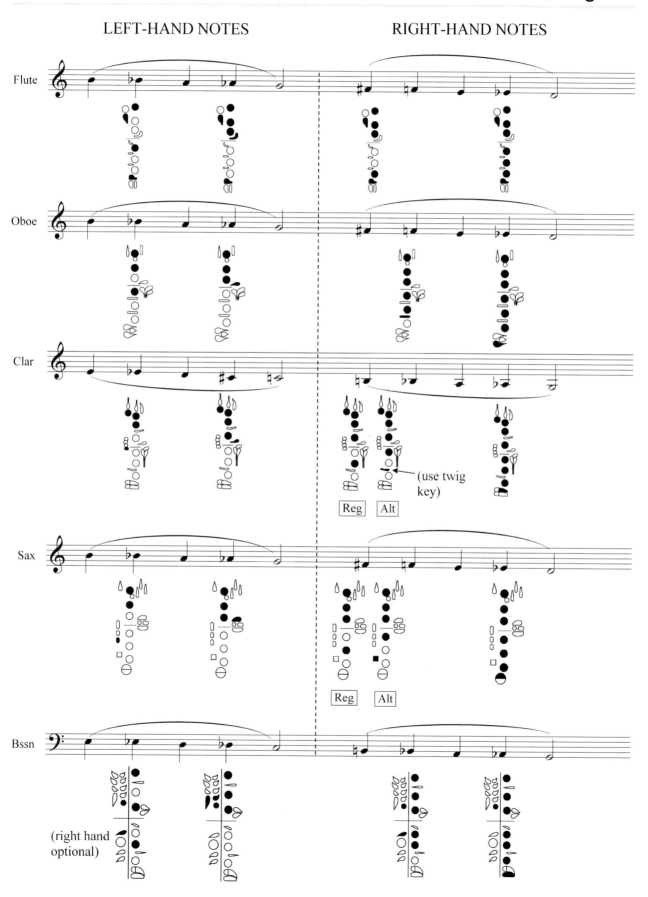

Flute

Oboe

Clar

(use twig key)

Reg   Alt

Sax

Reg   Alt

Bssn

(right hand optional)

Basic Scale: Chromatic—Middle Registers

As in the previous exercise, the chromatic version of the basic scale in the middle register reveals similar fingering patterns for the five woodwind instruments (see opposite page).

General

- Practice each hand separately.
- Practice slowly and accurately in order to develop reliable finger reflex without thought.
- Observe the slurs—breathe after half notes only.
- Do not take in too much air—use a singing impulse to guide the intake of air.

Flute

- Left forefinger should be raised for D and E♭.
- E♭ key is down on all notes except D.
- As you ascend, cover more embouchure hole with the lower lip and increase the air speed.
- Control both the inner and outer part of the lip when guiding the air stream.

Oboe

- Use half-hole fingering on D and E♭.
- Use TOK (thumb octave key) on E, F, F♯, G, and A♭.
- Add SOK (side octave key) on A, B♭, and B♮.
- For higher notes, check speed, distance (of reed in mouth), and lip cushioning.

Clarinet

- Note the similarity between the clarinet and saxophone fingerings.
- Note that the RK (register key) is down throughout this exercise.
- Use the alternate F♯ fingering in order to avoid cross fingering (adjacent fingers moving in opposite directions).
- Keep embouchure and air speed constant throughout.

Saxophone

- Note the similarity between the clarinet and saxophone fingerings.
- Note that the OK (octave key) is down throughout this exercise.
- Use the alternate F♯ fingering in order to avoid cross fingering (see clarinet).
- Keep embouchure and air speed constant throughout.

Bassoon

- Use half-hole fingerings on G and A♭.
- Use WK (whisper key) on G and A♭.
- Practice each hand separately.

Basic Scale: Chromatic—Middle Registers

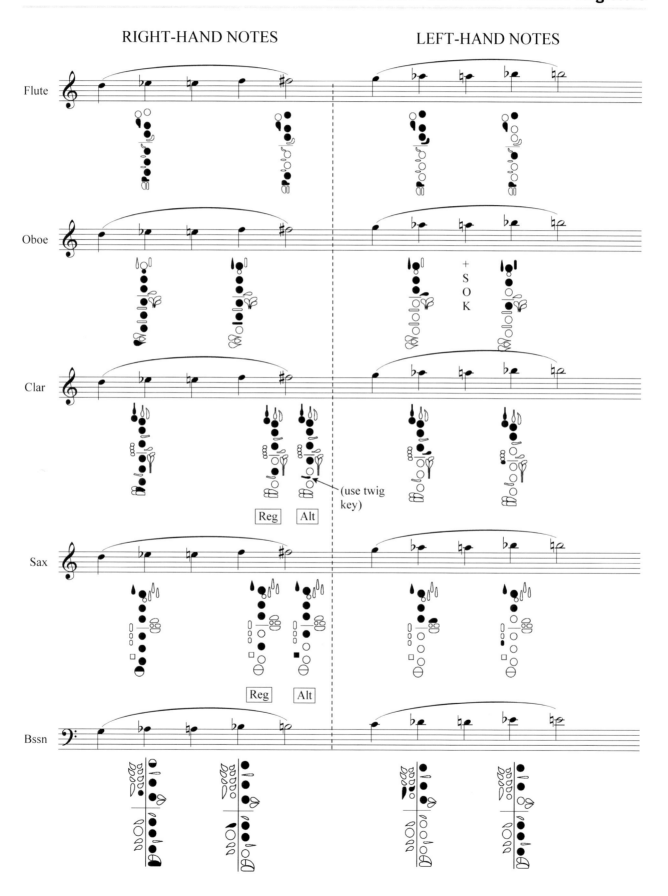

RIGHT-HAND NOTES

LEFT-HAND NOTES

Flute

Oboe

Clar

(use twig key)

Reg   Alt

Sax

Reg   Alt

Bssn

Clarinet Throat Tones: Training the Left Hand

The clarinet student must develop unique left-hand skills in order to fill in the notes between the chalumeau and clarion registers.

These notes are called *throat tones* and it is essential that the clarinet student spend time developing the tone, intonation, and the left-hand positioning required for these notes.

The left-hand position on the clarinet is unique. It is the only woodwind instrument on which the left hand is *not anchored* to the body of the instrument while performing.

- Flute—The left hand is anchored at the base of the left forefinger.
- Oboe—The left thumb is anchored just below the thumb octave key.
- Saxophone—The left thumb is anchored on the pearl thumb rest.
- Bassoon—The left hand is anchored at the base of the left forefinger.

Mirror Practice

- While practicing these exercises, keep fingers hovering over their respective keys and tone holes.
- Keep the left pinky close to (or lightly touching) the low E key throughout.
- Check intonation of these throat tones. They are often sharp and require that the barrel be pulled out slightly.
- Time invested in these exercises will enable the student to progress more easily into the clarion register of the clarinet.

The exercises on page 81 address the technique required for maintaining the left-hand position on the clarinet as well as acquaint the student with the left forefinger cluster.

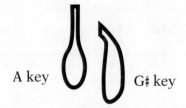

A key   G♯ key

The primary goal of these exercises is to acquire a "floating" and relaxed left-hand position while operating these keys.

Clarinet Throat Tones: Training the Left Hand

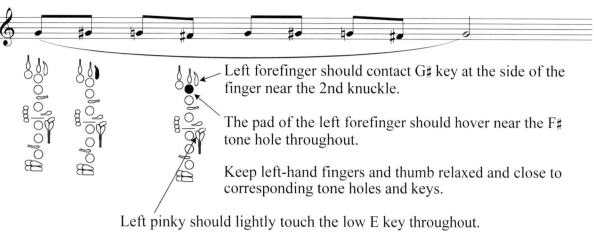

Left forefinger should contact G♯ key at the side of the finger near the 2nd knuckle.

The pad of the left forefinger should hover near the F♯ tone hole throughout.

Keep left-hand fingers and thumb relaxed and close to corresponding tone holes and keys.

Left pinky should lightly touch the low E key throughout.

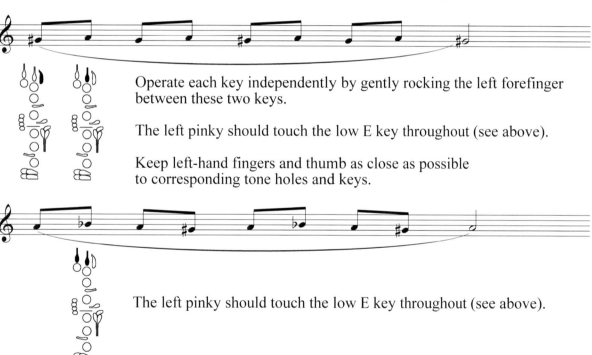

Operate each key independently by gently rocking the left forefinger between these two keys.

The left pinky should touch the low E key throughout (see above).

Keep left-hand fingers and thumb as close as possible to corresponding tone holes and keys.

The left pinky should touch the low E key throughout (see above).

Break Crossing Preparation

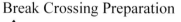

The finger movement required in these two exercises prepares the fingers for "crossing the break" (see the next lesson). Roll (*DO NOT LIFT*) the forefinger between A and F♯. This is similar to rolling or rocking the forefinger downward for the half hole on oboe. The thumb movement required for the B♭ to E interval is also a rolling (pivoting) motion. The left pinky should lightly touch the low E key throughout.

Break Crossings: Chromatic

General
- Practice slowly and observe the slurs—breathe after half notes only.
- Develop a singing impulse: sing first, then play.

Flute
- The flute should not move—finger movement should not jar the flute.
- Check the holding fulcrum (chin, left forefinger, right thumb/pinky).
- Control both inner and outer parts of the lip in order to adjust lip coverage, aperture size, air direction, and air speed.
- Match the tone quality and intonation of open tones C and C♯ with that of D.
- E♭ key is down on C and C♯, up on D.

Oboe
- Use half-hole fingering on C♯ and D—roll left forefinger to and from C.
- Be aware of embouchure factors: cushion, distance, and speed—see p. 22.
- Use a slow but well-supported air stream.
- Circular cushion on tip of reed is important.
- Match tone quality of open tone C with tone quality of the full fingerings for C♯ and D.
- Keep the throat open—see p. 22.

Clarinet
- THIS IS A LEFT-HAND EXERCISE—move the left hand only.
- The right hand stays in place (RHD—right hand down).
- Keep left hand close to the keys for smooth break crossing.
- Left thumb is at approximately a 2 o'clock position; left pinky touches low E key.
- The following exercise will help train the left hand (see previous lesson):

- The right thumb (on the thumb rest) pushes mouthpiece against upper teeth.
- Keep throat tones full and open. Don't bite; allow the lower lip to flex.

Saxophone
- Keep fingers close.
- Check the holding fulcrum.
- Match tone qualities for C♯ and D.
- Check left-thumb movement.

Bassoon
- Use half-hole fingering on F♯ and G.
- The WK (whisper key) should be down throughout this exercise.
- Be aware of embouchure factors: cushion, distance, and speed. See pp. 22–23.
- Match tone quality of open F with the tone of full fingerings on F♯ and G.

Break Crossings: Chromatic

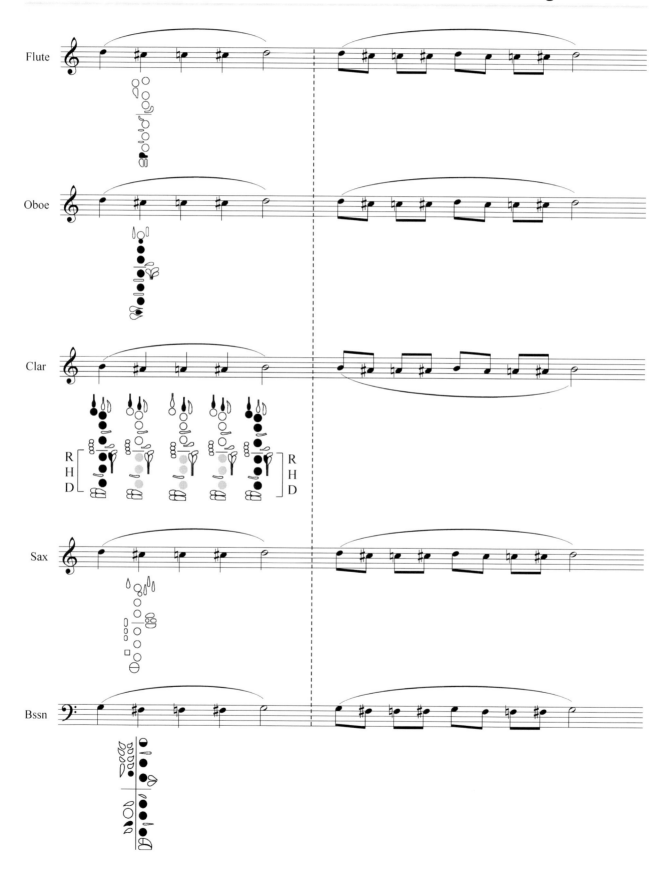

Right Pinky Key Clusters—Low Registers

- All woodwind instruments have right-pinky key clusters.
- These key clusters can be isolated, compared, and easily memorized.
- *On clarinet and oboe, avoid playing two consecutive notes in the same key cluster.*

Procedure

1. Practice the descending (memorized) basic scales that end on D (flute, oboe, sax) or G (clarinet, bassoon), which are the first notes of this exercise.
2. Using that note as a starting tone, practice these right-pinky key clusters.

If Low Notes Do Not Speak

- Check embouchure, finger coverage, and air streams.
- Check alignment of the connecting levers.
- Make certain reeds are wet—use pop tests. See p. 25.
- In general, lower notes speak more readily with a softer reed.
- Low notes on the flute may jump an octave or they may be soft and airy at first—use less lip coverage, slower air stream, and aim the air stream downward by receding the lower lip slightly. Reducing the aperture size will help create more "edge" or "buzz" in the tone in order to increase projection.
- Low notes on oboe and saxophone tend to be more resistive to the air stream and initially may have to be played louder in order to have these notes speak.
- The notes in this exercise should speak readily on the clarinet and bassoon. If not, check finger coverage.

Right Pinky Key Clusters—Low Registers

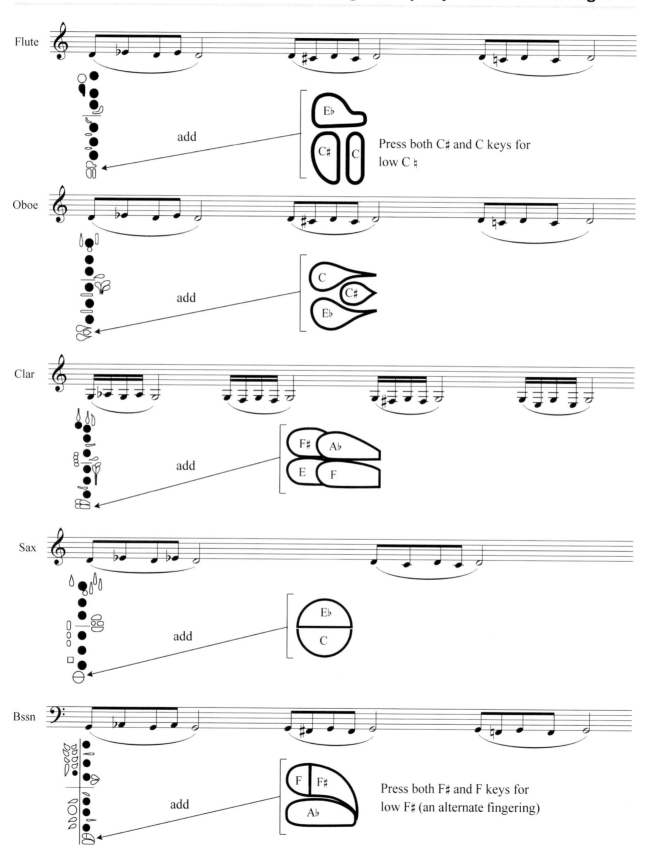

Left Pinky Key Clusters—Low Registers

General

- The flute has only one left-pinky key.
- Left-pinky key clusters on saxophone and bassoon are primarily for the production of low notes.
- *Keys in left-hand pinky clusters on oboe and clarinet are used in alternation with right-hand pinky clusters.*

Flute

- While practicing this exercise before a mirror, check the guide position for the right hand.

Oboe

- These fingerings involve *alternating key clusters* between the right and left clusters.
- Low notes may be resistive at the bottom of the oboe's range—make certain the reed is soaked with a "pop test" (see p. 25) and, if necessary open the tip of the reed very slightly with pressure applied sideways near the string wrapping with the thumb and forefinger. (See p. 48 for photo.)
- *Do not allow the pinky to slide within a cluster*—avoid by alternating clusters as shown.

Clarinet

- These fingerings involve the *alternation of key clusters* between the right and left pinkies.
- Pinky alternation occurs frequently on the clarinet.
- One often sees "L" and "R" marked in clarinet parts to indicate this alternation.
- *Do not allow the pinky to slide within a cluster*—avoid by alternating clusters as shown.

Saxophone

- Unlike oboe and clarinet, the keys in the saxophone clusters are not for alternating—they simply extend the saxophone's range downward.
- The low notes may require loud playing in order to make them speak at first.
- Except for the A♭ key, all other keys in this cluster are for the large keys covering the large tone holes in the upward curve of the bell of the instrument. If the large pads covering these tone holes leak, low notes will be difficult to achieve (see repairs p. 51).

Bassoon

- Keep the throat open and the lower jaw receded.
- If the low notes do not speak, check finger coverage.
- Check closure of connecting levers between the boot, tenor joint, and bocal.
- Make certain the reed is thoroughly soaked, and relax the embouchure cushion. See pp. 22–23.
- If reed seems too closed for these low notes, open the reed blades by squeezing the sides of the reed blades near the first wire with the thumb and forefinger. See p. 48.

Left Pinky Key Clusters—Low Registers

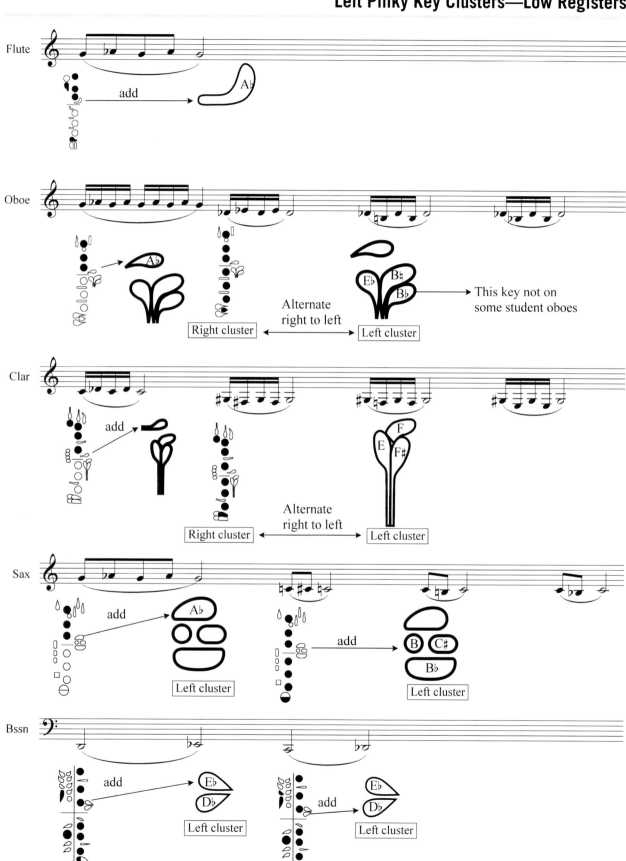

Right Pinky Key Clusters—Middle Registers

As with the lower basic scale, right-pinky key clusters are also applicable to the middle registers of the five woodwind instruments.

General

- When practicing these clusters, retain the given fingering and add the appropriate key within the key cluster.
- It is recommended that one practice these clusters until memorized so that one may check body, holding, and finger coverage in a mirror.

Flute

- Note that the left forefinger is raised for both D and E♭—this is an important fingering habit to develop from the very beginning.
- The E♭ key on the flute also serves as a *resonance key* throughout most of the flute's range as well as a balancing element in holding the flute.

Oboe

- Note that these three notes—the 3 Ds (D♭, D♮, and D♯)—are the only notes which require half-hole fingerings in the middle register of the oboe.
- It is important for the beginning student to memorize the correct fingering for the 3 Ds early in his/her studies.

Clarinet

- Relax the hands and check finger coverage if notes do not speak.
- These notes are all in the clarion register of the clarinet and, like their corresponding notes in the chalumeau register, are notes on which the student can achieve a warm and focused sound.
- Memorizing this key cluster is essential in the early stages of developing one's technique on the clarinet.

Saxophone

- Only one note is involved here in the middle register.
- Practice the exercise in front of a mirror in order to check embouchure (see pp. 20–21) and holding position.

Bassoon

- Note that these three notes—the 3 Gs (G♭, G♮, and G♯) are the only notes which require half-hole fingerings in the middle register of the bassoon.
- It is important for the beginning bassoon student to memorize the 3 Gs early in his/her studies.

Right Pinky Key Clusters—Middle Registers

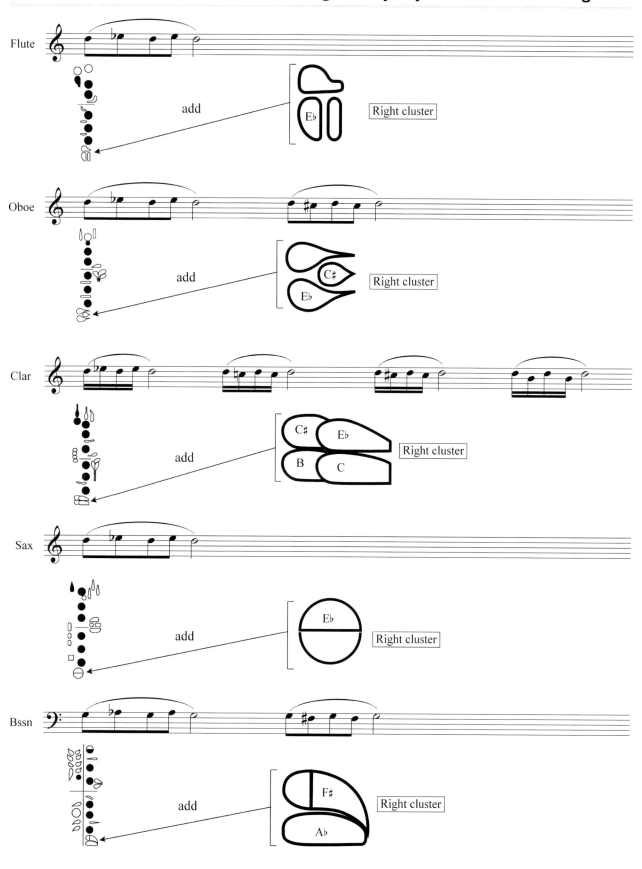

Left Pinky Key Clusters—Middle Registers

All five woodwind instruments utilize left-pinky keys in the middle registers. Before beginning, check the embouchures and air streams with the following:

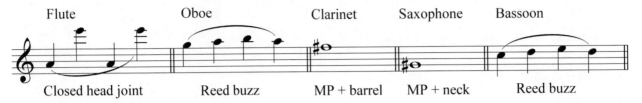

Flute

- The flute does not really have a left-pinky cluster, but it is essential to teach a left-hand position which allows easy pinky access to the A♭ key.
- Be aware of the right-hand position and its role in holding the flute when playing this short exercise.
- Memorize and use a mirror to check.

Oboe

- The alternate left-hand pinky fingering for E♭ is used in both the lower and middle registers.
- It is used with key signatures containing four or more flats or sharps.

Clarinet

- These notes are all in the clarion register and the student should try to play with a tone that is characteristic of this register.
- Alternation of right- and left-pinky clusters is an important part of a clarinetist's technique.

Saxophone

- Be aware of the right-hand guide positioning over key pearls when playing this short exercise.

Bassoon

- The E♭ key is used on middle G to stabilize the pitch.
- Using the E♭ resonator key in the upper register increases the resonance of the bassoon similar to the E♭ key on flute, which is used to add resonance throughout most of its range—see the previous lesson.

Left Pinky Key Clusters—Middle Registers

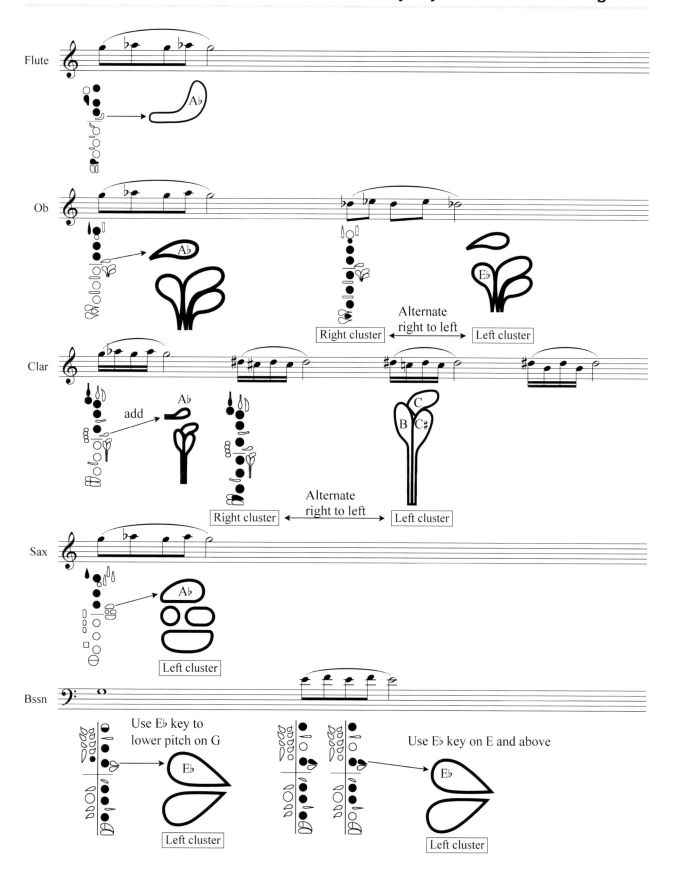

Right Forefinger Clusters

Right forefinger clusters are found on the saxophone, clarinet, and oboe. These keys are operated by the first knuckle of the right forefinger.

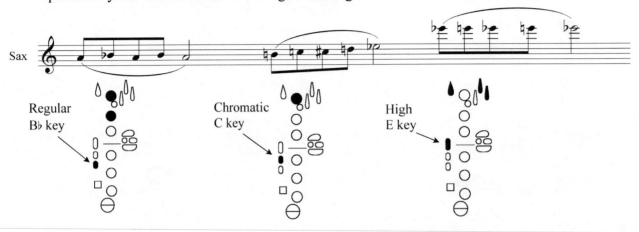

Sax

Regular
B♭ key

Chromatic
C key

High
E key

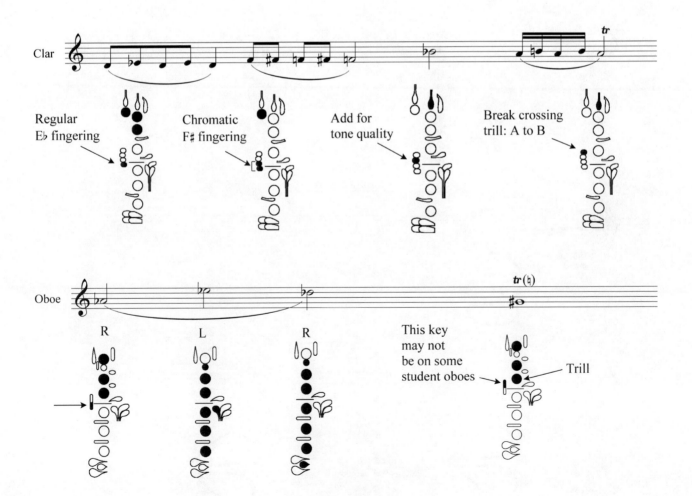

Clar

Regular
E♭ fingering

Chromatic
F♯ fingering

Add for
tone quality

Break crossing
trill: A to B

Oboe

R   L   R

This key
may not
be on some
student oboes

Trill

Left Forefinger Clusters

Left forefinger clusters are found on the saxophone. These Palm Keys (PKs) are cumulative. *Avoid* rotating left wrist and lifting other fingers when pressing PKs.

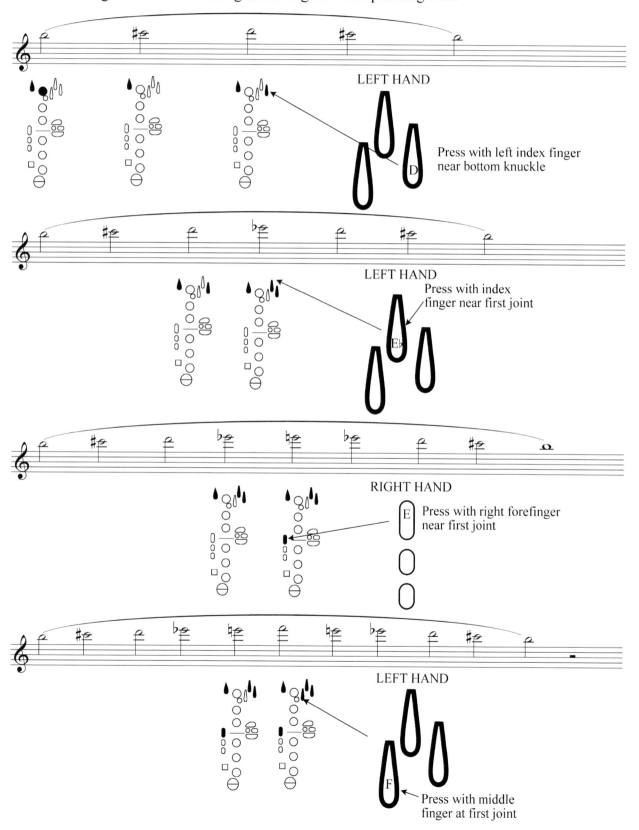

Twig Keys

Twig keys are not part of key clusters. They are found *between* the finger positions used for playing the six-note basic scales.

Flute

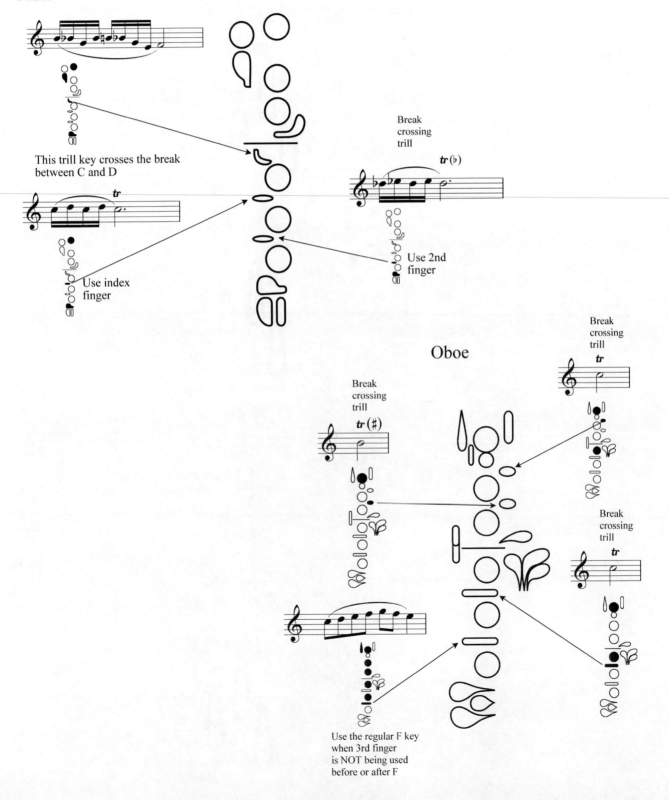

This trill key crosses the break between C and D

Use index finger

Break crossing trill

tr (♭)

Use 2nd finger

Oboe

Break crossing trill

tr

Break crossing trill

tr (♯)

Break crossing trill

tr

Use the regular F key when 3rd finger is NOT being used before or after F

Twig Keys

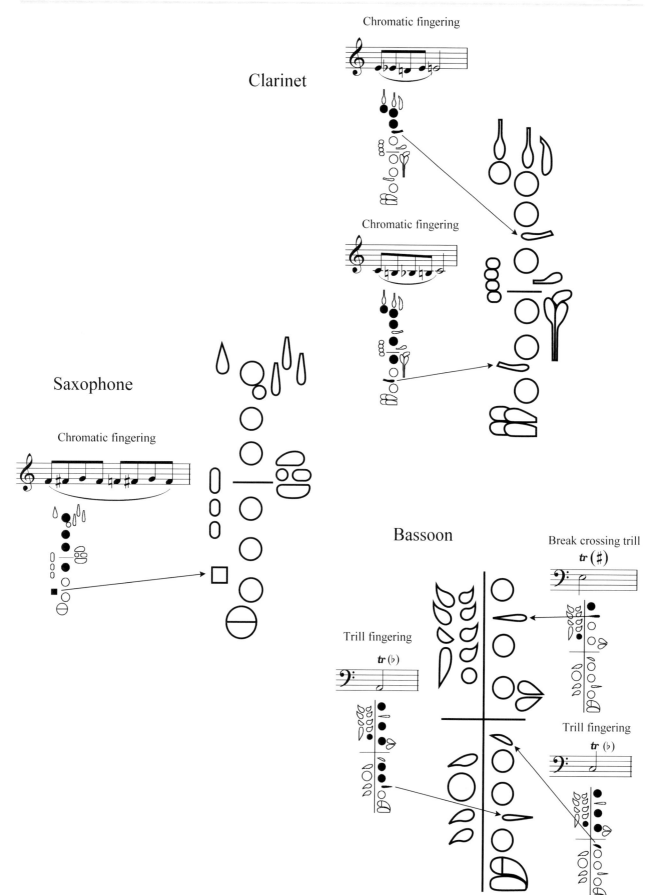

Clarinet

Chromatic fingering

Chromatic fingering

Saxophone

Chromatic fingering

Bassoon

Break crossing trill

$tr\ (\sharp)$

Trill fingering

$tr\ (\flat)$

Trill fingering

$tr\ (\flat)$

Role of the Thumbs

There are thirteen thumb keys on the bassoon including the whisper key (WK), two thumb keys on the flute (B and B♭ keys), and one thumb key on the saxophone (OK), clarinet (RK), and oboe (TOK).

Flute

- On flute, the left thumb is on the B key much of the time. Note that the left thumb *does not* support the flute while playing.
- In holding the flute, the three points of contact *with hands* are: (1) the right thumb, (2) the E♭ resonator key, and (3) the left forefinger.
- Maintain this holding position when playing the following:

Thumb B key

Thumb B♮-Key down on all notes except C

- If the above passage is changed to the key of E♭, it is advantageous to use the thumb B♭ key instead of the B key.
- Use thumb B♭ when B♮s are not present, especially in keys of F, B♭, E♭, and A♭ major.

Thumb B♭ key

Thumb B♭-Key down on all notes except C

Oboe

- The left thumb on the oboe operates the thumb octave key (TOK).
- The thumb can rest on the body of the oboe directly below the TOK or it can hover over the TOK.
- It is used on these notes:

Add TOK (Thumb Octave Key) on upper notes:

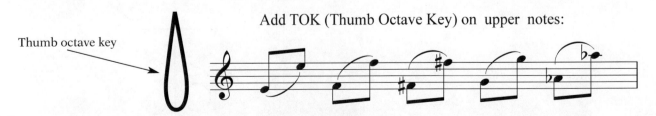

Thumb octave key

- Upper notes will be flat unless embouchure and air adjustments are made. See p. 22.
- Use the touch-tone-teaching exercise to check air flow and intonation. See p. 26.

Role of the Thumbs

Clarinet

• The only woodwind instrument with an actual **thumb hole** is the clarinet.

• Keep the left-hand fingers close to the instrument while practicing the following:

Thumb hole

• The only instrument with a **register key** is the clarinet.

• Place the left thumb diagonally over the thumb hole and pivot the tip of the thumb on the tip of register key.

• Unlike flute, oboe, and bassoon, there should be no adjustment to the air flow or the embouchure.

• Use the touch-tone-teaching concept to illustrate this technique. See p. 27.

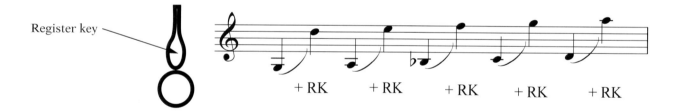

Register key

+ RK   + RK   + RK   + RK   + RK

Saxophone

• The octave key (OK) on the saxophone is operated by the left thumb much the same way as the RK on the clarinet.

• The left thumb should be placed diagonally on the pearl thumb rest so that the tip of the thumb operates the OK with a simple pivoting movement.

• Use the touch-tone-teaching concept to illustrate this technique. See p. 27.

Octave key

+ OK   + OK   + OK   + OK   + OK

Bassoon Thumb Clusters

Summary and Sequence of Teaching Steps

STEP 1   The first thumb key taught to bassoon students should be the **whisper key**. The WK is used on the following notes. (Note that the WK remains in place for the octave exercises used for introducing high registers.)

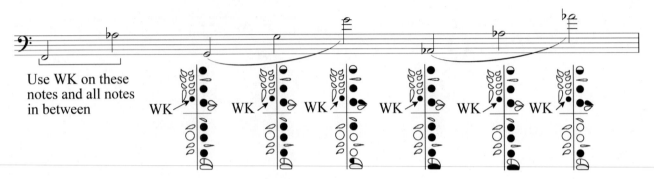

Use WK on these notes and all notes in between

STEP 2   Introduce the student to the thumb keys used for the **C♯s**.

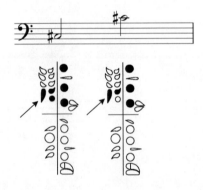

STEP 3   Introduce the student to the thumb keys used in the **right-thumb-cluster** (see the opposite page).

STEP 4   Teach/learn the low notes utilizing the **left-thumb-cluster** (see the opposite page).

STEP 5   Introduce the use of the **flick keys** (see the opposite page).

• Start the lower note with the WK down.

• On the second beat raise the thumb toward the flick key.

• On the third beat, "flick" (tap) the designated key and increase the air speed.

STEP 6   Introduce the **high-note fingerings** (see the opposite page). For the teaching sequence see pp. 110–111.

Bassoon Thumb Clusters

BASSOON: RIGHT-THUMB CLUSTER

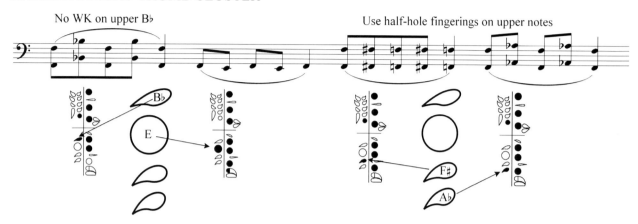

BASSOON: LEFT THUMB CLUSTER: LOW NOTES

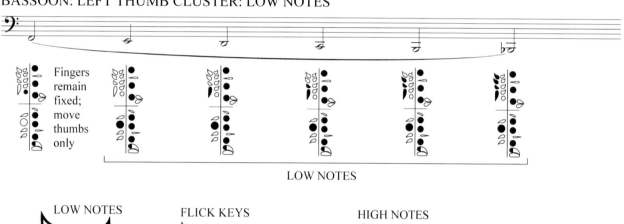

LOW NOTES

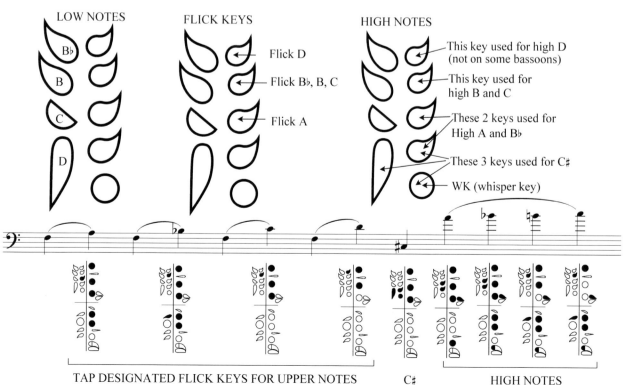

TAP DESIGNATED FLICK KEYS FOR UPPER NOTES   C♯   HIGH NOTES

5 Hands-on Overview: Part III

Introducing High Registers

Flute, Oboe, and Bassoon

A slurred octave approach is recommended in order to achieve the third and highest register on the flute, oboe, and bassoon. Note the similarity of fingerings—this is a *right-hand exercise* for all three instruments. Freeze the left hand and move only the right hand.

At first, remind students to produce the higher tones with simply faster airstreams. The upper notes will probably be louder and sharper until students add embouchure elements to these exercises—see pages 18–19 (flute) and pages 22–23 (oboe and bassoon).

Clarinet

- Review pp. 20–21.
- A slurred ascending passage is used to introduce the altissimo register of the clarinet.
- Keep the air stream constant.
- The lower teeth support the lower lip, but do not bite upwards.
- Keep chin flat.
- Allow the lower lip to flex against the reed.
- Gently push the MP against the upper teeth with the right thumb. Avoid biting.
- One may have to change to a harder reed for this exercise.

Saxophone

- Review pp. 20–21.
- Review the introduction of palm keys on p. 93.
- Establish a firm holding fulcrum: left thumb pushes MP out of mouth; right thumb pushes MP into mouth. See p. 13.
- Keep the air stream constant and raise the neck strap in order to keep the MP pressed firmly against the upper teeth.
- The lower teeth should support the lower lip, but should not bite upwards.
- Allow muscles in the lower lip to flex against the reed.
- One may have to change to a harder reed for this exercise.
- Using slightly more MP in the mouth may help control high notes.

Introducing High Registers

RIGHT-HAND EXERCISES

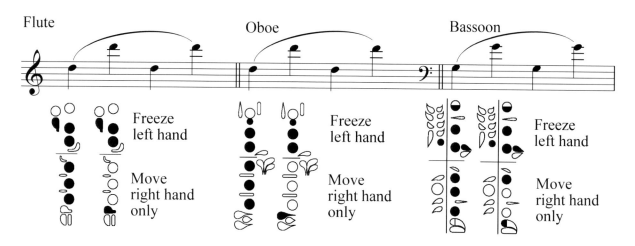

Flute

Freeze
left hand

Move
right hand
only

Oboe

Freeze
left hand

Move
right hand
only

Bassoon

Freeze
left hand

Move
right hand
only

TWO-FINGER EXERCISE

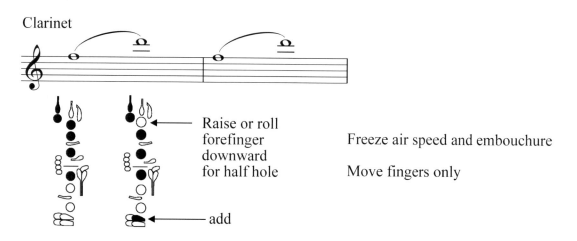

Clarinet

Raise or roll
forefinger
downward
for half hole

add

Freeze air speed and embouchure

Move fingers only

LEFT-HAND EXERCISE

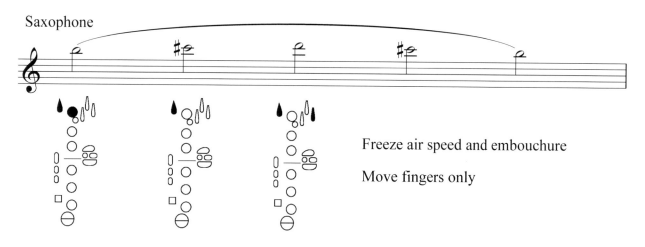

Saxophone

Freeze air speed and embouchure

Move fingers only

Introducing Secondary Break Crossings

General
Slurring ascending octaves/registers is helpful in learning the fingerings and achieving embouchure/air control of the high register.

Flute
For high D and C try the following:
- High notes will be louder at first. Increase *air speed* by using a smaller aperture.
- Cover *more* of the embouchure hole with the lower lip.
- Pucker slightly in order to increase the lip coverage and raise the air stream.
- Turn lower lip outward so that air passes over the inner lip tissue.

Oboe
For high D and C try the following:
- Use faster *air speeds*.
- Increase the amount of reed in mouth.
- Decrease the reed aperture. Use a firmer lip cushion—think circular.
- Review the 3-D octave exercise on 22.

Clarinet
For high D and C try the following:
- The right thumb pushes MP pressure toward the upper teeth.
- Don't bite (this chokes the tone). Allow the muscles in the lower lip to flex.
- Keep the air stream and embouchure constant.
- Try rolling the left forefinger downward for the half hole.
- One may have to change to a harder reed for these exercises.
- If the student continues to choke the tone, the teacher can place thumb and forefinger on the barrel and *gently* pull MP upwards (against the student's upper teeth) while the student plays.

Saxophone
For high D and C try the following:
- Keep the air stream and embouchure constant. Do not overblow high notes.
- Avoid rotating the left-hand wrist when playing the high D palm key. See p. 93.
- The palm key is depressed with the left index finger near the bottom knuckle. See p. 93.
- Do not bite, the lower teeth should allow the muscles of the lower lip to flex.
- One may have to change to a harder reed for these exercises.

Bassoon
For high G and F try the following:
- Use faster *air speeds*.
- Increase the amount of reed in the mouth.
- Decrease the reed aperture. Use a firmer lip cushion—think circular.
- Review the 3-G octave exercise on p. 23.

Introducing Secondary Break Crossings

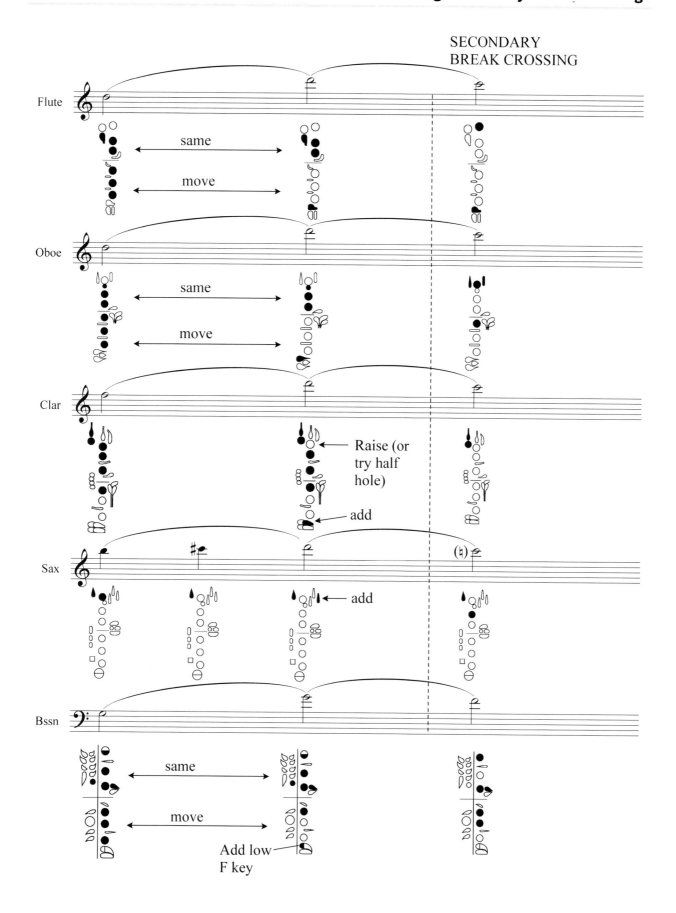

Connecting the Three Registers—Flute

FLUTE: CONNECTING THE THREE REGISTERS (TEN STEPS)

1. Practice 3-Ds

2. Introduce high C♯

3. Extended exercise

4. Practice D major scale (2 octaves)

5. Introduce high E♭

6. Extended exercise

7. Practice E♭ major scale (2 octaves)

8. Introduce high F

9. Extended exercise (as above)

10. Practice F major scale (2 octaves)

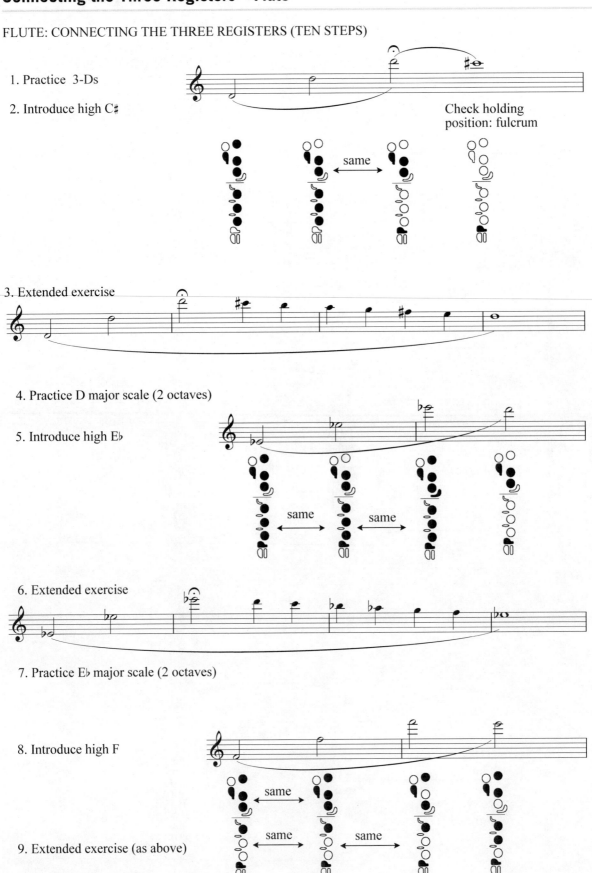

Connecting the Three Registers—Oboe

OBOE: CONNECTING THE THREE REGISTERS (SEVEN STEPS)

1. Practice 3-Ds

2. Introduce high C♯

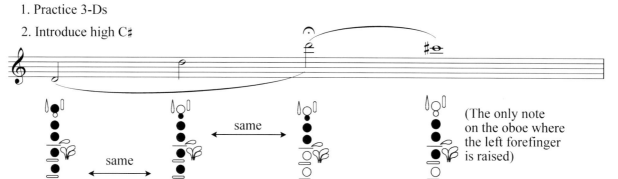

(The only note
on the oboe where
the left forefinger
is raised)

3. Extended exercise

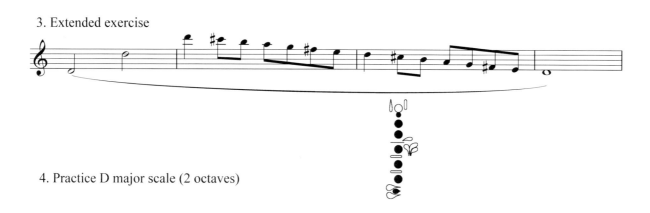

4. Practice D major scale (2 octaves)

5. Introduce high E♭

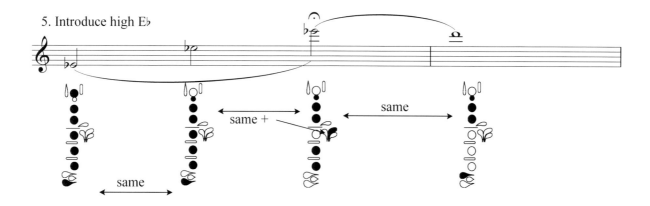

6. Extended exercise

7. Practice E♭ major scale (2 octaves)

Connecting the Three Registers—Clarinet

CLARINET: CONNECTING THE THREE REGISTERS (FIVE STEPS)

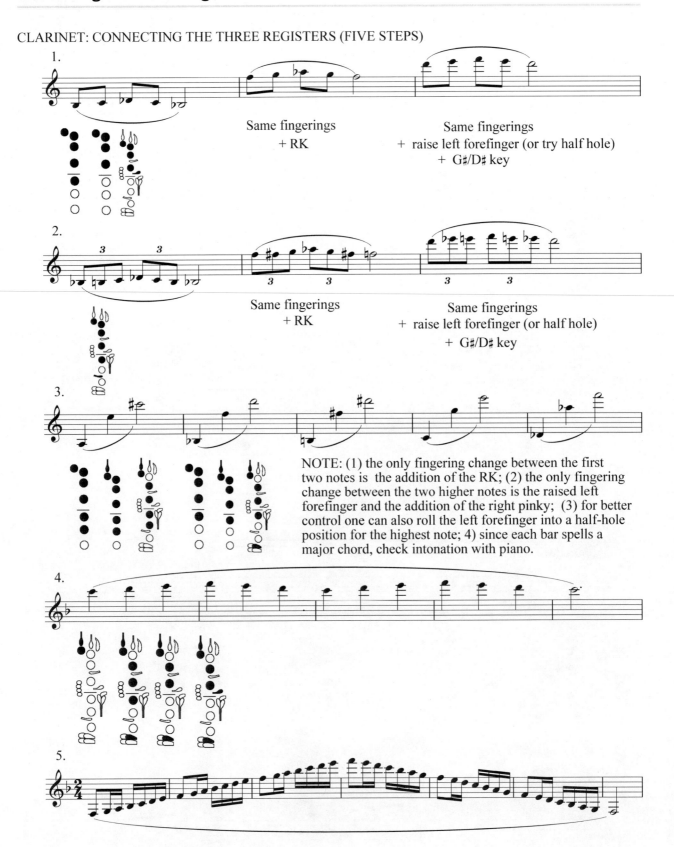

Same fingerings
+ RK

Same fingerings
+ raise left forefinger (or try half hole)
+ G♯/D♯ key

Same fingerings
+ RK

Same fingerings
+ raise left forefinger (or half hole)
+ G♯/D♯ key

NOTE: (1) the only fingering change between the first two notes is the addition of the RK; (2) the only fingering change between the two higher notes is the raised left forefinger and the addition of the right pinky; (3) for better control one can also roll the left forefinger into a half-hole position for the highest note; 4) since each bar spells a major chord, check intonation with piano.

Connecting the Three Registers—Saxophone

SAXOPHONE: CONNECTING THE THREE REGISTERS (FOUR STEPS)

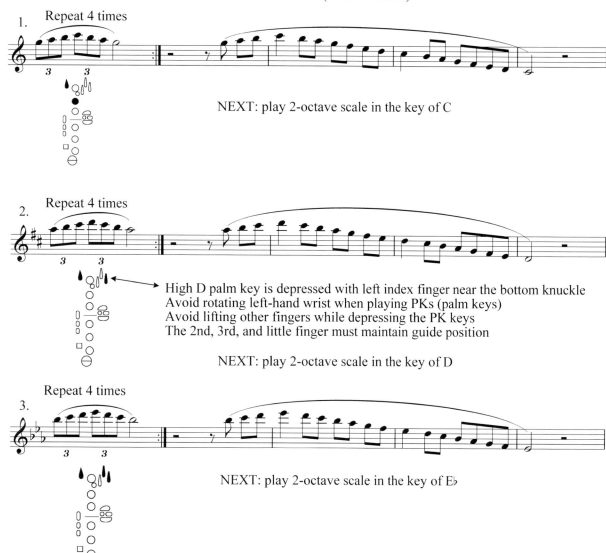

NEXT: play 2-octave scale in the key of C

High D palm key is depressed with left index finger near the bottom knuckle
Avoid rotating left-hand wrist when playing PKs (palm keys)
Avoid lifting other fingers while depressing the PK keys
The 2nd, 3rd, and little finger must maintain guide position

NEXT: play 2-octave scale in the key of D

NEXT: play 2-octave scale in the key of E♭

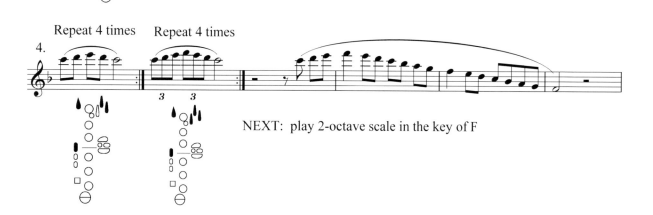

NEXT: play 2-octave scale in the key of F

Connecting the Three Registers—Bassoon

BASSOON: CONNECTING THE THREE REGISTERS (SEVEN STEPS)

1. Teach 3-Gs

2. Introduce high F♯

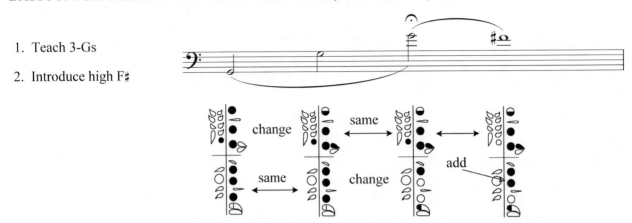

3. Combining Registers

4. Practice G major scale (2 octaves)

5. Introduce high A♭

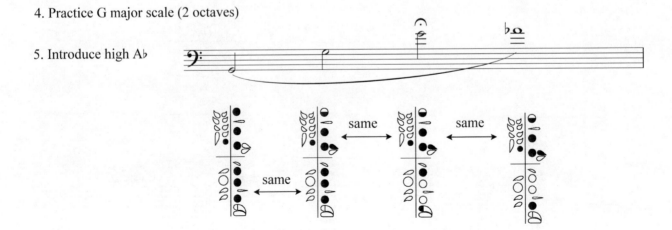

6. Combining Registers

7. Practice A♭ major scale (2 octaves)

Connecting the Three Registers—Bassoon

BASSOON: EXPANDING THE UPPER REGISTER (FIVE STEPS)

1. Start with 3-Gs

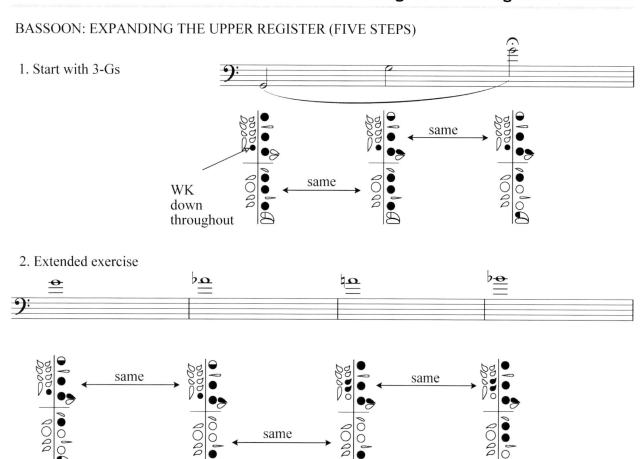

2. Extended exercise

3. Practice until fluent

Move RH only   Move LH only   Move RH only

4. Practice descending B♭ major scale

5. Practice 2-octave B♭ major scale

6 Fingering Review

Seven Steps For Learning/Teaching Fingerings

The following seven steps summarize the material presented in chapters 3, 4, and 5.

STEP 1   Introduce the basic six-note scales (low register) (refer to pp. 60–61)

STEP 2   Introduce break crossings and the seven register (octave) mechanisms (refer to pp. 64–65)

   1. **RK**—register key (clarinet)

   2. **OK**—octave key (saxophone)

   3. **TOK**—thumb octave key (oboe)

   4. **SOK**—side octave key (oboe)

   5. **¹/₂ H**—half hole (oboe and bassoon)

   6. **WK**—whisper key (bassoon)

   7. **FLK**—flick or speaker keys (bassoon)

STEP 3   Introduce the basic six-note scales (middle registers) (refer to pp. 68–69)

STEP 4   Introduce the basic chromatic scales and the chromatic break crossings (refer to pp. 76–79; 82–83)

STEP 5   Introduce key clusters and twig keys (refer to pp. 84–95)

STEP 6   Introduce high-note exercises and secondary break crossings (refer to pp. 102–105)

STEP 7   Connecting the three registers (refer to pp. 106–111)

Fingering Charts for the Basic Fingerings—Flute

Flute

Regular normal fingerings—teach first

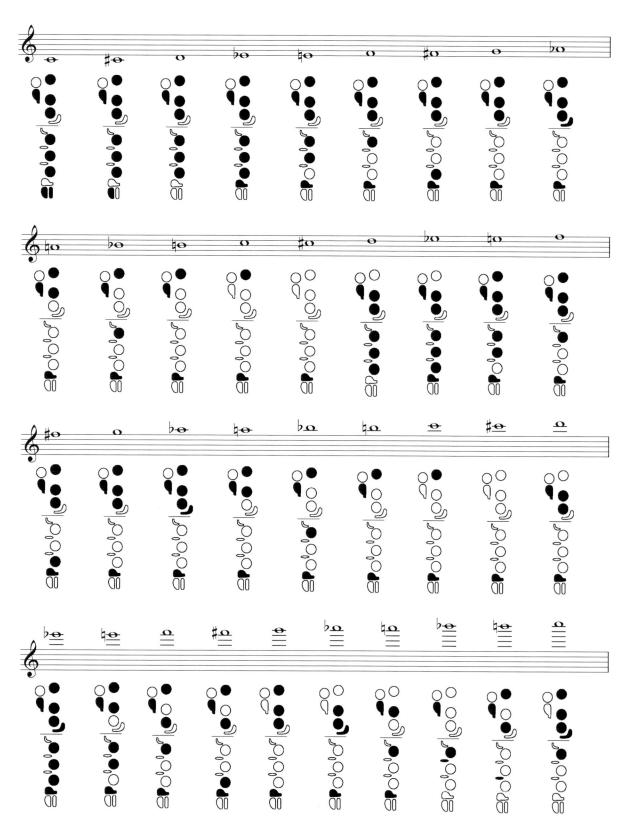

Fingering Charts for the Basic Fingerings—Oboe

Oboe

Regular normal fingerings—teach first

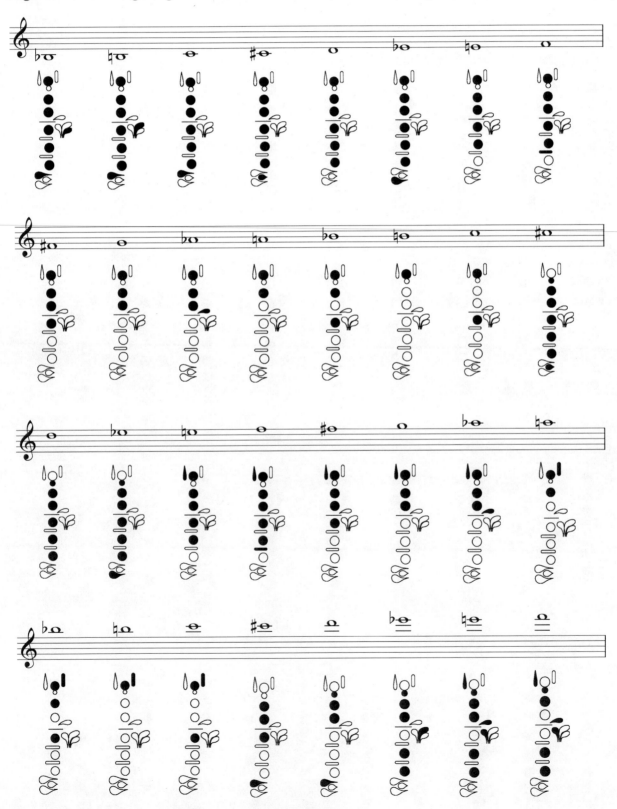

Fingering Charts for the Basic Fingerings—Clarinet

Clarinet

Regular normal fingerings—teach first

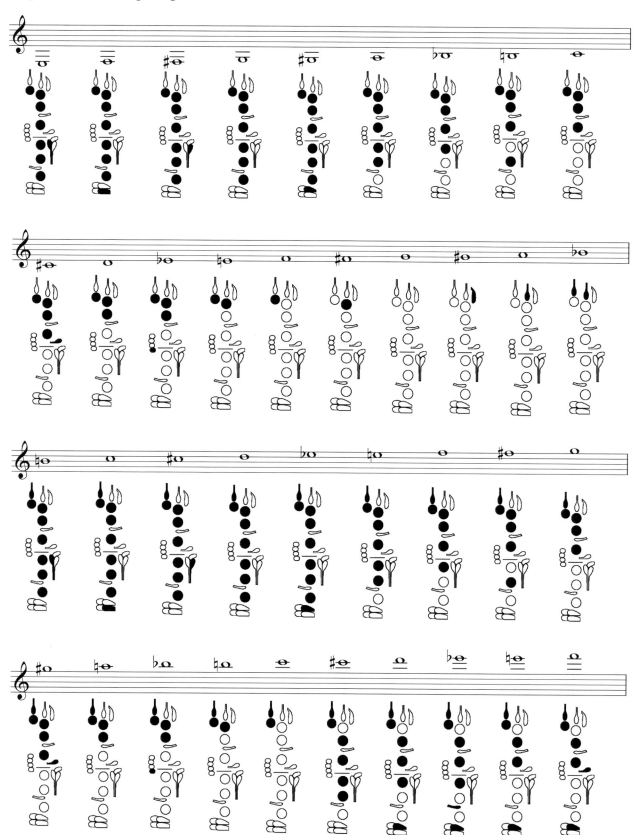

Fingering Charts for the Basic Fingerings—Saxophone

Saxophone

Regular normal fingerings—teach first

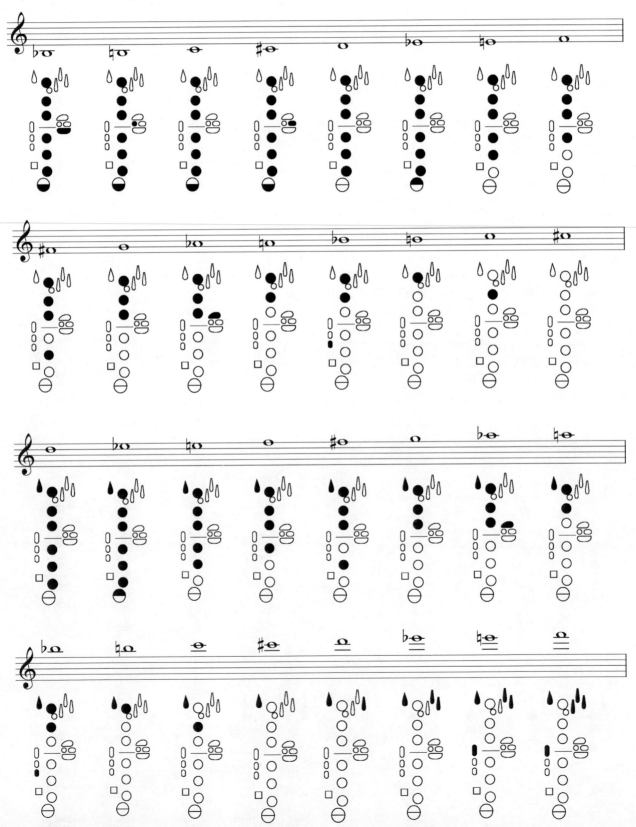

Fingering Charts for the Basic Fingerings—Bassoon

Bassoon

Regular normal fingerings—teach first

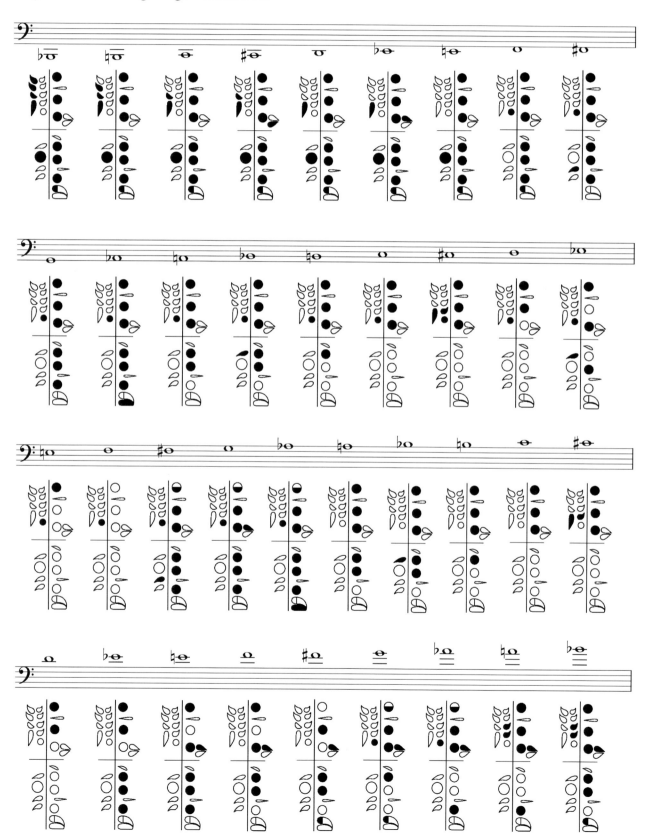

Hands-on Review: Major Scales

Scale Review: Major Scales

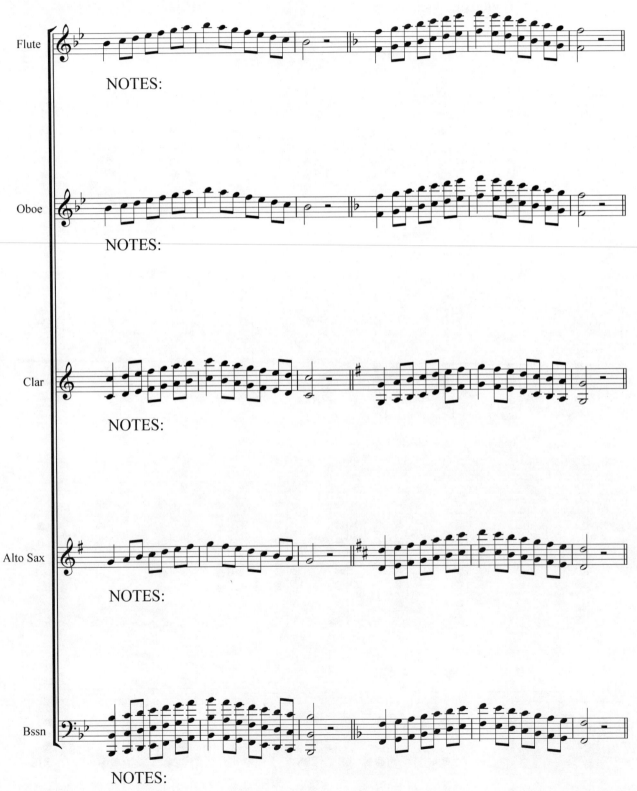

Flute

NOTES:

Oboe

NOTES:

Clar

NOTES:

Alto Sax

NOTES:

Bssn

NOTES:

Hands-on Review: Major Scales

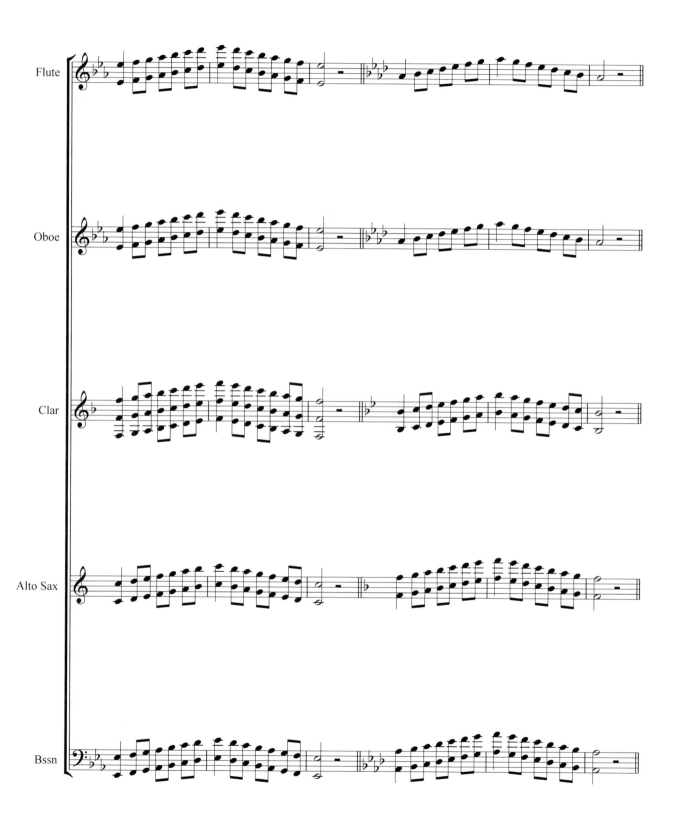

Hands-on Review: Minor Scales

Scale Review: Minor Scales

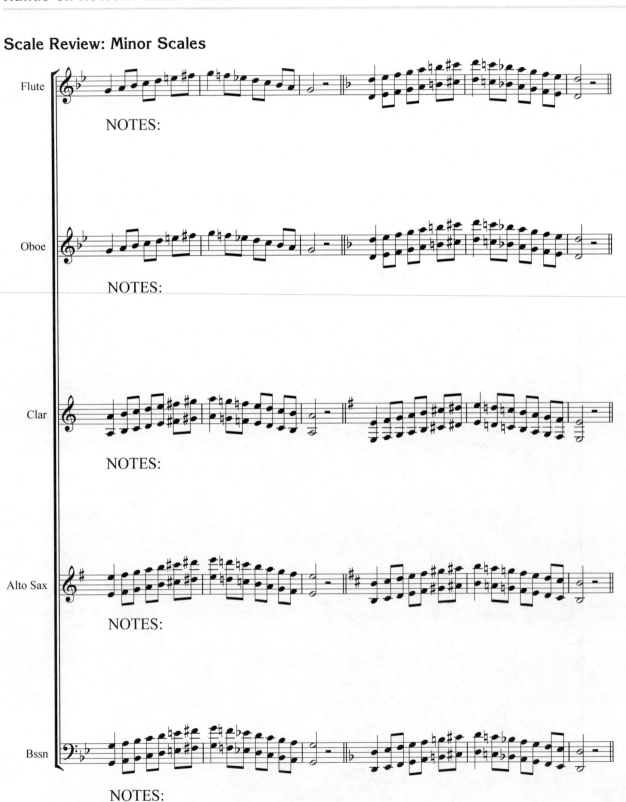

Flute

NOTES:

Oboe

NOTES:

Clar

NOTES:

Alto Sax

NOTES:

Bssn

NOTES:

Hands-on Review: Minor Scales

Hands-on Review: Chromatic Scales

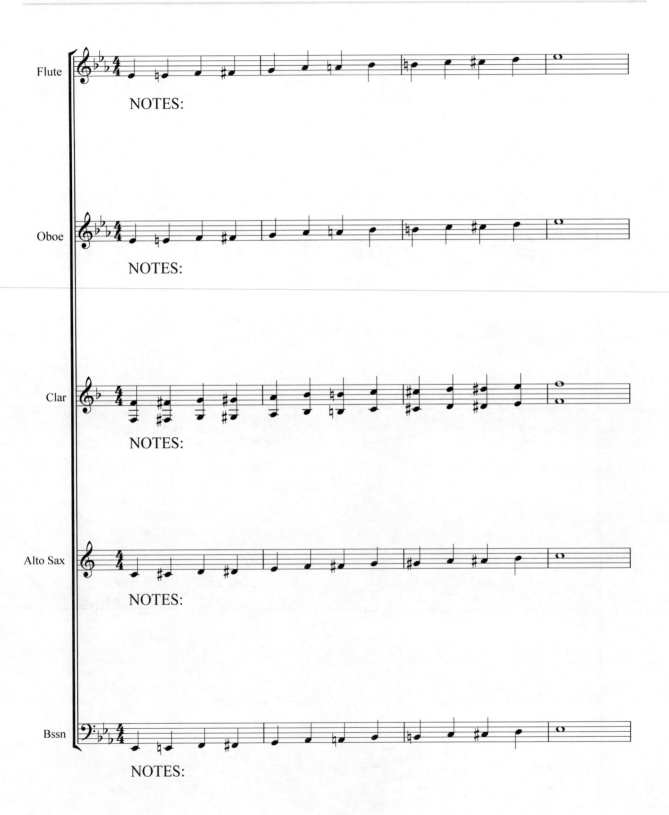

Flute

NOTES:

Oboe

NOTES:

Clar

NOTES:

Alto Sax

NOTES:

Bssn

NOTES:

Hands-on Review: Chromatic Scales

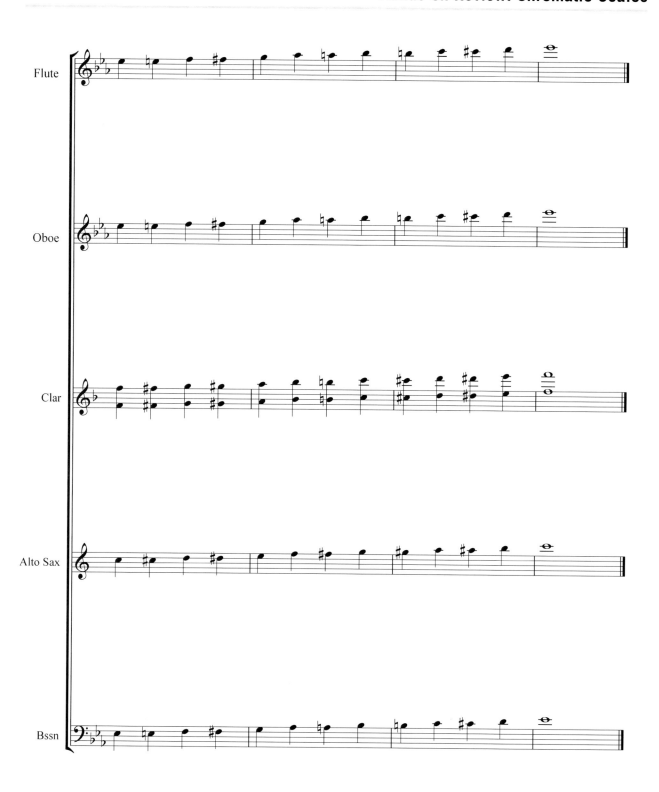

Hands-on Review: Chromatic Scales

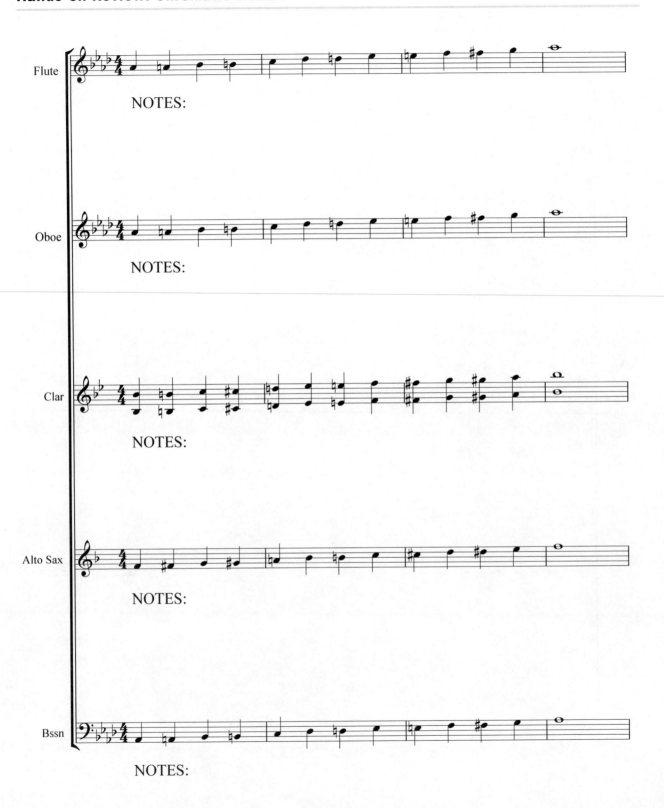

Flute

NOTES:

Oboe

NOTES:

Clar

NOTES:

Alto Sax

NOTES:

Bssn

NOTES:

Hands-on Review: Chromatic Scales

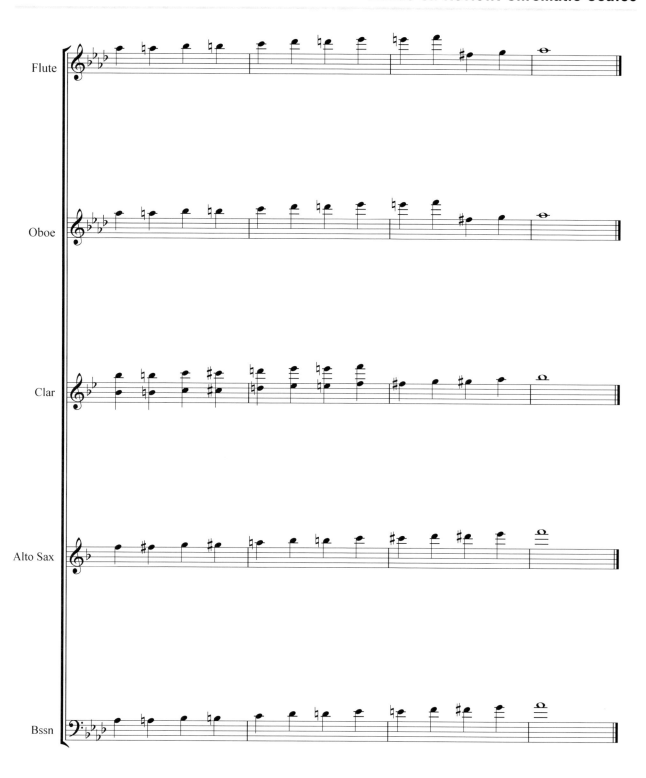

Blank Fingering Charts—Flute

Flute

Fill in the regular normal fingerings (answers on p. 115)

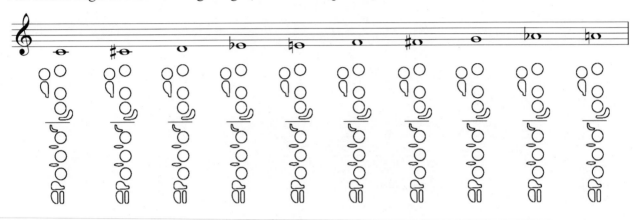

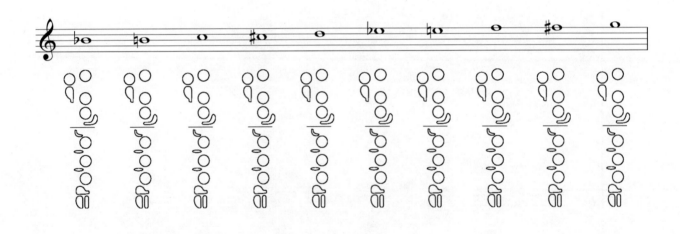

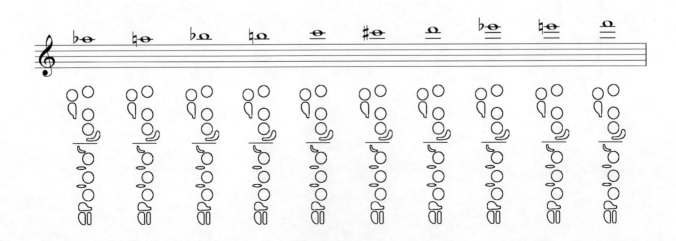

Blank Fingering Charts—Oboe

Oboe

Fill in the regular normal fingerings (answers on p. 116)

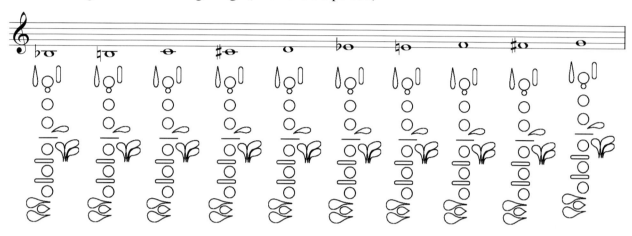

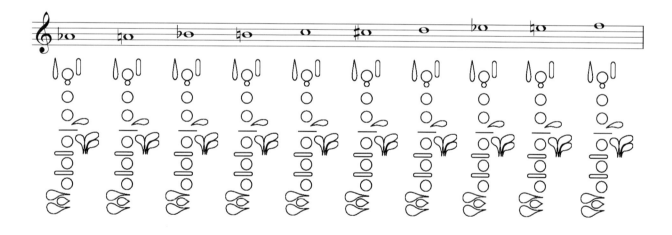

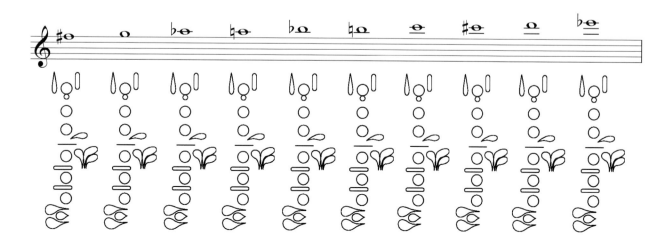

Blank Fingering Charts—Clarinet

Clarinet

Fill in the regular normal fingerings (answers on p. 117)

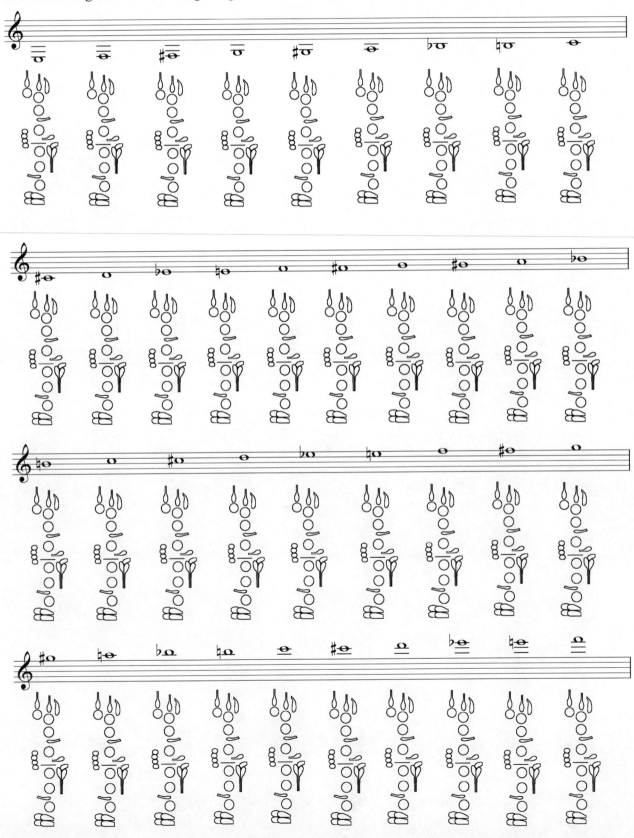

Blank Fingering Charts—Saxophone

Saxophone

Fill in the regular normal fingerings (answers on p. 118)

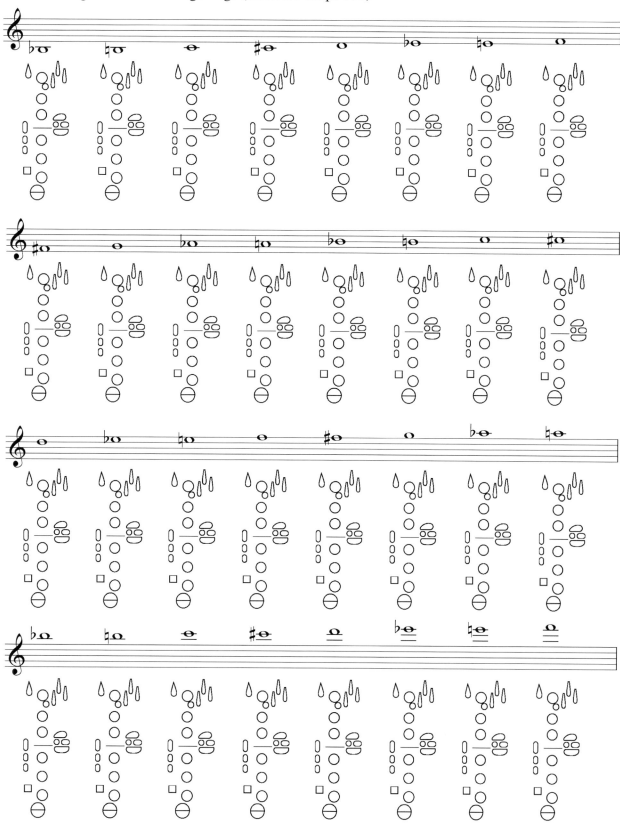

Blank Fingering Charts—Bassoon

Bassoon

Fill in the regular normal fingerings (answers on p. 119)

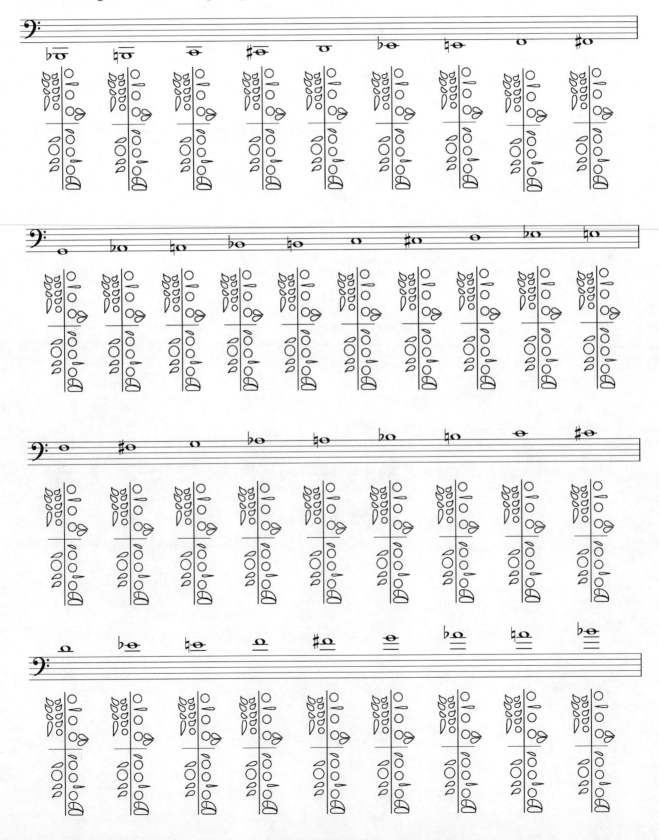

7 Technique/Tunes: Twenty-five Class Lessons

Technique/Tunes—Introduction

- In these twenty-five lessons, previously discussed pedagogy is applied to actual tunes commonly found in band method books.

- The opposite-page format introduces the user to fingerings and pedagogical exercises on the left page, which are directly applicable to the tune on the right page.

- The "Practice Tips" (see p. 57) for individual preparation are also applicable to directing ensembles.

- A teacher uses *visual analysis* by observing student embouchures and hand/body position.

- At the same time the teacher uses *aural analysis* by observing tone quality, articulation, intonation, and general expression of the ensemble.

- As mentioned earlier, the definition of practice (rehearsing) is "accurate repetition." The key is to practice slowly and accurately and avoid practicing mistakes. This also applies to ensemble rehearsals.

- Fragmenting passages and repeating them accurately is effective for individuals as well as for ensembles.

- Identifying the problem spots is the first step. Applying the required pedagogical steps, such as analysis of mouthpiece pitches, scales, break crossing, and so on, is the second step. Putting it all back together again is the third step.

- Above all, maintain a singing impulse.

  N O T E :

  These lessons follow the pacing found in band method books. The introduction of the clarion register on the clarinet follows the practice used in most band method books, i.e., it is delayed in order to give students time to develop their left-hand playing positions. (The clarinet is the only woodwind instrument on which the left hand is not anchored to the body of the instrument.)

  N O T E :

  If students have oboes equipped with left-hand F keys (see page 42), use the left F fingerings instead of forked F fingerings in the lessons. The left F fingering produces better tone quality and intonation than the forked F fingering.

Lesson 1

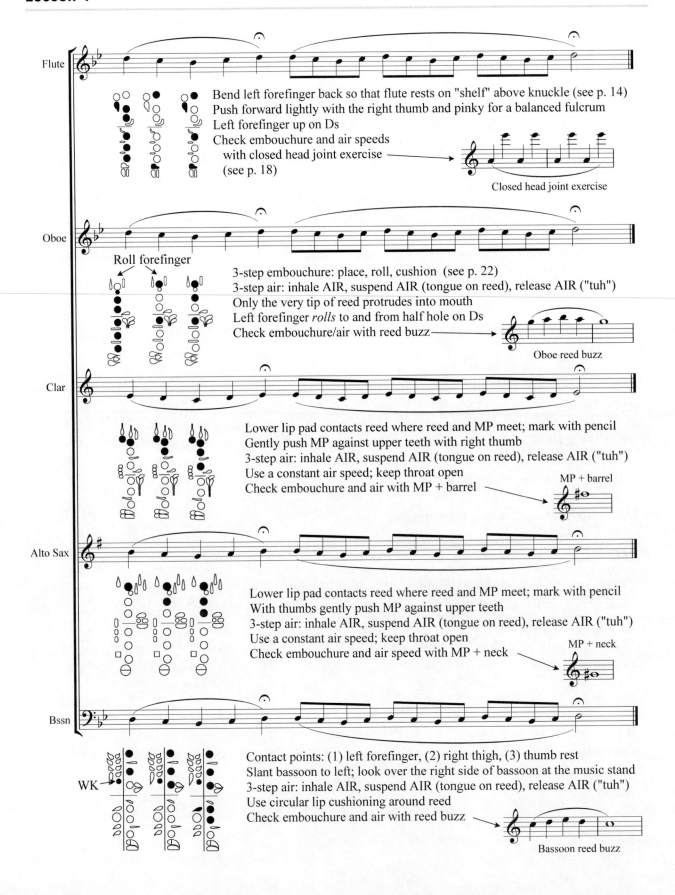

Flute

Bend left forefinger back so that flute rests on "shelf" above knuckle (see p. 14)
Push forward lightly with the right thumb and pinky for a balanced fulcrum
Left forefinger up on Ds
Check embouchure and air speeds
  with closed head joint exercise
  (see p. 18)

Closed head joint exercise

Oboe

Roll forefinger

3-step embouchure: place, roll, cushion (see p. 22)
3-step air: inhale AIR, suspend AIR (tongue on reed), release AIR ("tuh")
Only the very tip of reed protrudes into mouth
Left forefinger *rolls* to and from half hole on Ds
Check embouchure/air with reed buzz

Oboe reed buzz

Clar

Lower lip pad contacts reed where reed and MP meet; mark with pencil
Gently push MP against upper teeth with right thumb
3-step air: inhale AIR, suspend AIR (tongue on reed), release AIR ("tuh")
Use a constant air speed; keep throat open
Check embouchure and air with MP + barrel

MP + barrel

Alto Sax

Lower lip pad contacts reed where reed and MP meet; mark with pencil
With thumbs gently push MP against upper teeth
3-step air: inhale AIR, suspend AIR (tongue on reed), release AIR ("tuh")
Use a constant air speed; keep throat open
Check embouchure and air speed with MP + neck

MP + neck

Bssn

WK →

Contact points: (1) left forefinger, (2) right thigh, (3) thumb rest
Slant bassoon to left; look over the right side of bassoon at the music stand
3-step air: inhale AIR, suspend AIR (tongue on reed), release AIR ("tuh")
Use circular lip cushioning around reed
Check embouchure and air with reed buzz

Bassoon reed buzz

Hot Cross Buns—English Folk Song

Lesson 2

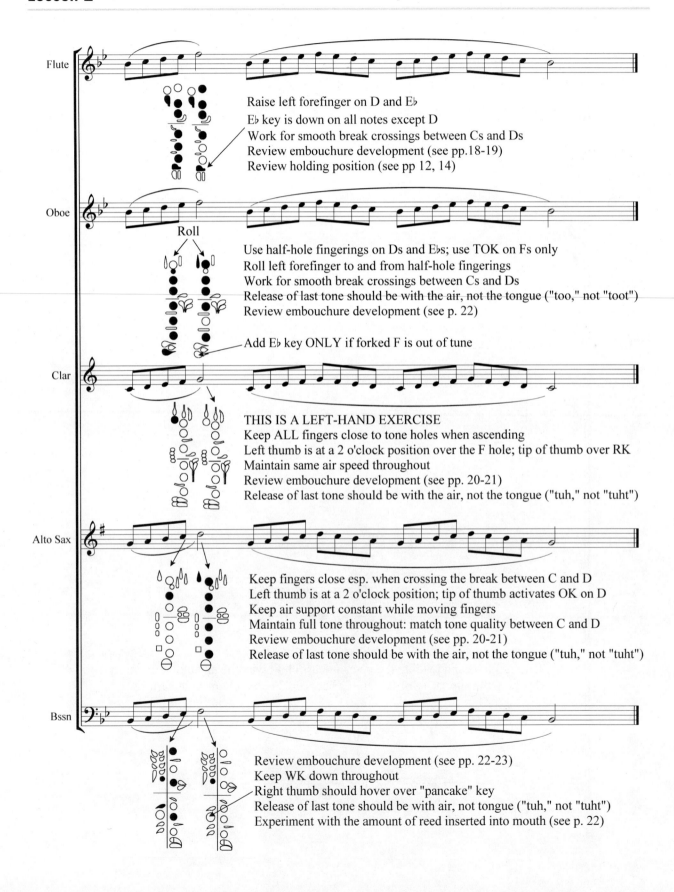

Flute

Raise left forefinger on D and E♭
E♭ key is down on all notes except D
Work for smooth break crossings between Cs and Ds
Review embouchure development (see pp.18-19)
Review holding position (see pp 12, 14)

Oboe

Roll

Use half-hole fingerings on Ds and E♭s; use TOK on Fs only
Roll left forefinger to and from half-hole fingerings
Work for smooth break crossings between Cs and Ds
Release of last tone should be with the air, not the tongue ("too," not "toot")
Review embouchure development (see p. 22)

Add E♭ key ONLY if forked F is out of tune

Clar

THIS IS A LEFT-HAND EXERCISE
Keep ALL fingers close to tone holes when ascending
Left thumb is at a 2 o'clock position over the F hole; tip of thumb over RK
Maintain same air speed throughout
Review embouchure development (see pp. 20-21)
Release of last tone should be with the air, not the tongue ("tuh," not "tuht")

Alto Sax

Keep fingers close esp. when crossing the break between C and D
Left thumb is at a 2 o'clock position; tip of thumb activates OK on D
Keep air support constant while moving fingers
Maintain full tone throughout: match tone quality between C and D
Review embouchure development (see pp. 20-21)
Release of last tone should be with the air, not the tongue ("tuh," not "tuht")

Bssn

Review embouchure development (see pp. 22-23)
Keep WK down throughout
Right thumb should hover over "pancake" key
Release of last tone should be with air, not tongue ("tuh," not "tuht")
Experiment with the amount of reed inserted into mouth (see p. 22)

Lesson 2

Go Tell Aunt Rhodie—American Folk Song

Lesson 3

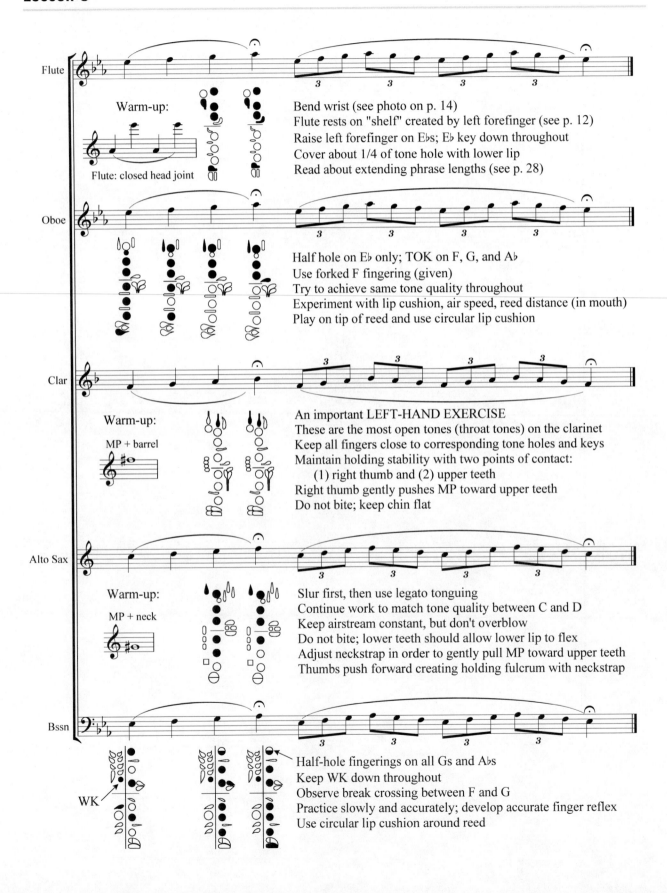

Flute

Warm-up:

Flute: closed head joint

Bend wrist (see photo on p. 14)
Flute rests on "shelf" created by left forefinger (see p. 12)
Raise left forefinger on E♭s; E♭ key down throughout
Cover about 1/4 of tone hole with lower lip
Read about extending phrase lengths (see p. 28)

Oboe

Half hole on E♭ only; TOK on F, G, and A♭
Use forked F fingering (given)
Try to achieve same tone quality throughout
Experiment with lip cushion, air speed, reed distance (in mouth)
Play on tip of reed and use circular lip cushion

Clar

Warm-up:

MP + barrel

An important LEFT-HAND EXERCISE
These are the most open tones (throat tones) on the clarinet
Keep all fingers close to corresponding tone holes and keys
Maintain holding stability with two points of contact:
　　(1) right thumb and (2) upper teeth
Right thumb gently pushes MP toward upper teeth
Do not bite; keep chin flat

Alto Sax

Warm-up:

MP + neck

Slur first, then use legato tonguing
Continue work to match tone quality between C and D
Keep airstream constant, but don't overblow
Do not bite; lower teeth should allow lower lip to flex
Adjust neckstrap in order to gently pull MP toward upper teeth
Thumbs push forward creating holding fulcrum with neckstrap

Bssn

WK

Half-hole fingerings on all Gs and A♭s
Keep WK down throughout
Observe break crossing between F and G
Practice slowly and accurately; develop accurate finger reflex
Use circular lip cushion around reed

Lesson 3

Yankee Doodle—American Folk Song

Lesson 4

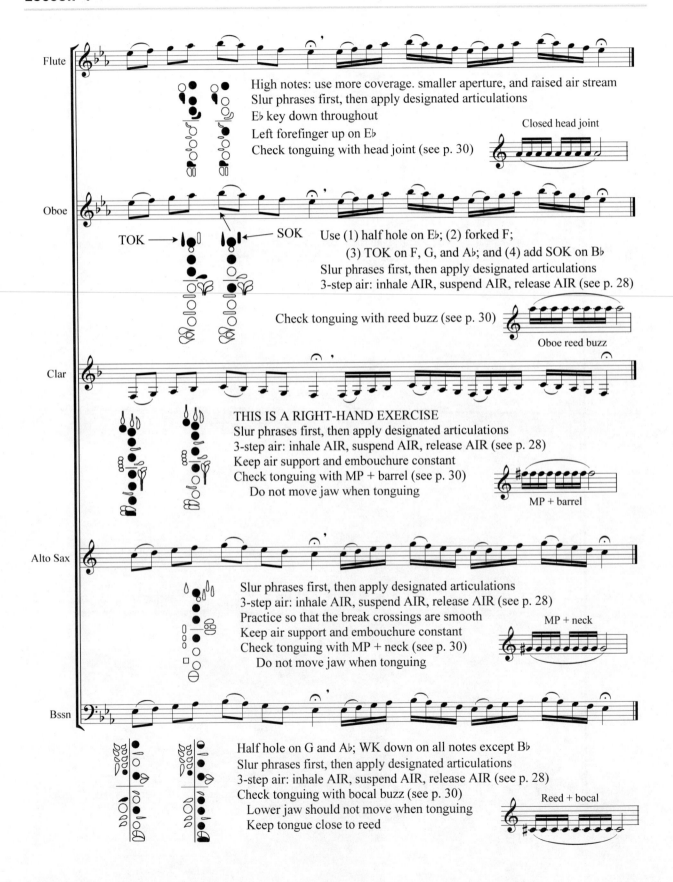

Flute

High notes: use more coverage. smaller aperture, and raised air stream
Slur phrases first, then apply designated articulations
E♭ key down throughout
Left forefinger up on E♭
Check tonguing with head joint (see p. 30)

Closed head joint

Oboe

TOK →   ← SOK

Use (1) half hole on E♭; (2) forked F;
   (3) TOK on F, G, and A♭; and (4) add SOK on B♭
Slur phrases first, then apply designated articulations
3-step air: inhale AIR, suspend AIR, release AIR (see p. 28)

Check tonguing with reed buzz (see p. 30)

Oboe reed buzz

Clar

THIS IS A RIGHT-HAND EXERCISE
Slur phrases first, then apply designated articulations
3-step air: inhale AIR, suspend AIR, release AIR (see p. 28)
Keep air support and embouchure constant
Check tonguing with MP + barrel (see p. 30)
   Do not move jaw when tonguing

MP + barrel

Alto Sax

Slur phrases first, then apply designated articulations
3-step air: inhale AIR, suspend AIR, release AIR (see p. 28)
Practice so that the break crossings are smooth
Keep air support and embouchure constant
Check tonguing with MP + neck (see p. 30)
   Do not move jaw when tonguing

MP + neck

Bssn

Half hole on G and A♭; WK down on all notes except B♭
Slur phrases first, then apply designated articulations
3-step air: inhale AIR, suspend AIR, release AIR (see p. 28)
Check tonguing with bocal buzz (see p. 30)
   Lower jaw should not move when tonguing
   Keep tongue close to reed

Reed + bocal

Lesson 4

Shepherd's Hey—English Folk Song

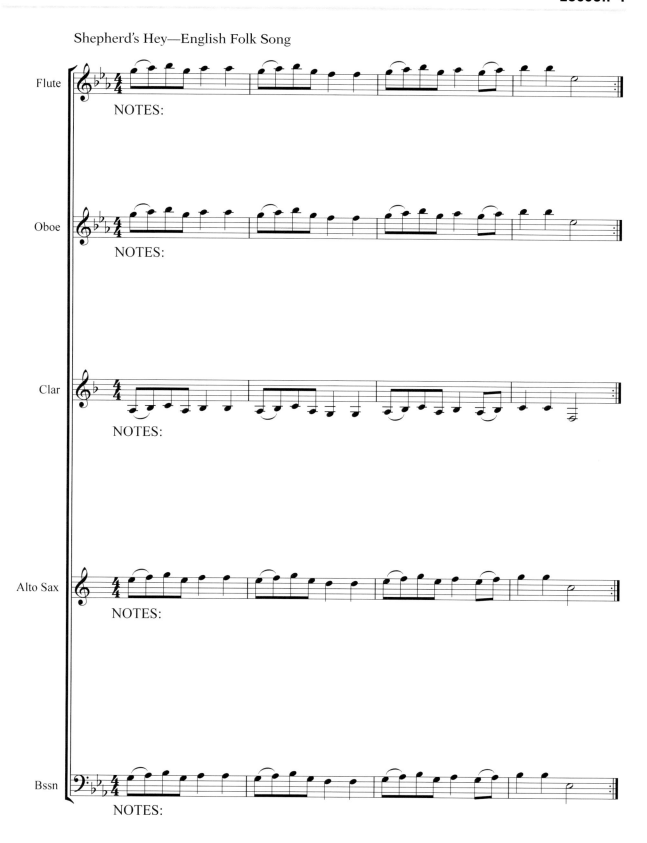

Lesson 5

This scale may also be performed as a Teacher/Student Duet—p. 190.

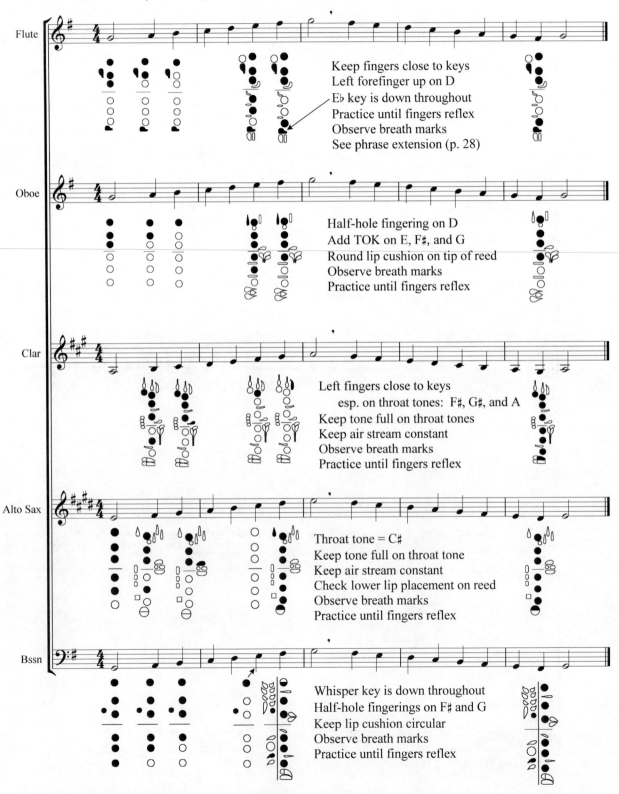

Flute

Keep fingers close to keys
Left forefinger up on D
Eb key is down throughout
Practice until fingers reflex
Observe breath marks
See phrase extension (p. 28)

Oboe

Half-hole fingering on D
Add TOK on E, F♯, and G
Round lip cushion on tip of reed
Observe breath marks
Practice until fingers reflex

Clar

Left fingers close to keys
   esp. on throat tones: F♯, G♯, and A
Keep tone full on throat tones
Keep air stream constant
Observe breath marks
Practice until fingers reflex

Alto Sax

Throat tone = C♯
Keep tone full on throat tone
Keep air stream constant
Check lower lip placement on reed
Observe breath marks
Practice until fingers reflex

Bssn

Whisper key is down throughout
Half-hole fingerings on F♯ and G
Keep lip cushion circular
Observe breath marks
Practice until fingers reflex

Rakes of Mallow—Traditional Irish Tune

Lesson 6

This scale may also be performed as a Teacher/Student Duet—p. 192.

Flute

Sing, then play
Slur first, then use legato tonguing
Raise left forefinger on high D
E♭ key is down on all notes except Ds
Check holding fulcrum when crossing break (see p. 12)

Oboe

Sing, then play
Slur first, then use legato tonguing
Keep lips on tip of reed; use circular cushion
Use regular F throughout, half hole on D, TOK on high E and F
Fragment and practice C, D, E, D, C until fingers reflex without thought
Work for smooth note connections

Clar

Sing, then play
Slur first, then use legato tonguing
Go slowly and establish accurate finger reflex
Check right thumb and upper teeth for holding stability
Fragment and practice D, E, F♯, and G; keep fingers close to tone holes
Keep air constant throughout

Alto Sax

Sing, then play
Slur first, then use legato tonguing
Keep air constant throughout
Fragment and practice the top 4 notes for accurate finger reflex
Holding fulcrum: work for balance between strap + 2 thumbs
    Right thumb pushes MP into mouth
    Left thumb pushes MP out of mouth

Bssn

Sing, then play
Slur first, then use legato tonguing
Check holding position: (1) left forefinger, (2) right thigh, (3) hand rest
WK down throughout
If low notes don't speak, check finger coverage
If top notes are flat, increase air speed

Lesson 6

Wearing of the Green—Irish Folk Song

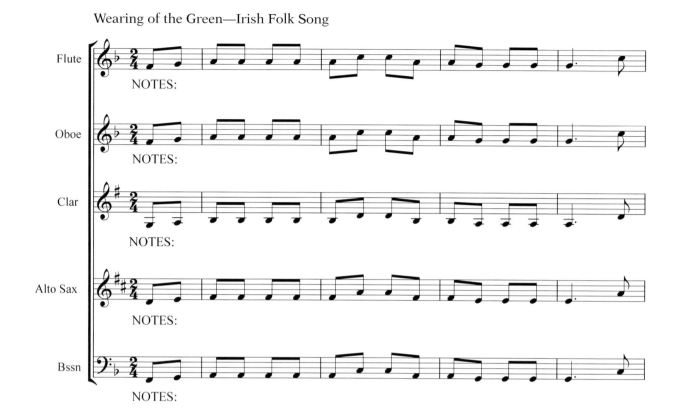

Lesson 7

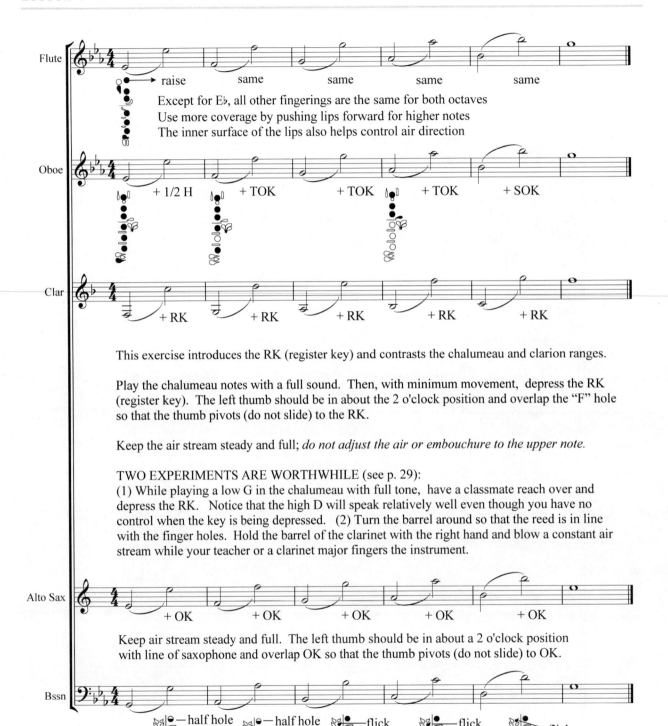

Flute

raise   same   same   same   same

Except for Eb, all other fingerings are the same for both octaves
Use more coverage by pushing lips forward for higher notes
The inner surface of the lips also helps control air direction

Oboe

+ 1/2 H   + TOK   + TOK   + TOK   + SOK

Clar

+ RK   + RK   + RK   + RK   + RK

This exercise introduces the RK (register key) and contrasts the chalumeau and clarion ranges.

Play the chalumeau notes with a full sound. Then, with minimum movement, depress the RK (register key). The left thumb should be in about the 2 o'clock position and overlap the "F" hole so that the thumb pivots (do not slide) to the RK.

Keep the air stream steady and full; *do not adjust the air or embouchure to the upper note.*

TWO EXPERIMENTS ARE WORTHWHILE (see p. 29):
(1) While playing a low G in the chalumeau with full tone, have a classmate reach over and depress the RK. Notice that the high D will speak relatively well even though you have no control when the key is being depressed. (2) Turn the barrel around so that the reed is in line with the finger holes. Hold the barrel of the clarinet with the right hand and blow a constant air stream while your teacher or a clarinet major fingers the instrument.

Alto Sax

+ OK   + OK   + OK   + OK   + OK

Keep air stream steady and full. The left thumb should be in about a 2 o'clock position with line of saxophone and overlap OK so that the thumb pivots (do not slide) to OK.

Bssn

—half hole   —half hole   —flick   —flick   —flick

Flick Keys (see p. 98): (1) start lower note with WK down, (2) on 2nd beat raise thumb toward flick key, (3) on 3rd beat "flick" (tap) the designated key and increase air speed for the upper tone.

Lesson 7

Aura Lee—American Folk Song
PRACTICE IN BOTH KEYS

Lesson 8

These notes may also be played as a Teacher/Student Duet—p. 194.

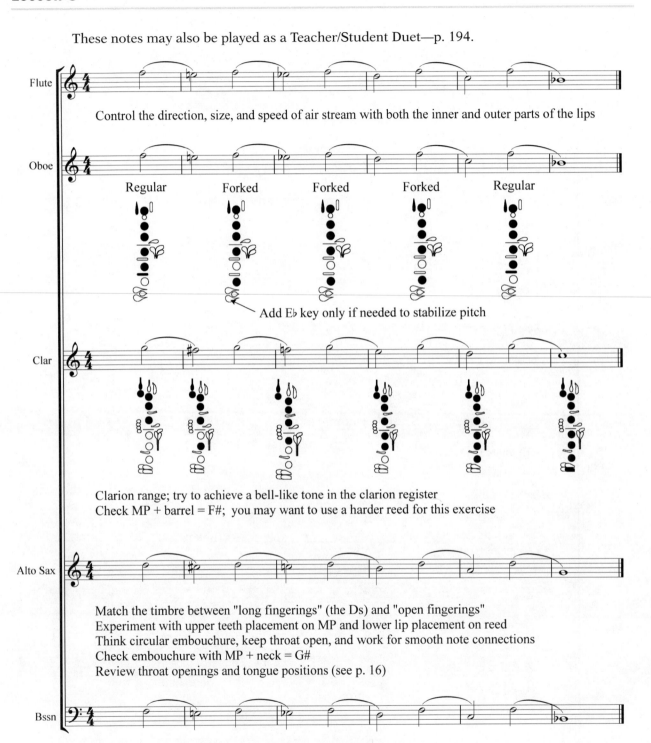

Flute

Control the direction, size, and speed of air stream with both the inner and outer parts of the lips

Oboe

Regular   Forked   Forked   Forked   Regular

Add E♭ key only if needed to stabilize pitch

Clar

Clarion range; try to achieve a bell-like tone in the clarion register
Check MP + barrel = F#; you may want to use a harder reed for this exercise

Alto Sax

Match the timbre between "long fingerings" (the Ds) and "open fingerings"
Experiment with upper teeth placement on MP and lower lip placement on reed
Think circular embouchure, keep throat open, and work for smooth note connections
Check embouchure with MP + neck = G#
Review throat openings and tongue positions (see p. 16)

Bssn

Match the tone quality between the open Fs and the other notes
Watch hand position; keep fingers close to instrument
Think circular embouchure, keep throat open, and work for smooth note connections
Review throat openings and tongue positions (see p. 16)

Lesson 8

Theme from"New World Symphony"—Antonin Dvorak (1841–1904)

Lesson 9

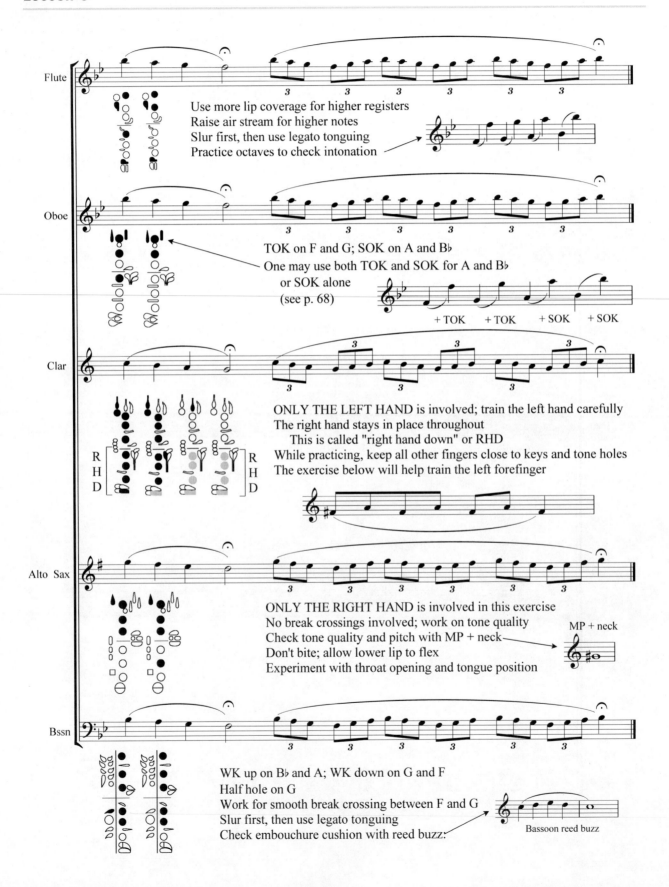

Flute

Use more lip coverage for higher registers
Raise air stream for higher notes
Slur first, then use legato tonguing
Practice octaves to check intonation

Oboe

TOK on F and G; SOK on A and B♭
One may use both TOK and SOK for A and B♭
or SOK alone
(see p. 68)

+ TOK   + TOK   + SOK   + SOK

Clar

ONLY THE LEFT HAND is involved; train the left hand carefully
The right hand stays in place throughout
    This is called "right hand down" or RHD
While practicing, keep all other fingers close to keys and tone holes
The exercise below will help train the left forefinger

R
H
D

R
H
D

Alto Sax

ONLY THE RIGHT HAND is involved in this exercise
No break crossings involved; work on tone quality
Check tone quality and pitch with MP + neck
Don't bite; allow lower lip to flex
Experiment with throat opening and tongue position

MP + neck

Bssn

WK up on B♭ and A; WK down on G and F
Half hole on G
Work for smooth break crossing between F and G
Slur first, then use legato tonguing
Check embouchure cushion with reed buzz:

Bassoon reed buzz

Lesson 9

Chester—William Billings (1746–1800)

Lesson 10

This scale may also be performed as a Teacher/Student Duet—p. 196.

Flute

Sing first, then play
Slur first, then use legato tonguing
Try to play in one breath (slurred)
Raise left forefinger on D and E♭
E♭ key is down on all notes except D and E♭

Practice octaves to check intonation:

NOTE: fingerings are the same
for both octaves

Oboe

Sing first, then play
Slur first, then use legato tonguing
Adjust air stream, lip cushion,
    and reed distance for higher notes
Half hole on Ds and E♭s
Use forked F

Practice octaves to check intonation:

+ TOK   + TOK   + SOK   + SOK

NOTE: fingerings are the same except for the addition
of octave mechanisms

Clar

RHD

Sing first, then play
Slur first, then use legato tonguing
Keep air stream support constant throughout
You may have to use RHD on G and above until left hand is trained
Two points of holding support: (1) upper teeth and (2) right thumb
Experiment with throat opening and tongue position (see p. 16)

Alto Sax

Sing first, then play
Slur first, then use legato tonguing
Try to play in one breath
Keep air stream support constant throughout
Experiment with throat opening and
    tongue position (see p. 16)

Practice octaves to check intonation:

+ OK   + OK   + OK

NOTE: fingerings are the same except for
addition of OK

Bssn

Sing first, then play
Slur first, then use legato tonguing
Try to play in one breath
Half hole on G only
WK up on A
Experiment with throat opening and
    tongue position (see p. 16)

Lesson 10

Minuet—Johann Sebastian Bach (1685–1750)

Lesson 11

Flute

Continue working on extending phrase lengths (see p. 28)
Review the five primary factors regarding embouchure (see p. 18)
Slur first, then use legato tonguing
Warm up with B♭ octaves

Oboe

Use TOK throughout; Add SOK on B♭
Practice with regular F and forked F
Slur first, then use legato tonguing
Warm up with B♭ octaves

Clar

Another LEFT-HAND EXERCISE
Use RHD throughout; slur first, then use legato tonguing
If problematic, try descending first, then ascending
Isolate the interval: B♭ to C; the following exercise will help
    train the left-hand movement required for the break crossing:

RHD   RHD

Alto Sax

ONLY THE RIGHT HAND IS INVOLVED; focus on holding position
Slur first, then use legato tonguing
Make certain the lower jaw does not move when tonguing
No break crossing involved; work on tone quality
Use a mirror to check embouchure and holding position

Bssn

WK off on B♭ only

Half hole on Gs and A♭s

Practice first two notes alone for smooth break crossing
Practice 3rd and 4th notes for coordination between right pinky and thumb
Slur first, then use legato tonguing

Lesson 11

"Ode to Joy" from Symphony No. 9—Ludwig van Beethoven (1770–1827)

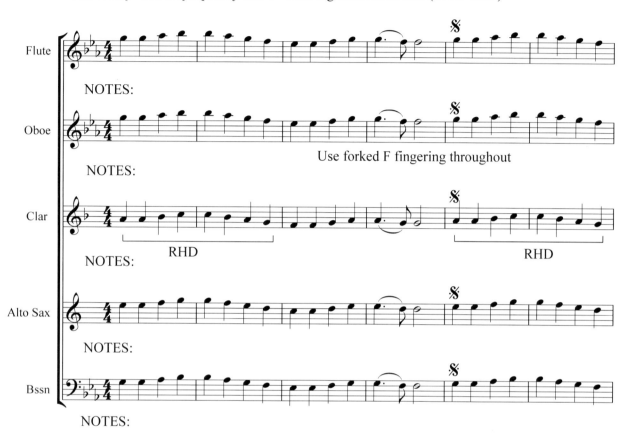

Use forked F fingering throughout

Lesson 12

This scale may also be performed as a Teacher/Student Duet—p. 198.

Flute

Check coverage, direction, and
  air speed with head joint exercise
Raise left forefinger on D and high E♭
Practice slurring entire exercise
  then use legato tonguing (see p. 31)

Legato Tonguing
Closed head joint

Oboe

Use half hole on high D and E♭
Fragment and practice top three notes
  for smooth break crossing
Practice slurring entire exercise,
  then use legato tonguing (see p. 31)

Legato Tonguing
Oboe reed buzz

If F is unstable, add right-hand E♭ key

Clar

Try this scale without RHD; if needed, use RHD on G, A, and B♭
Work for a smooth break crossing between B♭ and C
Slur entire exercise, then use legato tonguing (see p. 31)
3-step air: inhale AIR, suspend AIR, release AIR
Check lower lip placement (see p. 20)
Keep chin flat

Legato Tonguing
MP + barrel

Alto Sax

Reg   Alt

Legato Tonguing
MP + Neck

Use alternate fingering for high C
  (eliminates the cross fingering - see p. 216)
3-step air: inhale AIR, suspend AIR, release AIR
Check lower lip placement (see p. 20)
Keep chin flat
Don't bite upper notes; lower teeth
  should allow lower lip to flex
Slur entire exercise, then use legato tonguing
  (see p. 31)

Bssn

Legato Tonguing
Reed + bocal

WK off on B♭ and above
Use half-hole fingerings on G and A♭
High E♭ tends to be flat, use faster air
Slur entire exercise, then use legato tonguing
  (see p. 31)

Lesson 12

Barbara Allen—Scottish Song (1665)

Flute

NOTES:

Oboe

NOTES:

Clar

NOTES:

Alto Sax

NOTES:

Bssn

NOTES:

Flute

Oboe

Clar

Alto Sax

Bssn

Lesson 13

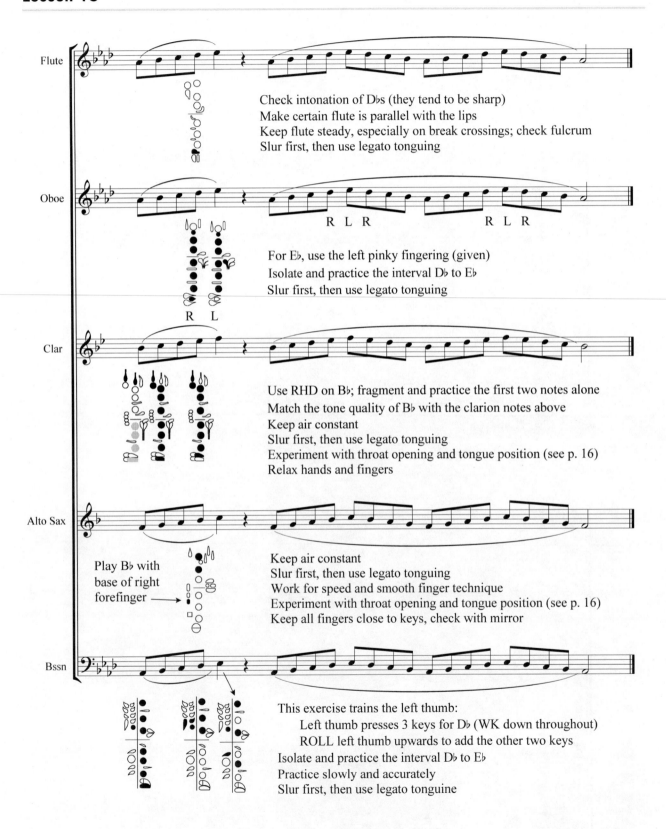

Flute

Check intonation of D♭s (they tend to be sharp)
Make certain flute is parallel with the lips
Keep flute steady, especially on break crossings; check fulcrum
Slur first, then use legato tonguing

Oboe

For E♭, use the left pinky fingering (given)
Isolate and practice the interval D♭ to E♭
Slur first, then use legato tonguing

Clar

Use RHD on B♭; fragment and practice the first two notes alone
Match the tone quality of B♭ with the clarion notes above
Keep air constant
Slur first, then use legato tonguing
Experiment with throat opening and tongue position (see p. 16)
Relax hands and fingers

Alto Sax

Play B♭ with base of right forefinger →

Keep air constant
Slur first, then use legato tonguing
Work for speed and smooth finger technique
Experiment with throat opening and tongue position (see p. 16)
Keep all fingers close to keys, check with mirror

Bssn

This exercise trains the left thumb:
Left thumb presses 3 keys for D♭ (WK down throughout)
ROLL left thumb upwards to add the other two keys
Isolate and practice the interval D♭ to E♭
Practice slowly and accurately
Slur first, then use legato tonguine

Lesson 13

Frère Jacques—French Folk Song

Lesson 14

This scale may also be performed as a Teacher/Student Duet—p. 200.

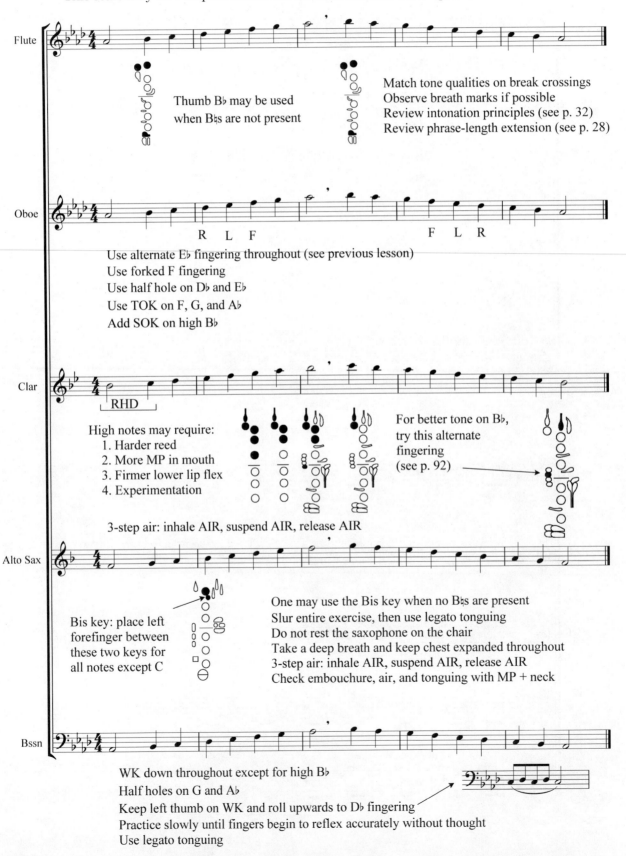

Flute

Thumb B♭ may be used
when B♮s are not present

Match tone qualities on break crossings
Observe breath marks if possible
Review intonation principles (see p. 32)
Review phrase-length extension (see p. 28)

Oboe

R   L   F   F   L   R

Use alternate E♭ fingering throughout (see previous lesson)
Use forked F fingering
Use half hole on D♭ and E♭
Use TOK on F, G, and A♭
Add SOK on high B♭

Clar

RHD

High notes may require:
1. Harder reed
2. More MP in mouth
3. Firmer lower lip flex
4. Experimentation

For better tone on B♭,
try this alternate
fingering
(see p. 92)

3-step air: inhale AIR, suspend AIR, release AIR

Alto Sax

Bis key: place left
forefinger between
these two keys for
all notes except C

One may use the Bis key when no B♮s are present
Slur entire exercise, then use legato tonguing
Do not rest the saxophone on the chair
Take a deep breath and keep chest expanded throughout
3-step air: inhale AIR, suspend AIR, release AIR
Check embouchure, air, and tonguing with MP + neck

Bssn

WK down throughout except for high B♭
Half holes on G and A♭
Keep left thumb on WK and roll upwards to D♭ fingering
Practice slowly until fingers begin to reflex accurately without thought
Use legato tonguing

Lesson 14

Scarborough Fair—English Folk Song

Lesson 15

This scale may also be performed as a Teacher/Student Duet—p. 202.

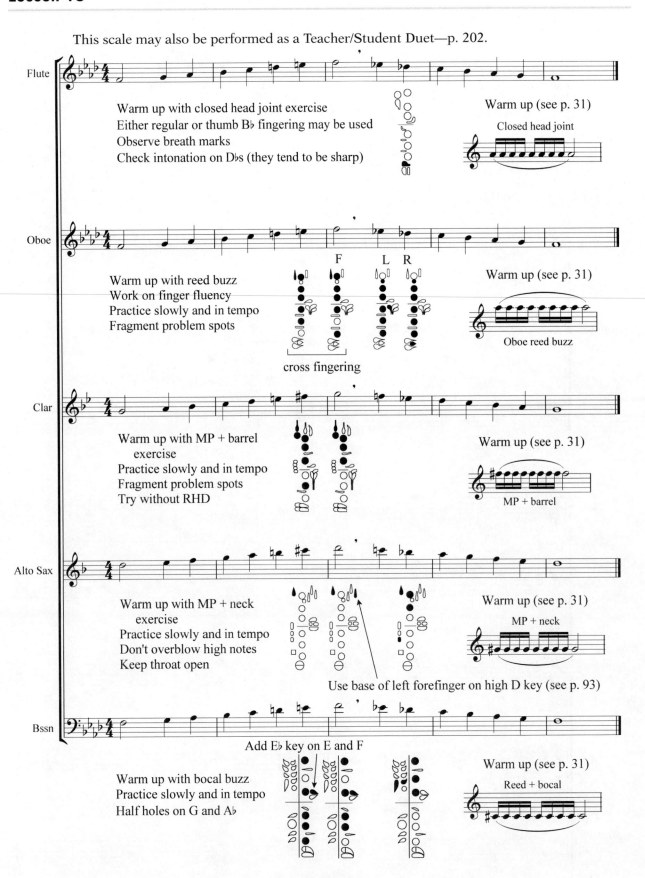

Flute

Warm up with closed head joint exercise
Either regular or thumb B♭ fingering may be used
Observe breath marks
Check intonation on D♭s (they tend to be sharp)

Warm up (see p. 31)

Closed head joint

Oboe

Warm up with reed buzz
Work on finger fluency
Practice slowly and in tempo
Fragment problem spots

cross fingering

Warm up (see p. 31)

Oboe reed buzz

Clar

Warm up with MP + barrel
  exercise
Practice slowly and in tempo
Fragment problem spots
Try without RHD

Warm up (see p. 31)

MP + barrel

Alto Sax

Warm up with MP + neck
  exercise
Practice slowly and in tempo
Don't overblow high notes
Keep throat open

Use base of left forefinger on high D key (see p. 93)

Warm up (see p. 31)

MP + neck

Bssn

Add E♭ key on E and F

Warm up with bocal buzz
Practice slowly and in tempo
Half holes on G and A♭

Warm up (see p. 31)

Reed + bocal

Lesson 15

Wayfaring Stranger—American Folk Ballad

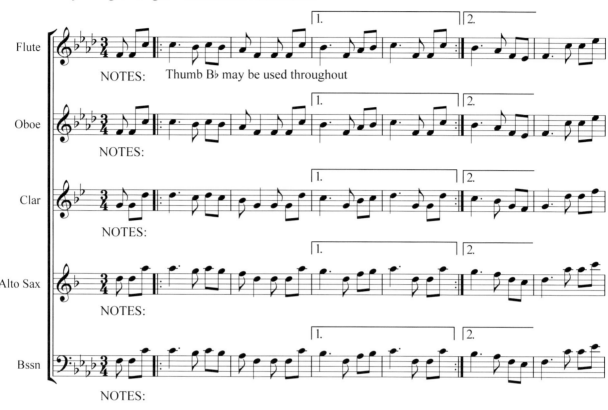

NOTES: Thumb B♭ may be used throughout

NOTES:

NOTES:

NOTES:

NOTES:

Lesson 16

This scale may also be performed as a Teacher/Student Duet—p. 204.

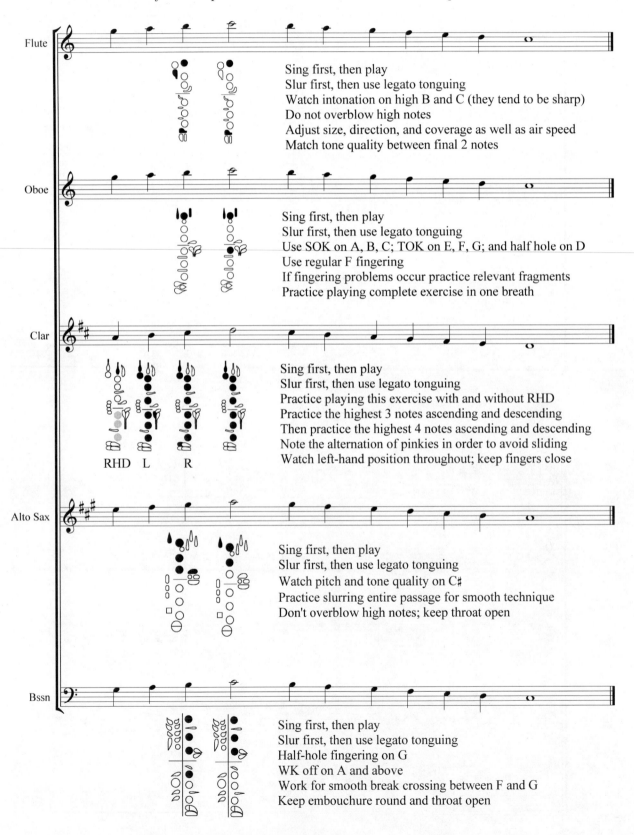

Flute

Sing first, then play
Slur first, then use legato tonguing
Watch intonation on high B and C (they tend to be sharp)
Do not overblow high notes
Adjust size, direction, and coverage as well as air speed
Match tone quality between final 2 notes

Oboe

Sing first, then play
Slur first, then use legato tonguing
Use SOK on A, B, C; TOK on E, F, G; and half hole on D
Use regular F fingering
If fingering problems occur practice relevant fragments
Practice playing complete exercise in one breath

Clar

Sing first, then play
Slur first, then use legato tonguing
Practice playing this exercise with and without RHD
Practice the highest 3 notes ascending and descending
Then practice the highest 4 notes ascending and descending
Note the alternation of pinkies in order to avoid sliding
Watch left-hand position throughout; keep fingers close

RHD   L   R

Alto Sax

Sing first, then play
Slur first, then use legato tonguing
Watch pitch and tone quality on C♯
Practice slurring entire passage for smooth technique
Don't overblow high notes; keep throat open

Bssn

Sing first, then play
Slur first, then use legato tonguing
Half-hole fingering on G
WK off on A and above
Work for smooth break crossing between F and G
Keep embouchure round and throat open

Lesson 16

Triplet Song—French Folk Song

Lesson 17

This scale may also be performed as a Teacher/Student Duet—p. 206.

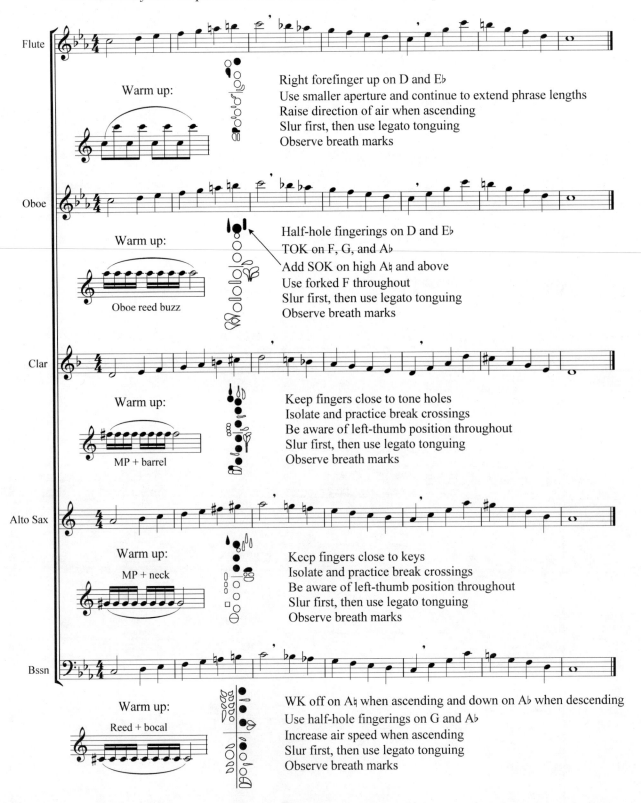

Flute

Warm up:

Right forefinger up on D and E♭
Use smaller aperture and continue to extend phrase lengths
Raise direction of air when ascending
Slur first, then use legato tonguing
Observe breath marks

Oboe

Warm up:

Oboe reed buzz

Half-hole fingerings on D and E♭
TOK on F, G, and A♭
Add SOK on high A♮ and above
Use forked F throughout
Slur first, then use legato tonguing
Observe breath marks

Clar

Warm up:

MP + barrel

Keep fingers close to tone holes
Isolate and practice break crossings
Be aware of left-thumb position throughout
Slur first, then use legato tonguing
Observe breath marks

Alto Sax

Warm up:

MP + neck

Keep fingers close to keys
Isolate and practice break crossings
Be aware of left-thumb position throughout
Slur first, then use legato tonguing
Observe breath marks

Bssn

Warm up:

Reed + bocal

WK off on A♮ when ascending and down on A♭ when descending
Use half-hole fingerings on G and A♭
Increase air speed when ascending
Slur first, then use legato tonguing
Observe breath marks

Lesson 17

Drunken Sailor—Sea Shanty

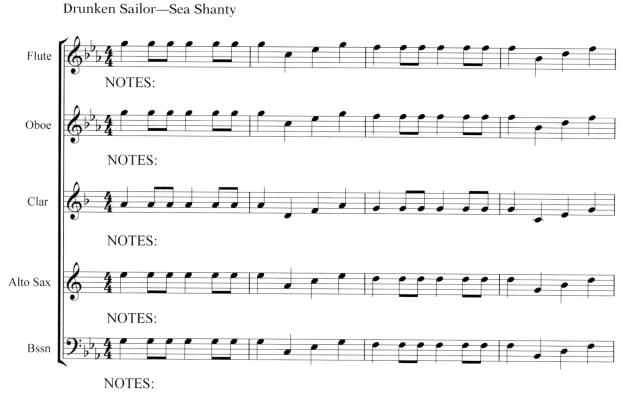

Flute

NOTES:

Oboe

NOTES:

Clar

NOTES:

Alto Sax

NOTES:

Bssn

NOTES:

Flute

Oboe

Clar

Alto Sax

Bssn

Lesson 18

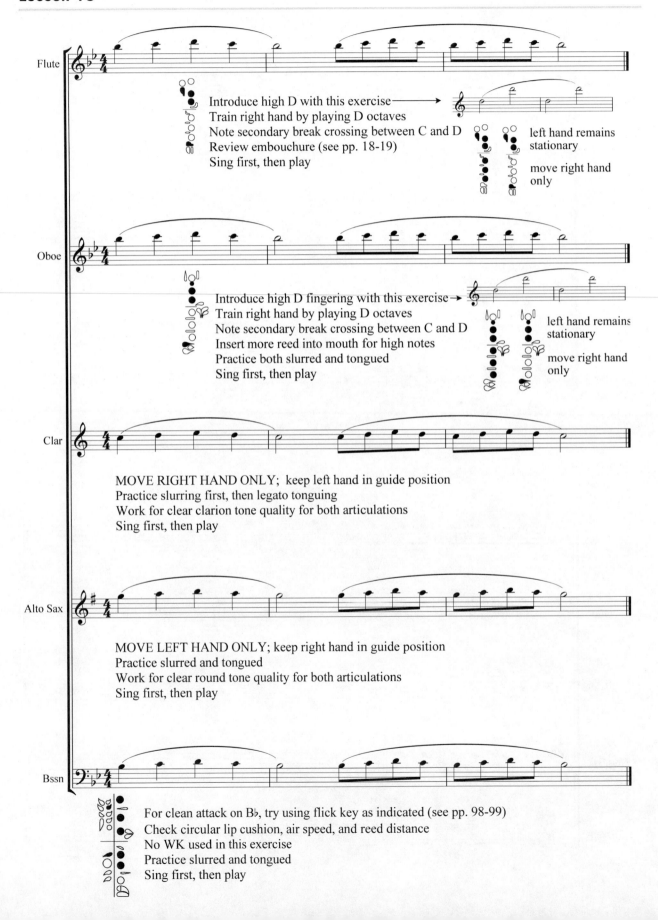

Flute

Introduce high D with this exercise⟶
Train right hand by playing D octaves
Note secondary break crossing between C and D
Review embouchure (see pp. 18-19)
Sing first, then play

left hand remains stationary

move right hand only

Oboe

Introduce high D fingering with this exercise→
Train right hand by playing D octaves
Note secondary break crossing between C and D
Insert more reed into mouth for high notes
Practice both slurred and tongued
Sing first, then play

left hand remains stationary

move right hand only

Clar

MOVE RIGHT HAND ONLY; keep left hand in guide position
Practice slurring first, then legato tonguing
Work for clear clarion tone quality for both articulations
Sing first, then play

Alto Sax

MOVE LEFT HAND ONLY; keep right hand in guide position
Practice slurred and tongued
Work for clear round tone quality for both articulations
Sing first, then play

Bssn

For clean attack on B♭, try using flick key as indicated (see pp. 98-99)
Check circular lip cushion, air speed, and reed distance
No WK used in this exercise
Practice slurred and tongued
Sing first, then play

Lesson 18

Alma Mater—Traditional

Flute

NOTES:

Oboe

NOTES:

Clar

NOTES: RHD

Alto Sax

NOTES:

Bssn

NOTES:

Lesson 19

This scale may also be performed as a Teacher/Student Duet—p. 208.

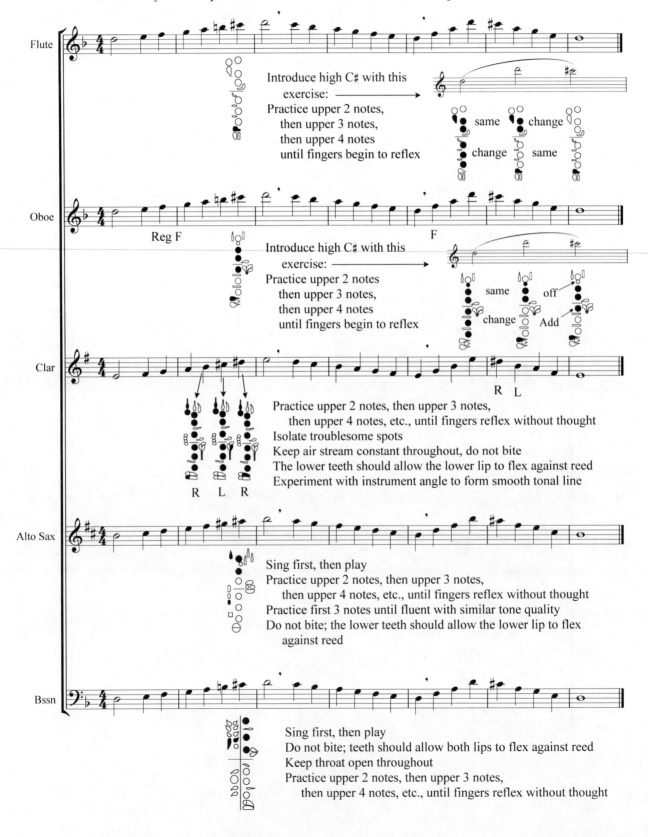

Three Ravens—Old English (1611)

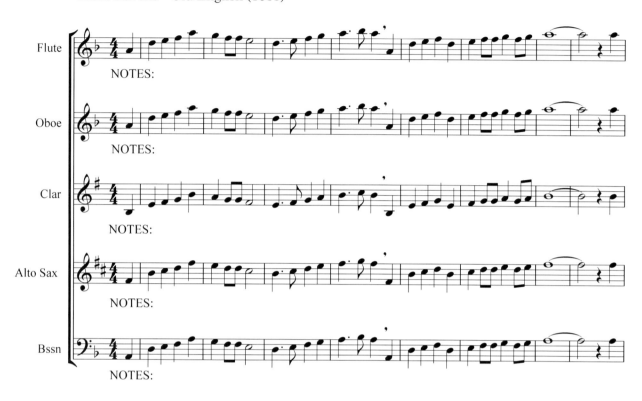

Flute
NOTES:

Oboe
NOTES:

Clar
NOTES:

Alto Sax
NOTES:

Bssn
NOTES:

Flute

Oboe

Clar

Alto Sax

Bssn

Lesson 20

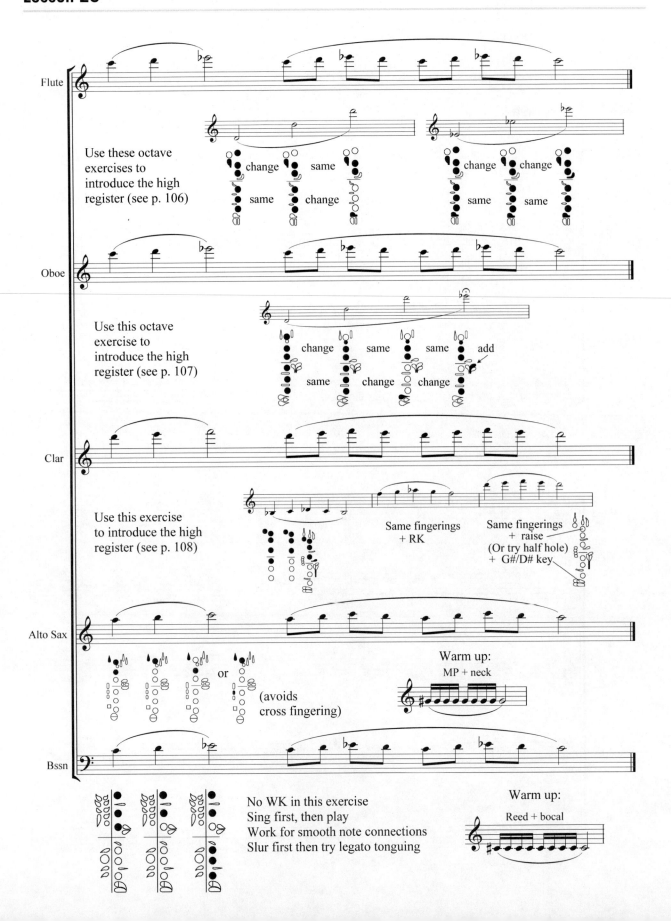

Lesson 20

Barcarolle—Jacques Offenbach (1819–1880)

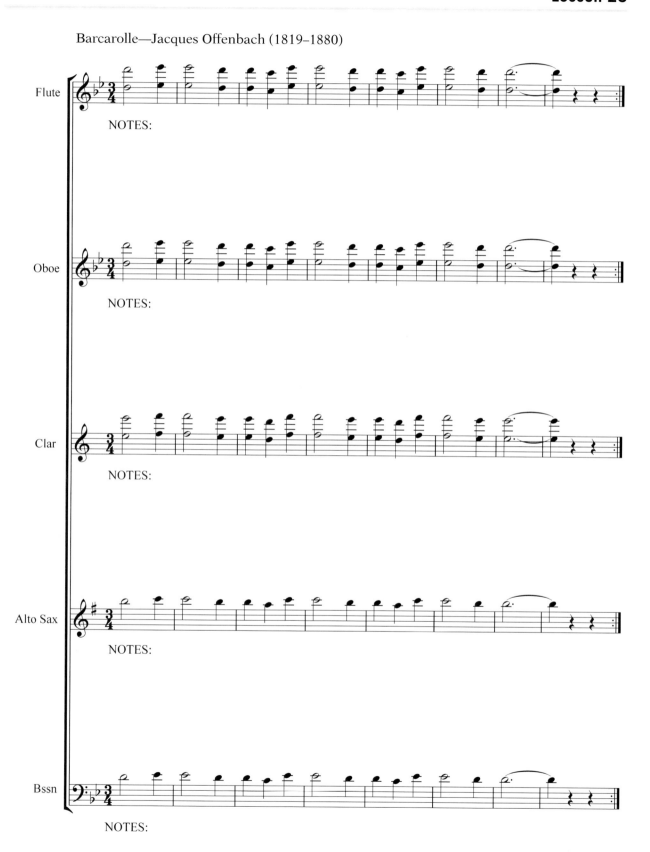

Flute

NOTES:

Oboe

NOTES:

Clar

NOTES:

Alto Sax

NOTES:

Bssn

NOTES:

Lesson 21

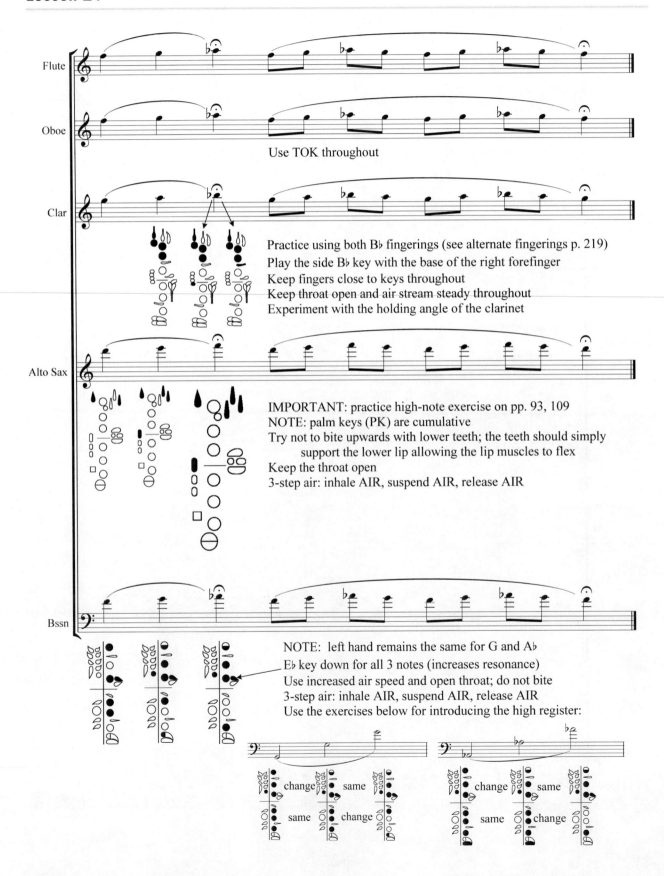

Use TOK throughout

Clar

Practice using both B♭ fingerings (see alternate fingerings p. 219)
Play the side B♭ key with the base of the right forefinger
Keep fingers close to keys throughout
Keep throat open and air stream steady throughout
Experiment with the holding angle of the clarinet

Alto Sax

IMPORTANT: practice high-note exercise on pp. 93, 109
NOTE: palm keys (PK) are cumulative
Try not to bite upwards with lower teeth; the teeth should simply
       support the lower lip allowing the lip muscles to flex
Keep the throat open
3-step air: inhale AIR, suspend AIR, release AIR

Bssn

NOTE: left hand remains the same for G and A♭
E♭ key down for all 3 notes (increases resonance)
Use increased air speed and open throat; do not bite
3-step air: inhale AIR, suspend AIR, release AIR
Use the exercises below for introducing the high register:

change   same
same   change

change   same
same   change

Lesson 21

Theme from Symphony No. 1—Johannes Brahms (1833–1897)

Lesson 22

This scale may also be performed as a Teacher/Student Duet—p. 210.

Flute

Before starting, review Lesson 20
  Left forefinger should be raised for all of the lower E♭s in this exercise
  Do not rely on faster air speed alone for high notes or high notes will be loud and shrill
  Instead use more coverage, higher direction, and smaller aperture (p. 18)
  Practice slurred, then use legato tonguing

Oboe

Before starting, review Lesson 20
  Use half hole on E♭
  Use forked F
  Use TOK on G and A♭
  Add SOK on B♭ and C
  Half hole on high D and E♭

Clar

Before starting, review Lesson 20
  Practice both registers; you may have to use a harder reed for this exercise
  Use 3-step air: inhale AIR, suspend AIR, release AIR
  Practice slurred, then use legato tonguing
  Do not bite; allow lower lip to flex
  Gently push MP against upper teeth with right thumb
  If RHD is needed, mark the appropriate notes in the score

Alto Sax

  Practice sustaining the low C with throat open
  Use 3 step-air: inhale AIR, suspend AIR, release AIR
  Play entire exercise in one breath
  Fingers should move by reflex; memorize this scale
  Practice slurred, then use legato tonguing
  If fingering problems occur; isolate and repeat problematic fragments of the scale

Bssn

  Practice sustaining the low E♭ with throat open
  Use 3 step-air: inhale AIR, suspend AIR, release AIR
  WK off on upper B♭; use half-hole fingerings on G and A♭
  High E♭ tends to be flat; use faster air stream and/or push reed into mouth slightly
  Practice slurred, then use legato tonguing

Lesson 22

Greensleeves—English Renaissance Song

Lesson 23

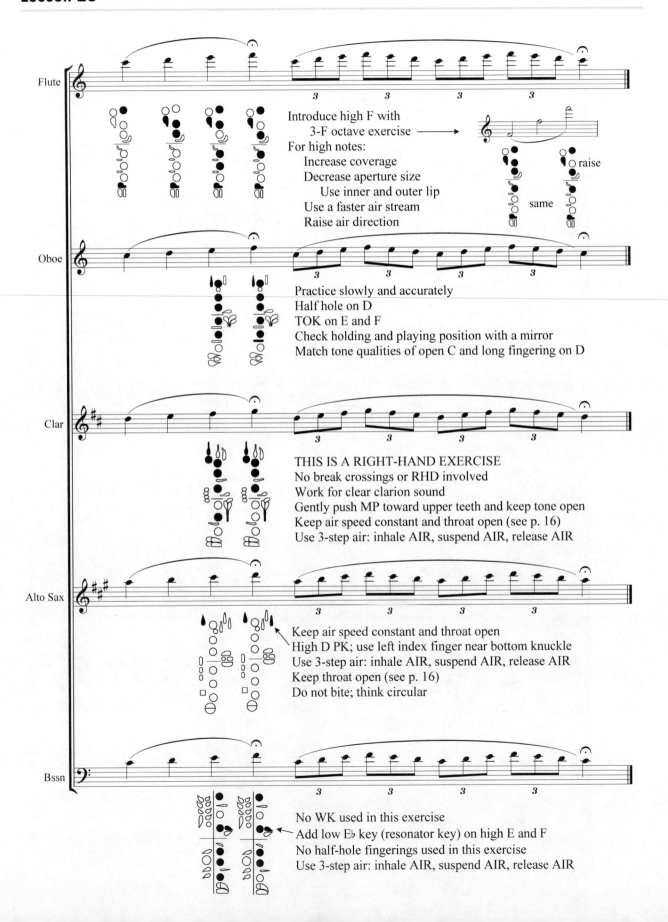

Flute

Introduce high F with
3-F octave exercise ———→
For high notes:
  Increase coverage
  Decrease aperture size
    Use inner and outer lip
  Use a faster air stream
  Raise air direction

same   raise

Oboe

Practice slowly and accurately
Half hole on D
TOK on E and F
Check holding and playing position with a mirror
Match tone qualities of open C and long fingering on D

Clar

THIS IS A RIGHT-HAND EXERCISE
No break crossings or RHD involved
Work for clear clarion sound
Gently push MP toward upper teeth and keep tone open
Keep air speed constant and throat open (see p. 16)
Use 3-step air: inhale AIR, suspend AIR, release AIR

Alto Sax

Keep air speed constant and throat open
High D PK; use left index finger near bottom knuckle
Use 3-step air: inhale AIR, suspend AIR, release AIR
Keep throat open (see p. 16)
Do not bite; think circular

Bssn

No WK used in this exercise
Add low Eb key (resonator key) on high E and F
No half-hole fingerings used in this exercise
Use 3-step air: inhale AIR, suspend AIR, release AIR

Lesson 23

America/God Save the Queen—Traditional

Lesson 24

This scale may also be performed as a Teacher/Student Duet—p. 212.

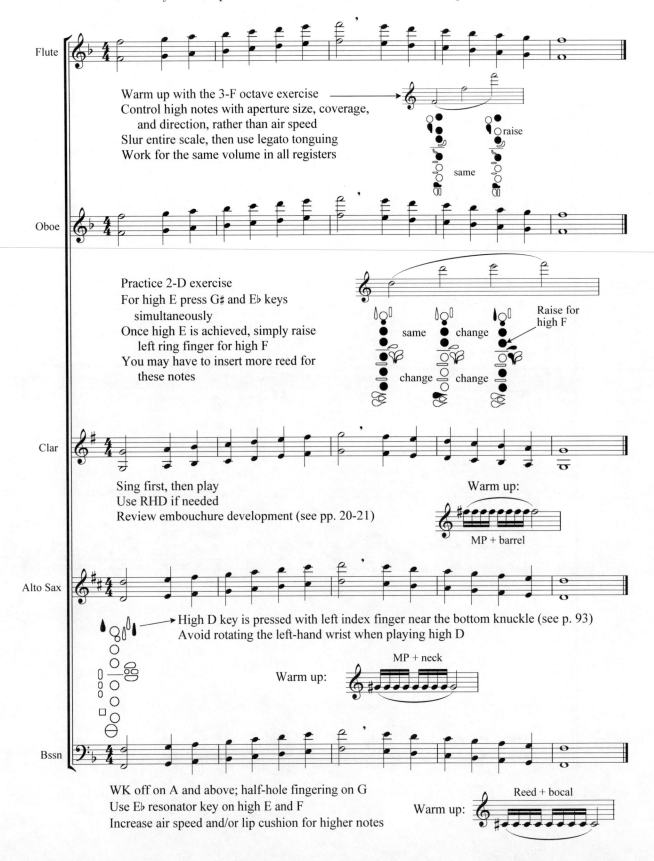

Flute

Warm up with the 3-F octave exercise
Control high notes with aperture size, coverage,
    and direction, rather than air speed
Slur entire scale, then use legato tonguing
Work for the same volume in all registers

raise

same

Oboe

Practice 2-D exercise
For high E press G♯ and E♭ keys
    simultaneously
Once high E is achieved, simply raise
    left ring finger for high F
You may have to insert more reed for
    these notes

same   change   Raise for high F

change   change

Clar

Sing first, then play
Use RHD if needed
Review embouchure development (see pp. 20-21)

Warm up:

MP + barrel

Alto Sax

High D key is pressed with left index finger near the bottom knuckle (see p. 93)
Avoid rotating the left-hand wrist when playing high D

MP + neck

Warm up:

Bssn

WK off on A and above; half-hole fingering on G
Use E♭ resonator key on high E and F
Increase air speed and/or lip cushion for higher notes

Reed + bocal

Warm up:

Lesson 24

Old Joe Clark—American Folk Song

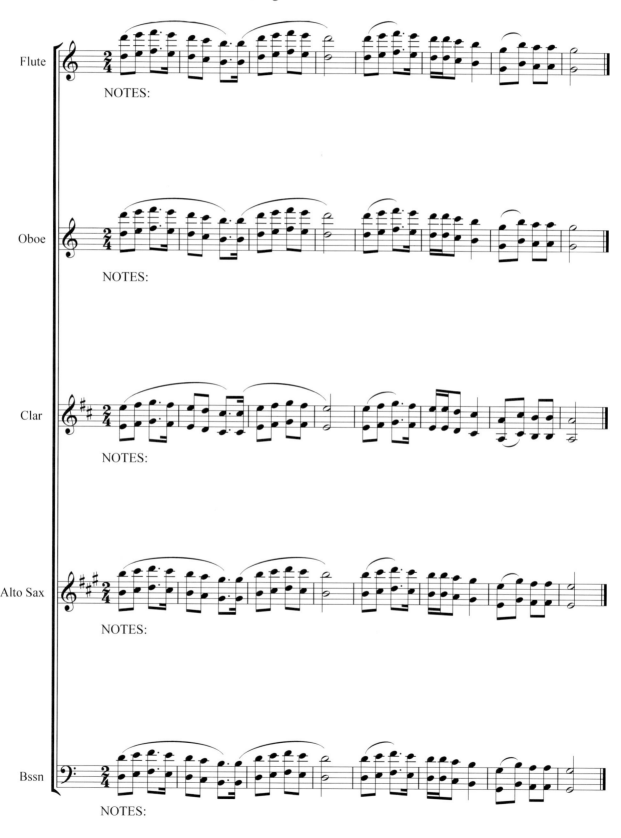

Lesson 25

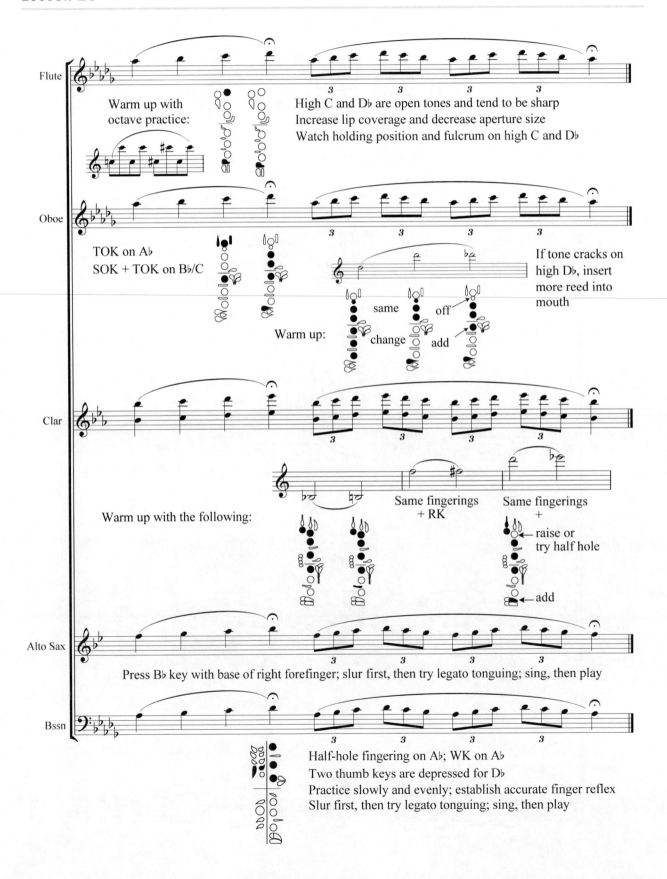

Flute

Warm up with octave practice:

High C and Db are open tones and tend to be sharp
Increase lip coverage and decrease aperture size
Watch holding position and fulcrum on high C and Db

Oboe

TOK on Ab
SOK + TOK on Bb/C

Warm up:
same   off
change   add

If tone cracks on high Db, insert more reed into mouth

Clar

Warm up with the following:

Same fingerings + RK

Same fingerings +
← raise or try half hole
← add

Alto Sax

Press Bb key with base of right forefinger; slur first, then try legato tonguing; sing, then play

Bssn

Half-hole fingering on Ab; WK on Ab
Two thumb keys are depressed for Db
Practice slowly and evenly; establish accurate finger reflex
Slur first, then try legato tonguing; sing, then play

Lesson 25

Turkey in the Straw—American Folk Tune

NOTES: Use alternate fingerings for A♭ and G♭ (see pages 99 and 221)

8 Student/Teacher Duets

Student/Teacher Duet 1

When practicing these duets with an advanced player, focus on what makes a "good tone." Listen for the following:

- General expression of the tone

- General tone quality (timbre) of the tone

- Flexibility of the tone

- Warmth of the tone

- Volume of the tone

- Attack and release of the tone

- Focus and center of the tone

- Intonation of the tone

Student/Teacher Duet 1

See Lesson 5—Technique/Tunes: Twenty-five Class Lessons

After Julius Weissenborn (1837–1888)

Student/Teacher Duet 1

Student/Teacher Duet 2

See Lesson 6—Technique/Tunes: Twenty-five Class Lessons

Carl Almenraeder (1786–1843)

Student/Teacher Duet 2

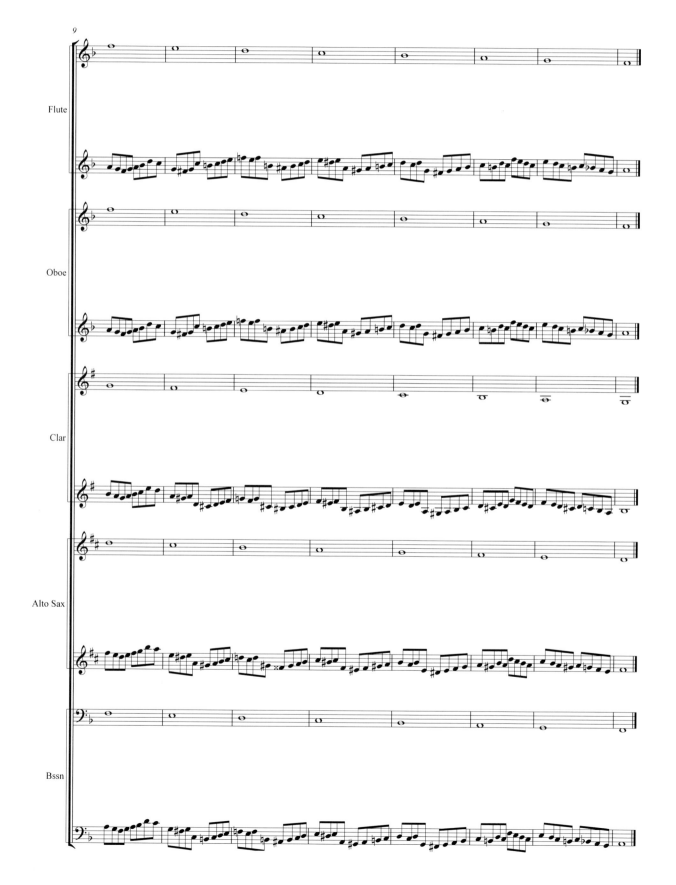

Student/Teacher Duet 3

See Lesson 8—Technique/Tunes: Twenty-five Class Lessons

After Carl Almenraeder (1786–1843)

Flute   NOTES:

Oboe   NOTES:

Clar   NOTES:

Alto Sax   NOTES:

Bssn   NOTES:

Student/Teacher Duet 3

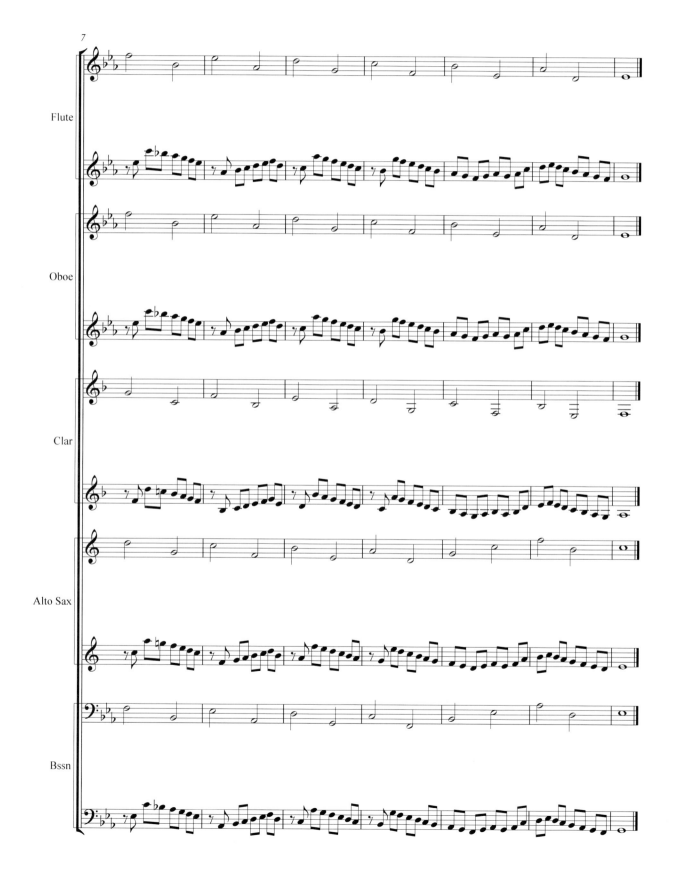

Student/Teacher Duet 4

See Lesson 10—Technique/Tunes: Twenty-five Class Lessons

Carl Almenraeder (1786–1843)

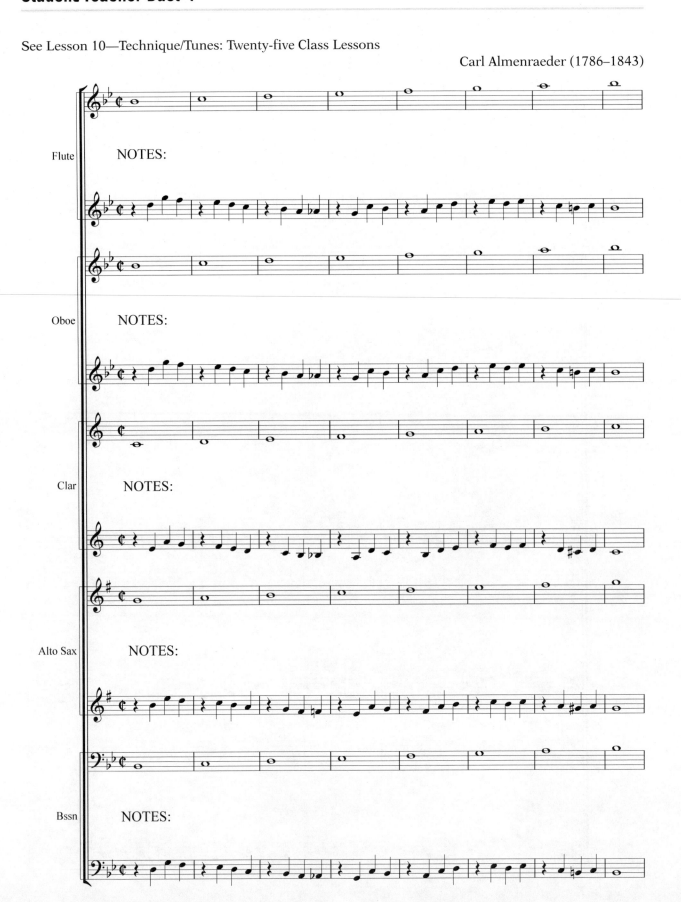

Student/Teacher Duet 4

Student/Teacher Duet 5

See Lesson 12—Technique/Tunes: Twenty-five Class Lessons

After Carl Almenraeder (1786–1843)

Student/Teacher Duet 5

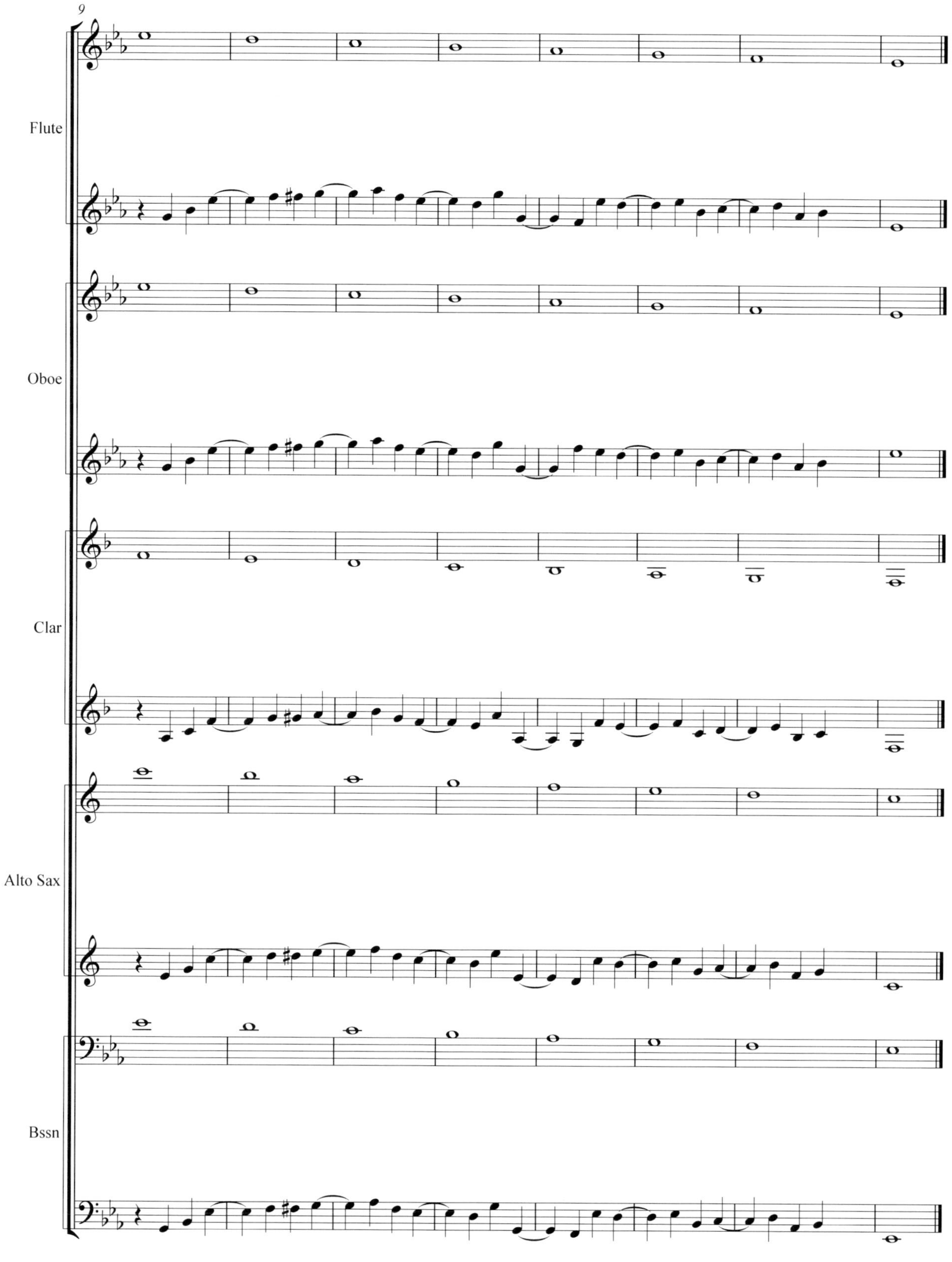

Student/Teacher Duet 6

See Lesson 14—Technique/Tunes: Twenty-five Class Lessons

After Carl Almenraeder (1786–1843)

Student/Teacher Duet 6

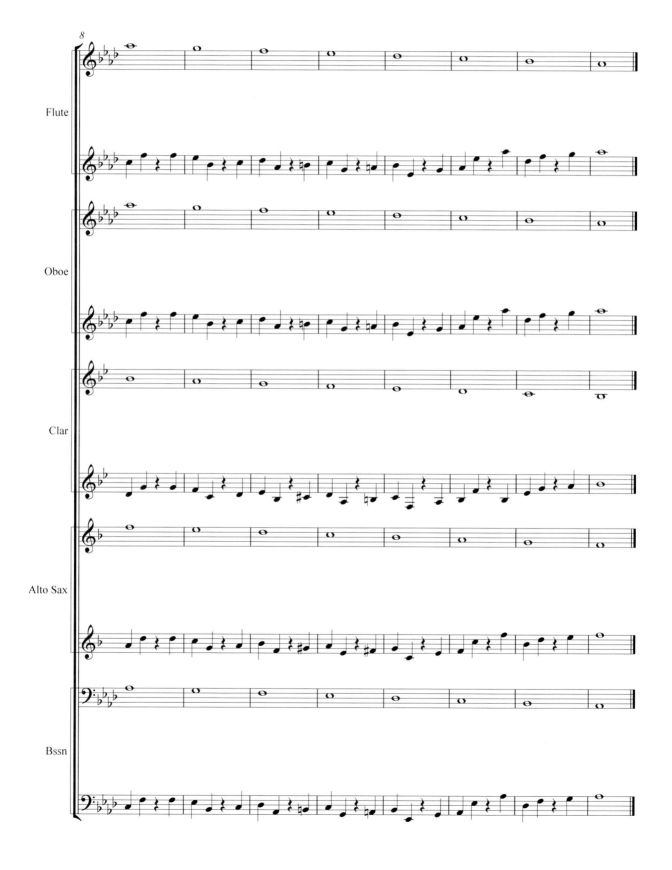

Student/Teacher Duet 7

See Lesson 15—Technique/Tunes: Twenty-five Class Lessons

After Carl Almenraeder (1786–1843)

Student/Teacher Duet 7

Student/Teacher Duet 8

See Lesson 16—Technique/Tunes: Twenty-five Class Lessons

After Carl Almenraeder (1786–1843)

Student/Teacher Duet 8

Student/Teacher Duet 9

See Lesson 17—Technique/Tunes: Twenty-five Class Lessons

After Carl Almenraeder (1786–1843)

Student/Teacher Duet 9

Student/Teacher Duet 10

See Lesson 19—Technique/Tunes: Twenty-five Class Lessons

After Carl Almenraeder (1786–1843)

Student/Teacher Duet 10

Student/Teacher Duet 11

See Lesson 22—Technique/Tunes: Twenty-five Class Lessons

After Carl Almenraeder (1786–1843)

Student/Teacher Duet 11

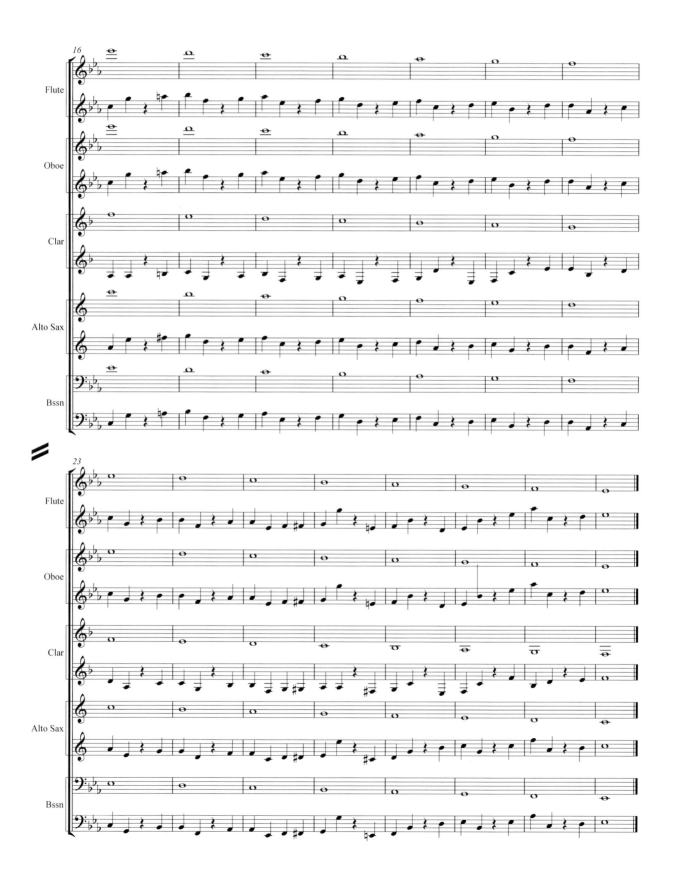

Student/Teacher Duet 12

See Lesson 24—Technique/Tunes: Twenty-five Class Lessons

After Carl Almenraeder (1786–1843)

Student/Teacher Duet 12

9 Alternate Fingerings

When to Teach

Beginning students should concentrate on standard fingerings. Alternate fingerings are used to solve technical problems when the normal fingerings are unsatisfactory.

If a student is playing a passage where the fingering sequence is so awkward that he/she cannot play it fast enough or smoothly enough, the problem may be solved with alternate fingerings.

Look and **listen** for the following problems:

- Is the student **sliding** a finger from one key to another?

- Is the student using a **cross-fingering**? (adjacent fingers going in opposite directions)

- Does the student **lack control** of dynamics and intonation on a **specific** high note?

Generally, the more advanced the student, the greater the need for alternate fingerings.

General Categories of Alternate Fingerings

- Chromatic passages
- Rapid movement between break crossings
- Trills
- Playing in specific keys
- Arpeggiated passages
- Dynamic and intonation control

Other Sources for Alternate Fingerings

Book:

Timm, Everett LeRoy. *The Woodwinds; Performance and Instructional Techniques*. Boston: Allyn and Bacon, 1964, 171.

Web sites:

http://www.wfg.woodwind.org/ (for all woodwind instruments—very comprehensive)

http://www.idrs.org/BSNFING/FINGHOME.HTM (bassoon fingerings by Terry B. Ewell)

Frequently Used Alternate Fingerings—Flute

THREE B♭'s

(1) Regular B♭
Teach first

(2) Thumb B♭
Use for flat keys

(3) Side B♭
B to B♭ to G combinations

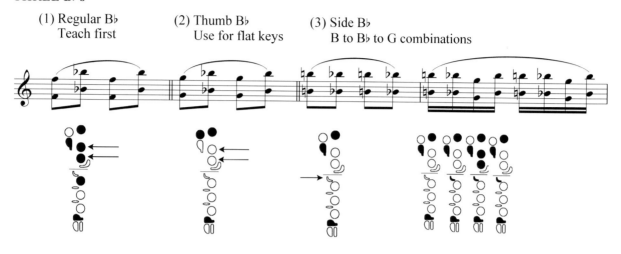

COMMON TRILLS (also for very fast passages)

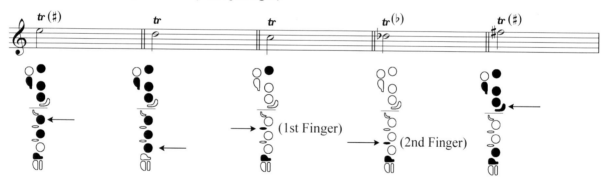

LEAPING TO HIGH E   HARMONICS: use in soft passages; also good for tone development

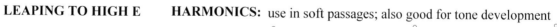

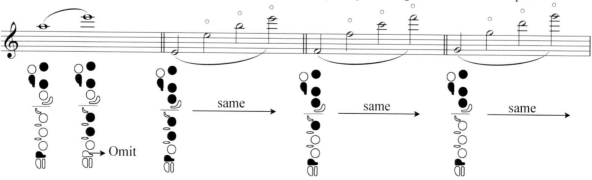

Frequently Used Alternate Fingerings—Oboe

TWO F FINGERINGS

(1) Regular (chromatic)   (2) Forked (Band methods books often introduce forked F first. Use this fingering when F is preceded or followed by a note using right ring finger.)

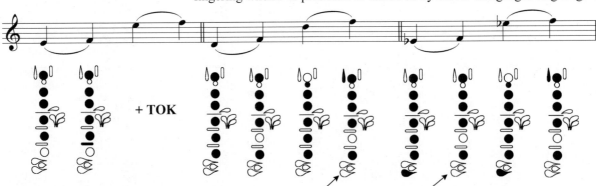

+ TOK

On forked Fs add E♭ key for pitch stability only if needed

TWO E♭ FINGERINGS

(1) Regular   (2) Alternate

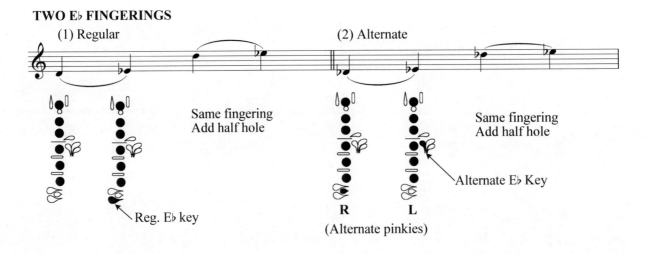

Same fingering
Add half hole

Same fingering
Add half hole

Alternate E♭ Key

Reg. E♭ key

R   L
(Alternate pinkies)

BREAK CROSSING TRILLS AND ARTICULATED G♯

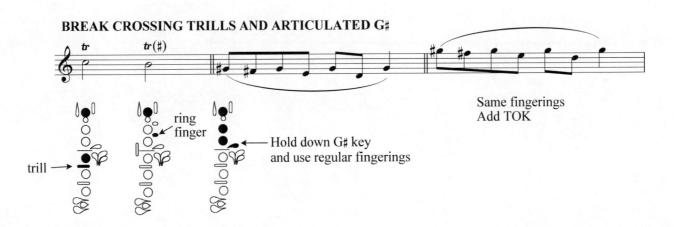

tr   *tr*(♯)

ring finger

Hold down G♯ key
and use regular fingerings

Same fingerings
Add TOK

trial → trill

Frequently Used Alternate Fingerings—Clarinet

PINKY KEY CLUSTERS RULE: always alternate clusters, do not slide pinky within clusters

Add register key (RK) for clarion notes

CHROMATIC ALTERNATES

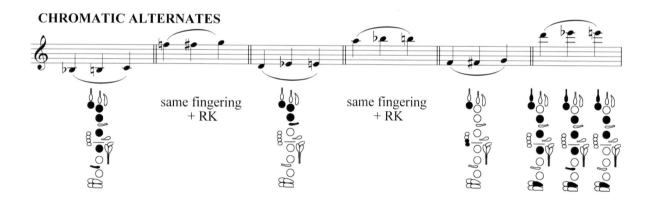

same fingering + RK

same fingering + RK

TRILLS   ARPEGGIOS

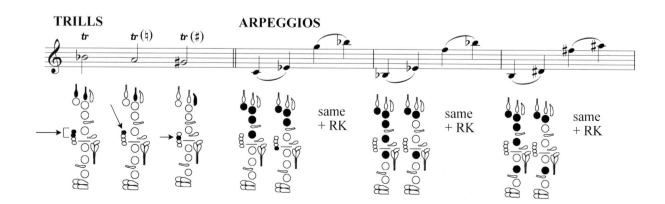

same + RK

same + RK

same + RK

Frequently Used Alternate Fingerings—Saxophone

FOUR B♭s (add OK for *8va*)

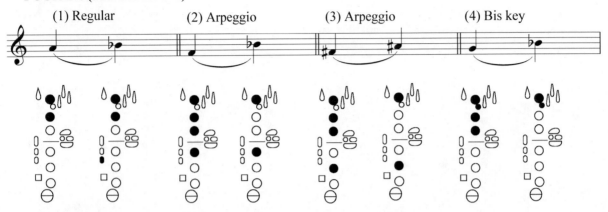

CHROMATIC AND HIGH-NOTE ARPEGGIOS

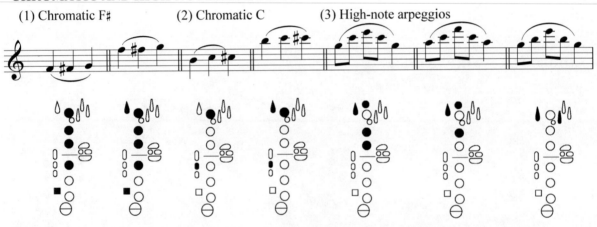

BREAK CROSSING TRILLS, ARTICULATED G♯, AND Bis KEY

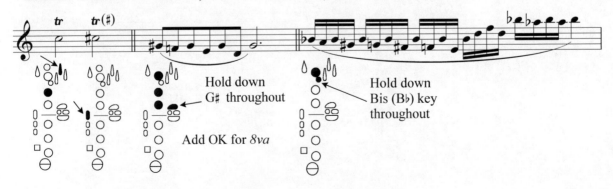

Hold down
G♯ throughout

Add OK for *8va*

Hold down
Bis (B♭) key
throughout

Frequently Used Alternate Fingerings—Bassoon

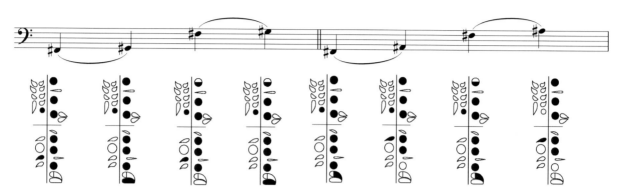

Alternate between right thumb and pinky   Alternate between right pinky and thumb

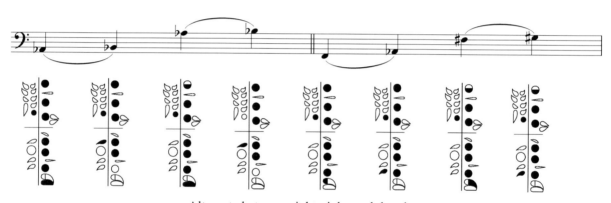

Alternate between right pinky and thumb

COMMON TRILL FINGERINGS

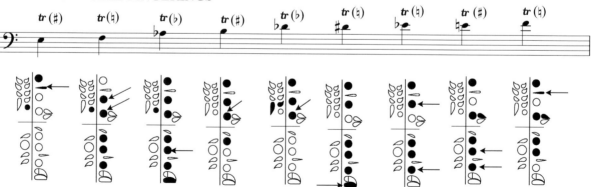

Application of Alternate Fingerings—Chromatic

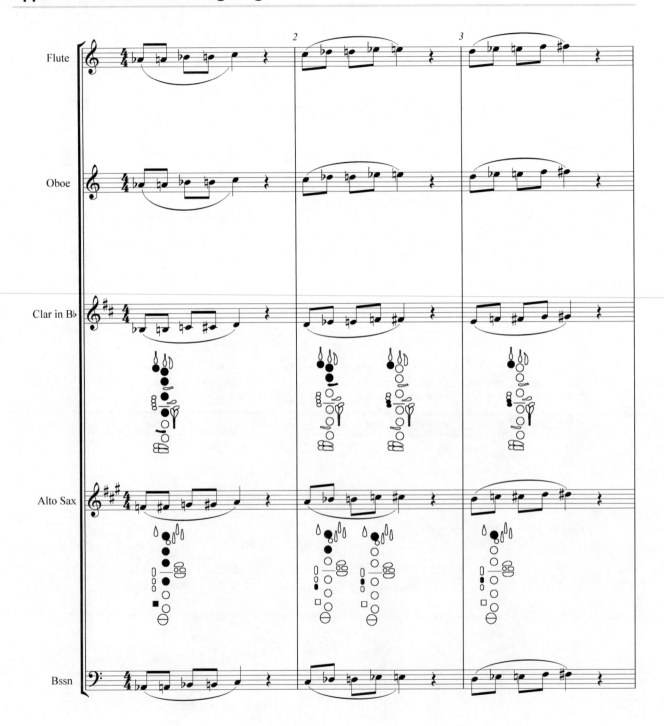

Application of Alternate Fingerings—Chromatic

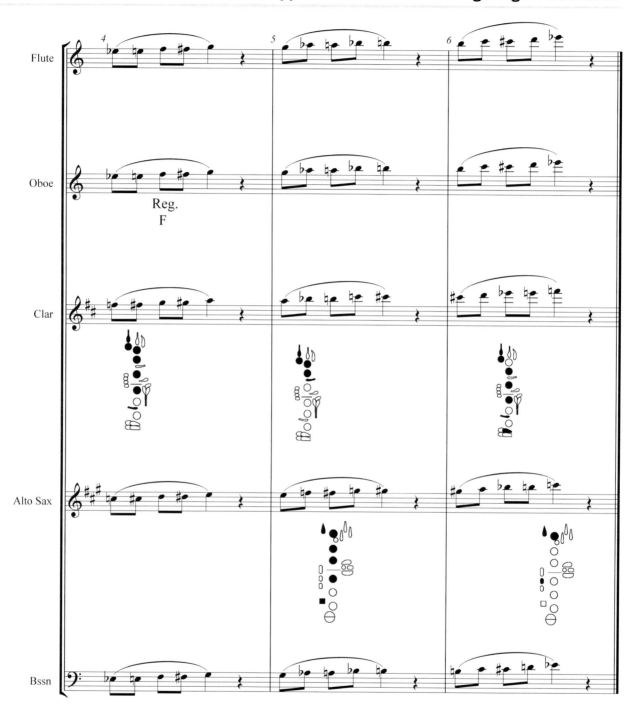

Application of Alternate Fingerings—Selected Arpeggios

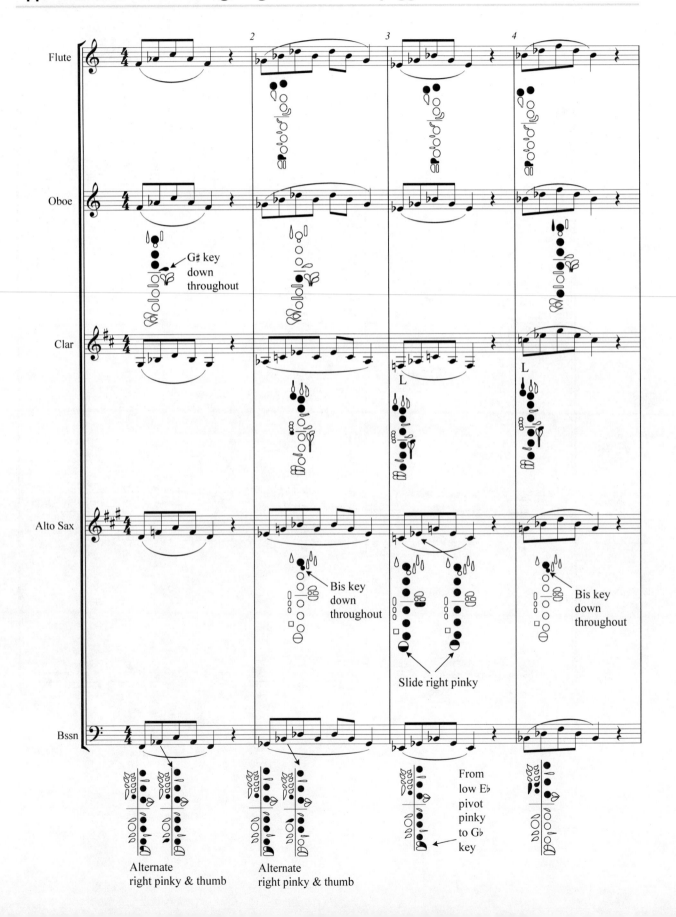

Flute

Oboe

G♯ key
down
throughout

Clar

L

L

Alto Sax

Bis key
down
throughout

Bis key
down
throughout

Slide right pinky

Bssn

Alternate
right pinky & thumb

Alternate
right pinky & thumb

From
low E♭
pivot
pinky
to G♭
key

Application of Alternate Fingerings—Selected Arpeggios

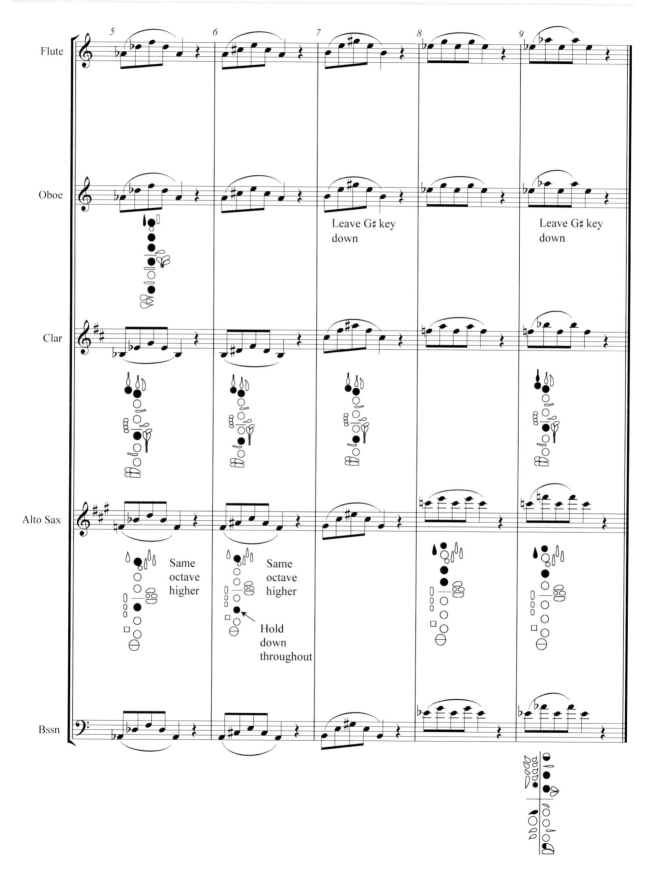

Application of Alternate Fingerings—Selected Trills

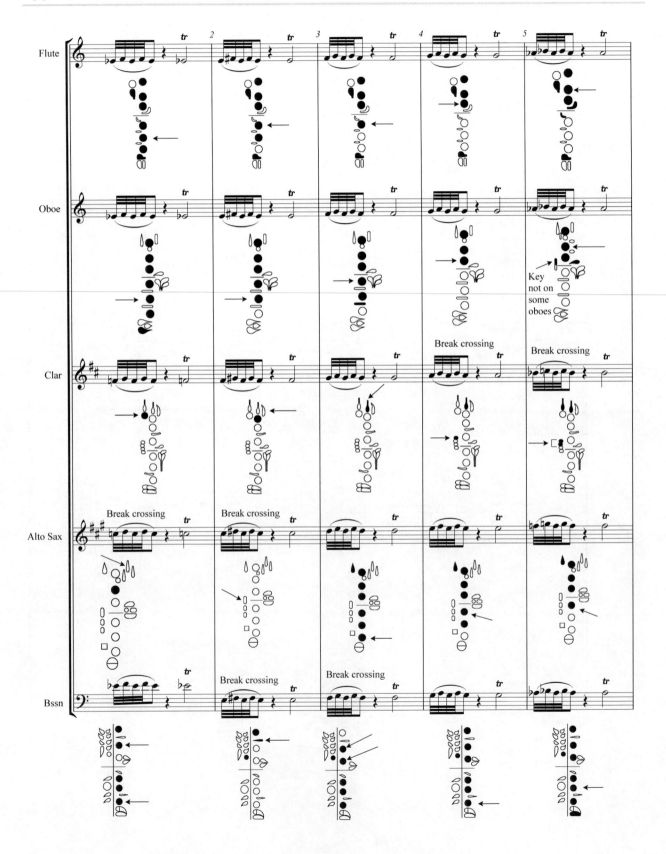

Application of Alternate Fingerings—Selected Trills

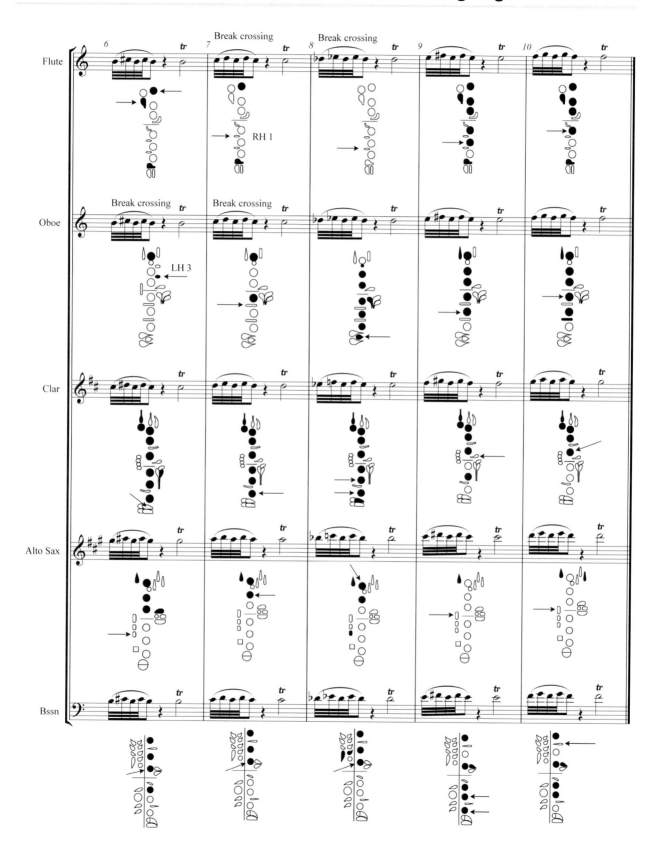

Application of Alternate Fingerings—Woodwind Quintet

This woodwind quintet is written at an advanced high school performance level. Prepare this music for a rehearsal by filling in the fingerings designated "A" (Alternate).

Write in the reason for using each alternate fingering—see p. 216.

(All fingerings may be found on pp. 217–221.)

A = ALTERNATE, T = THUMB, P = PINKY, R = RIGHT, L = LEFT

Application of Alternate Fingerings—Woodwind Quintet

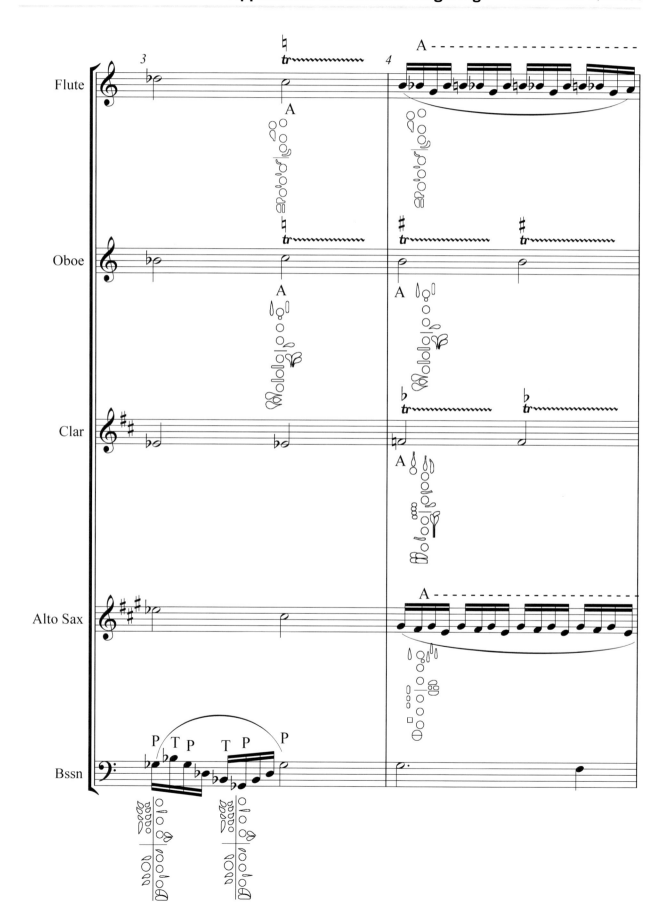

Application of Alternate Fingerings—Woodwind Quintet

Application of Alternate Fingerings—Woodwind Quintet

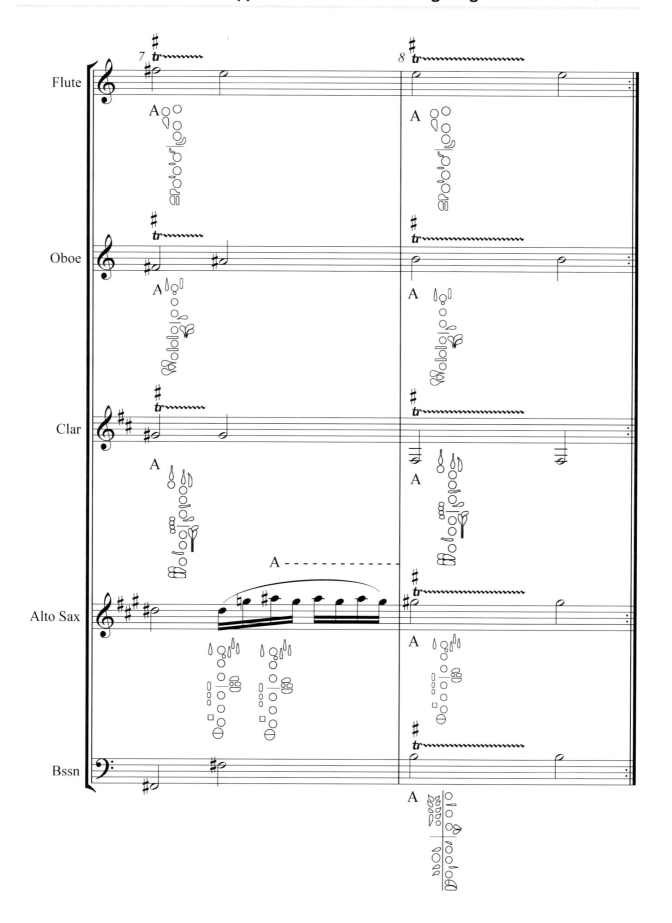

Application of Alternate Fingerings—Woodwind Quintet

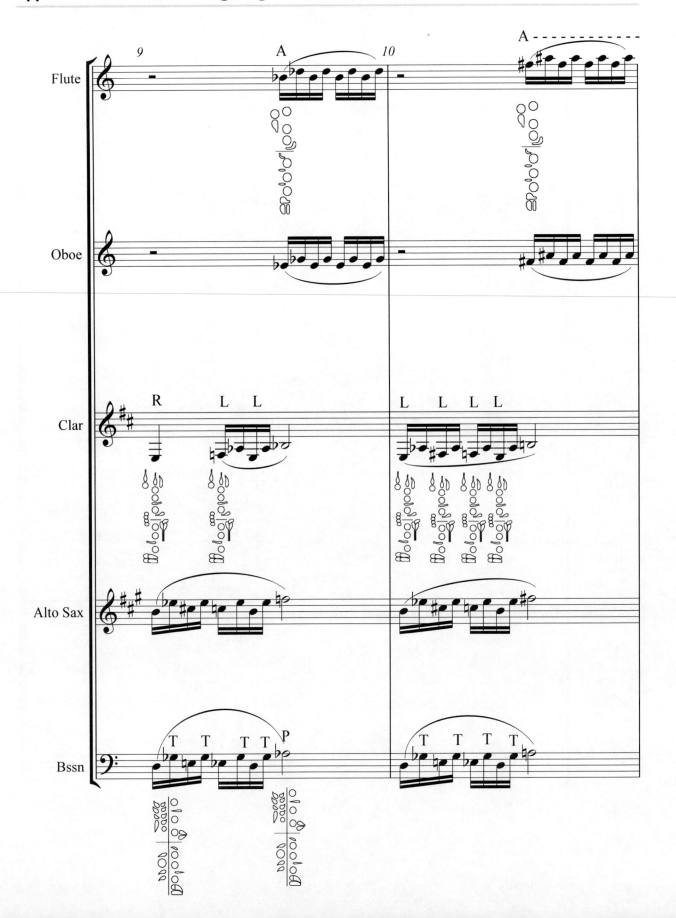

Application of Alternate Fingerings—Woodwind Quintet

Application of Alternate Fingerings—Woodwind Quintet

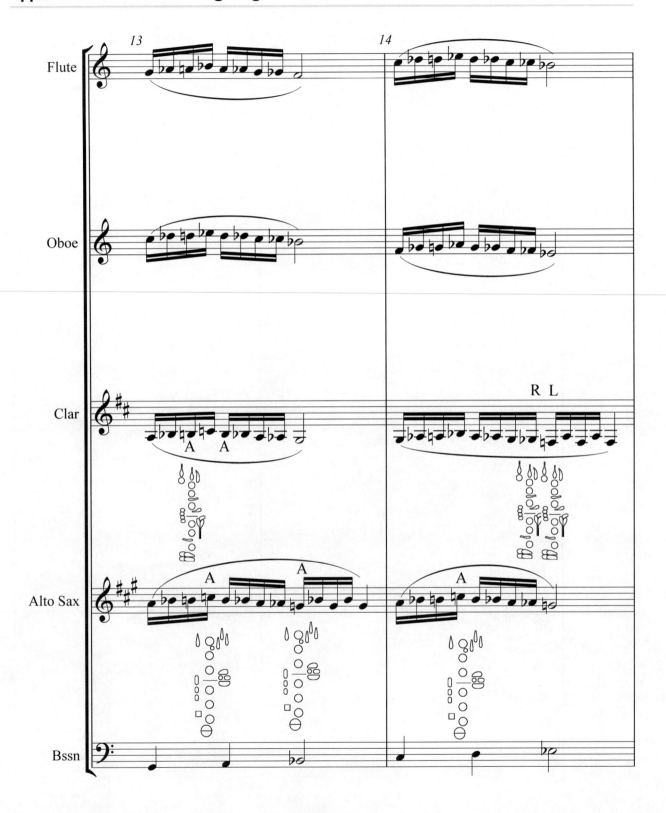

Application of Alternate Fingerings—Woodwind Quintet

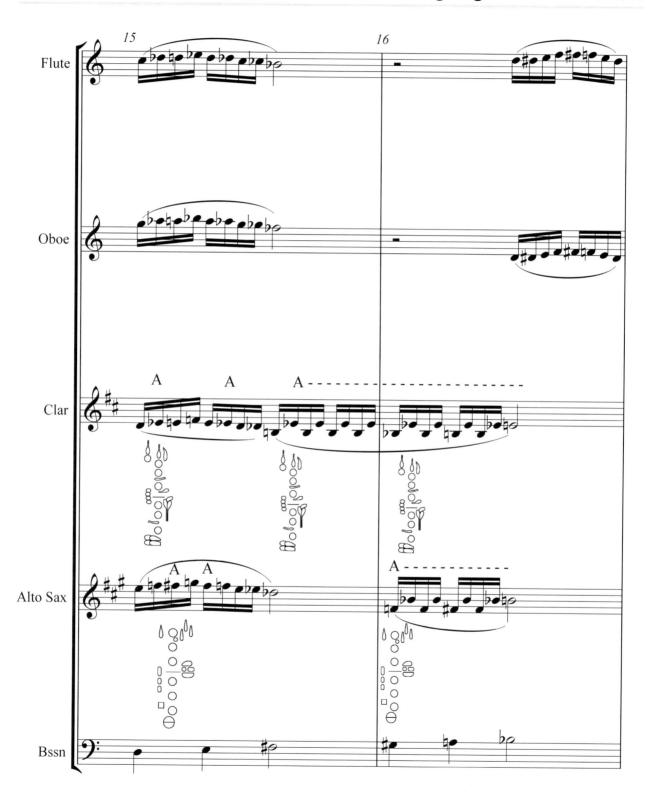

Application of Alternate Fingerings—Woodwind Quintet

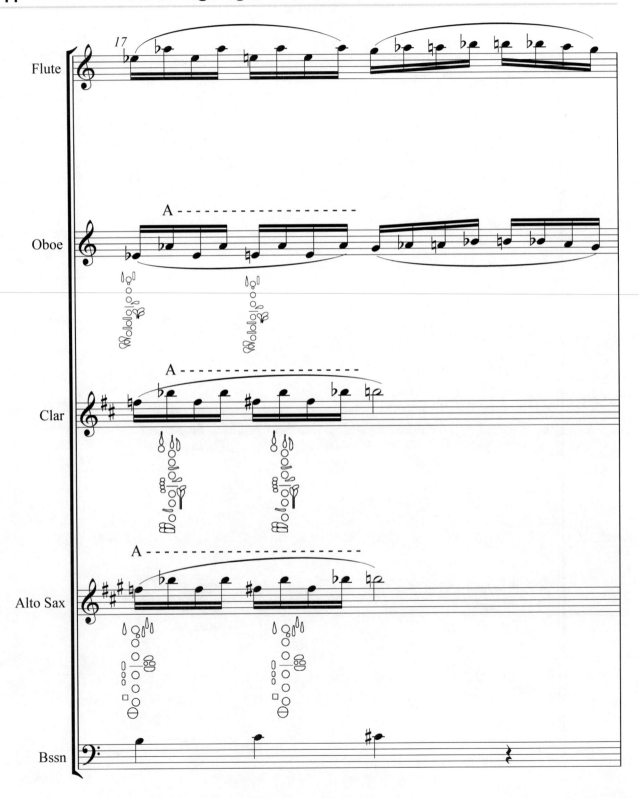

Application of Alternate Fingerings—Woodwind Quintet

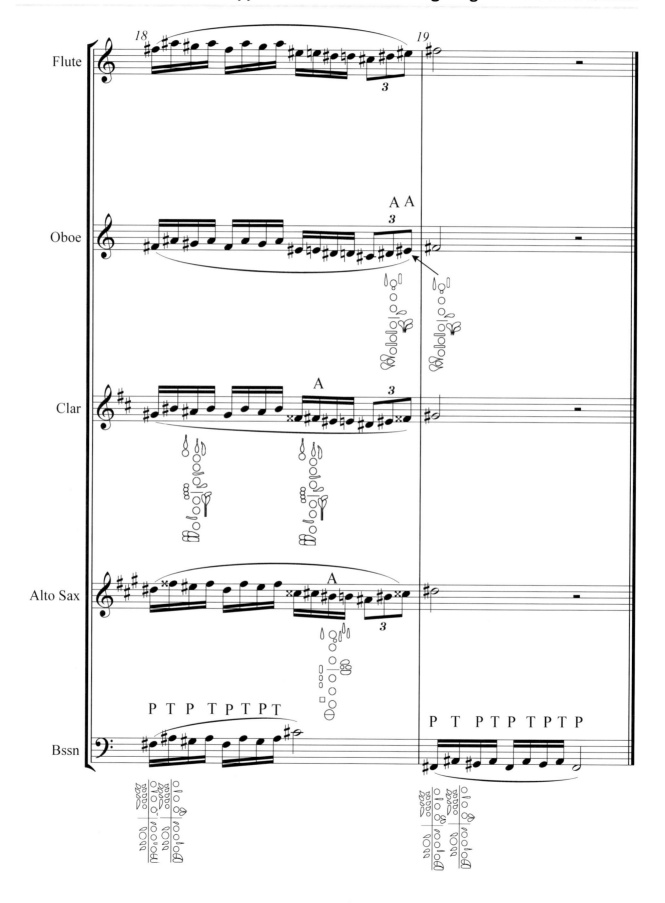

10 Review Questions

Ranges, Break Crossings, and Register—Octave Mechanisms (pp. 58–59)

1. Write the lowest and highest notes for each register
2. Using brackets, arrows, and noteheads, indicate the use of ALL octave and register keys

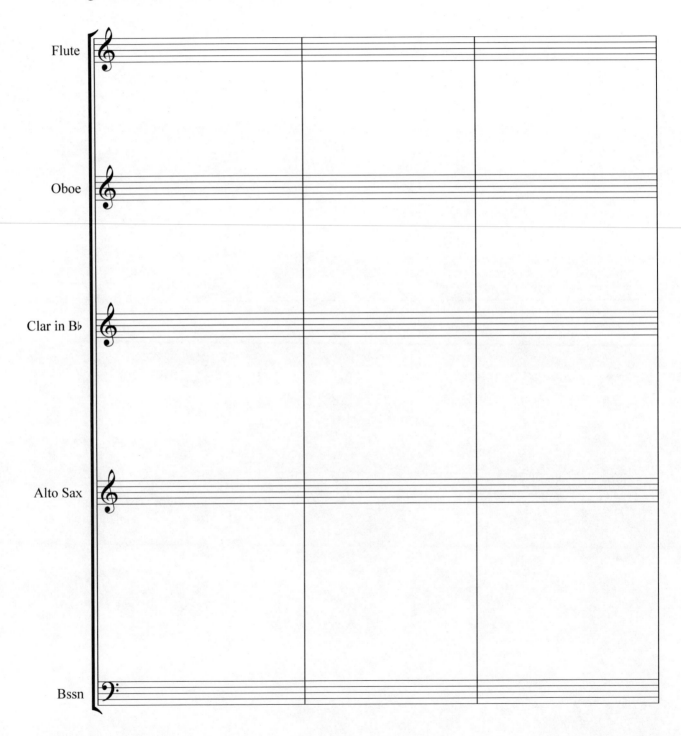

Ranges, Break Crossings, and Register—Octave Mechanisms (pp.58–59)

1. Notes requiring palm keys:

2. Lowest note of the middle register of the oboe:

3. Throat tones on the clarinet:

4. Half-hole notes on the bassoon:

5. Notes requiring flick keys:

6. Notes requiring the whisper key:

7. Lowest note of the bassoon's middle register:

8. Lowest note of the bassoon's lowest register:

9. Highest note of the saxophone's lowest register:

10. Highest note of the lowest register of the flute:

11. Lowest note of the altissimo register of the clarinet:

12. Lowest note of the chalumeau register of the clarinet:

13. Lowest note of the clarion register of the clarinet:

14. Notes requiring half-hole fingerings on oboe:

15. Notes requiring SOK:

16. Notes requiring TOK:

Basic Scale Fingerings (pp. 60–61)

Fill in and label: Thumb hole; E♭ resonance key, WK (whisper key), and the B key

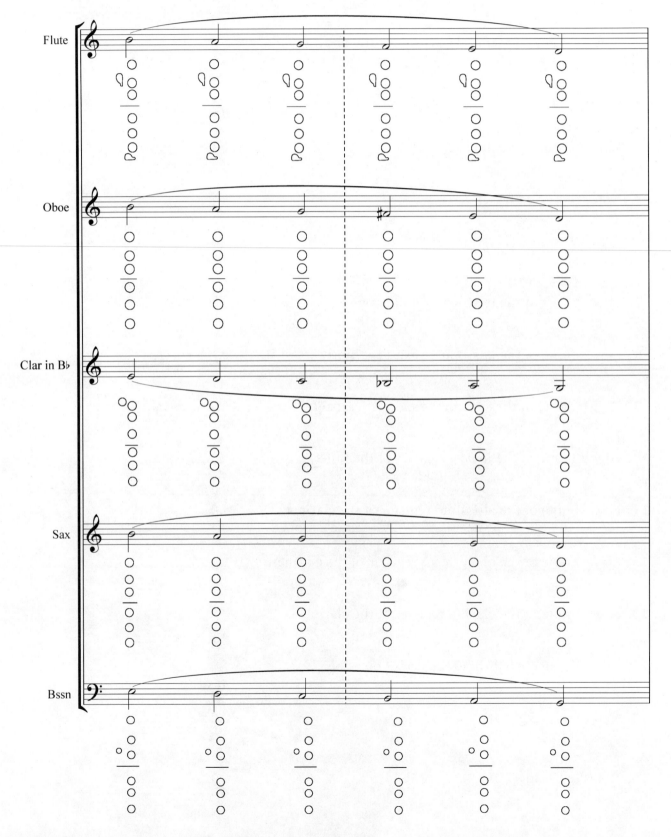

Basic Scale Fingerings (pp. 68–69)

Fill in and label: Thumb hole; E♭ resonance key, WK (whisper key), and the B key

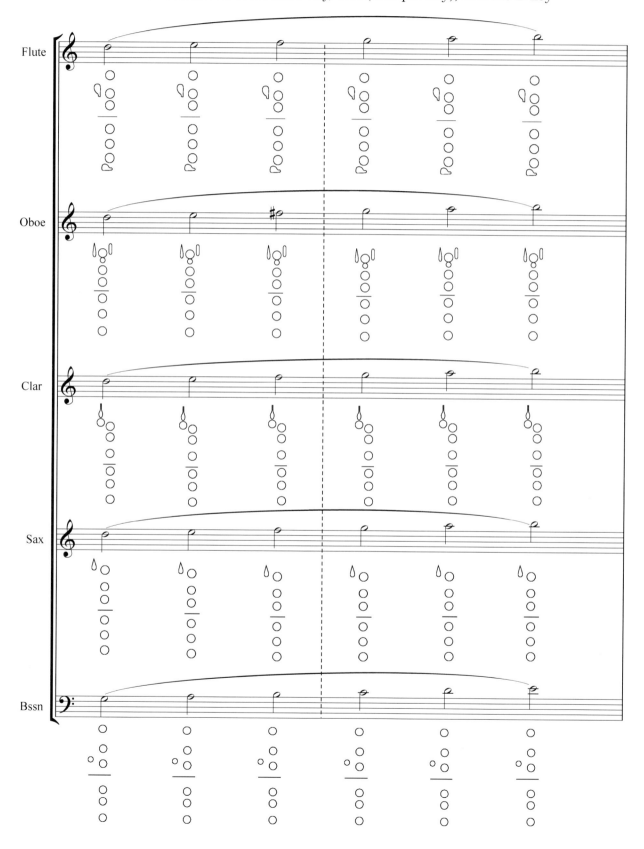

Thumbs in Woodwind Pedagogy (pp. 96–99)

There are thirteen thumb keys on the _____ including the whisper key (WK), two thumb keys on the _____ (B and B♭ keys), one thumb key on the _____ (OK), one thumb key on the _____ (TOK), and one thumb key (RK) and one thumb hole on the _____.

The WK on the _____ is operated with the left thumb.

T or F. The left thumb plays no role in supporting the flute while playing.

The only woodwind instrument where the right thumb is not involved with holding the instrument is the _____.

The only woodwind instrument where the left hand is not anchored to the body of the instrument is the _____.

On the _____, the left thumb must be anchored **at all times** on the pearl (plastic) thumb pad.

In holding the _____, the three points of contact with the hands are: (1) the right thumb, (2) the E♭ resonator key, and (3) the left forefinger.

The weight of the _____ is on the right thumb under the thumb rest and balanced between this point and the upper teeth with no other fingers involved in holding the instrument.

On the _____, the RK is operated by pivoting (not sliding) the tip of the left thumb.

On the _____, the left thumb must overlap onto the OK so that a simple pivotal motion is used to activate the OK, not a sliding motion.

The left thumb pushes the _____ out of the mouth, the right thumb pushes the mouthpiece into the mouth, and the neckstrap ring acts as a fulcrum.

Besides depressing keys, the left thumb on the _____ is also used for "flicking."

On the _____, students tend to "anchor" the right thumb on the body of the instrument rather than letting it "hover" over the appropriate key cluster.

On _____ and _____, the thumb rest lies against the side of the right thumb near the base of the thumbnail just above the first knuckle.

Key Clusters (pp. 84–99)

1. Identify the instrument for each cluster.
2. Write in the corresponding pitch on each individual key.

Right Pinky:

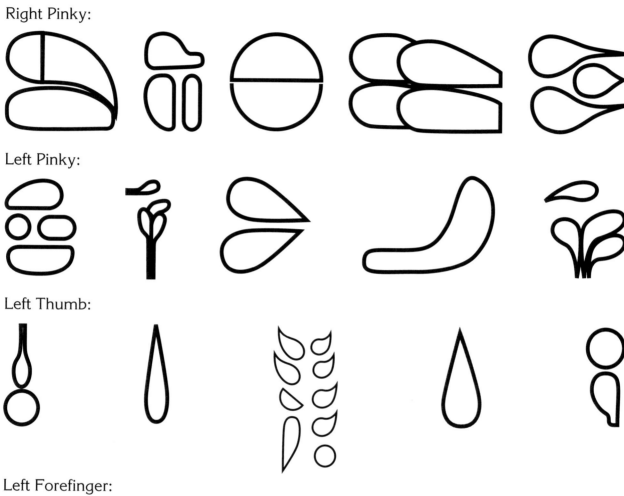

Left Pinky:

Left Thumb:

Left Forefinger:

Right Forefinger:  Right Thumb:

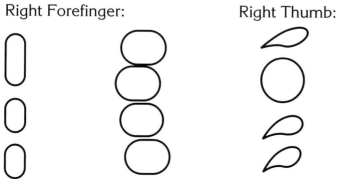

Fingerings—Flute

Label all keys/tone holes with corresponding pitch names. Use arrows if necessary. See pp. 57–99.

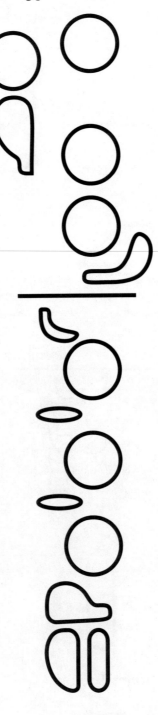

Fingerings—Oboe

Label all keys/tone holes with corresponding pitch names. Use arrows if necessary. See pp. 57–99.

Fingerings—Clarinet

Label all keys/tone holes with corresponding pitch names. Use arrows if necessary. See pp. 57–99.

Fingerings—Saxophone

Label all keys/tone holes with corresponding pitch names. Use arrows if necessary. See pp. 57–99.

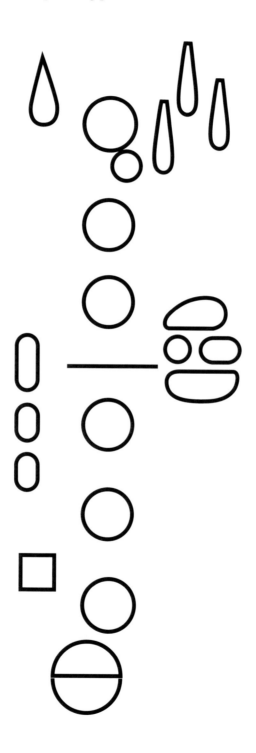

Fingerings—Bassoon

Label all keys/tone holes with corresponding pitch names. Use arrows if necessary. See pp. 57–99.

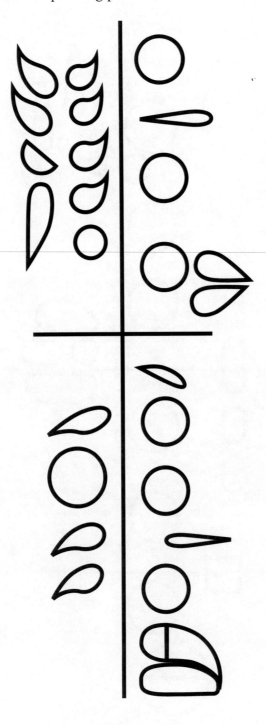

Arranging

You have been asked to arrange "The Star-Spangled Banner" for mixed woodwinds, saxophone ensemble, and clarinet ensemble. Consult the transposition chart on p. 53 and arrange the first phrase for the designated instruments.

The Star-Spangled Banner—John Smith (1750–1836)

Teaching Scales—Elementary School

While student teaching, your supervisory teacher asks you to rehearse the woodwind section of an elementary school band in a performance of a one-octave F major scale. Write a transposed score of the scale with key signatures. Include a break crossing in each part and mark all break crossings with brackets. Using abbreviations label all octave and register key mechanisms (RK, TOK, WK, etc.). Include pedagogical advice for performance problems your students might encounter such as RHD, alternate fingerings, embouchure/holding advice, and so forth (see pp. 53, 135–185).

Teaching Scales—Elementary School

While student teaching, your supervisory teacher asks you to rehearse the woodwind section of an elementary school band in a performance of a one-octave E♭ major scale. Write a transposed score of the scale with key signatures. Include a break crossing in each part and mark all break crossings with brackets. Using abbreviations label all octave and register key mechanisms (RK, TOK, WK, etc.). Include pedagogical advice for performance problems your students might encounter such as RHD, alternate fingerings, embouchure/holding advice, and so forth (see pp. 53, 135–185).

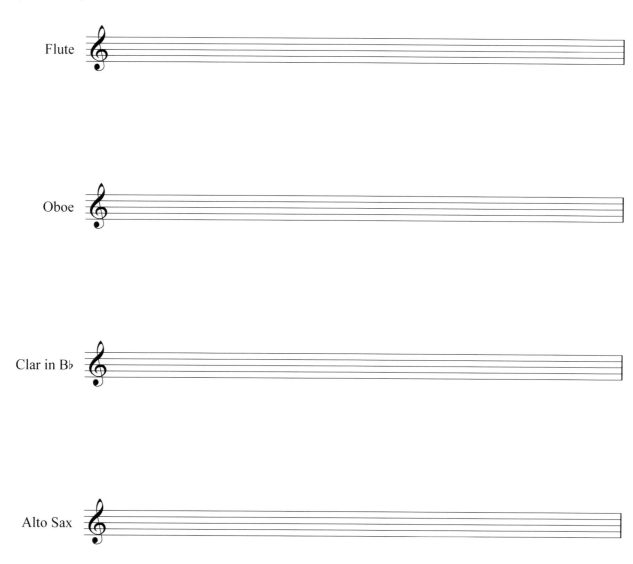

Teaching Tunes—Elementary School

Prepare this music for an elementary school band rehearsal by writing pedagogical notes below each staff. See pp. 135–185.

Donkey Round—American Folk Song

Teaching Tunes—Elementary School

Prepare this music for an elementary school band rehearsal by writing pedagogical notes below each staff. See pp. 135–185.

Au Clair de la Lune—French Folk Song

Teaching Tunes—Elementary School

Prepare this music for an elementary school band rehearsal by writing pedagogical notes below each staff. See pp. 135–185.

English Folk Song—Anonymous

Teaching Tunes—Elementary School

Prepare this music for an elementary school band rehearsal by writing pedagogical notes below each staff. See pp. 135–185.

Dreydl, Dreydl—Traditional Hanukkah Song

Teaching Tunes—Elementary School

Prepare this music for an elementary school band rehearsal by writing pedagogical notes below each staff. See pp. 135–185.

Ye Banks and Braes of Bonnie Doon—Scottish Folk Song

Teaching Tunes—Elementary School

Prepare this music for an elementary school band rehearsal by writing pedagogical notes below each staff. See pp. 135–185.

Molly Malone—Irish Folk Song

Teaching Scales—Junior High School

While student teaching, your supervisory teacher asks you to rehearse the woodwind section of a junior high school band in a performance of a one-octave B♭ major scale. Write a transposed score of the scale with key signatures. Include a break crossing in each part and mark all break crossings with brackets. Using abbreviations, label all octave and register key mechanisms (RK, TOK, WK, etc.). Include pedagogical advice for performance problems your students might encounter such as RHD, alternate fingerings, embouchure/holding advice, and so forth (see pp. 135–185).

Teaching Scales—Junior High School

While student teaching, your supervisory teacher asks you to rehearse the woodwind section of a junior high school band in a performance of a one-octave G major scale. Write a transposed score of the scale with key signatures. Include a break crossing in each part and mark all break crossings with brackets. Using abbreviations, label all octave and register key mechanisms (RK, TOK, WK, etc.). Include pedagogical advice for performance problems your students might encounter such as RHD, alternate fingerings, embouchure/holding advice, and so forth (see pp. 135–185).

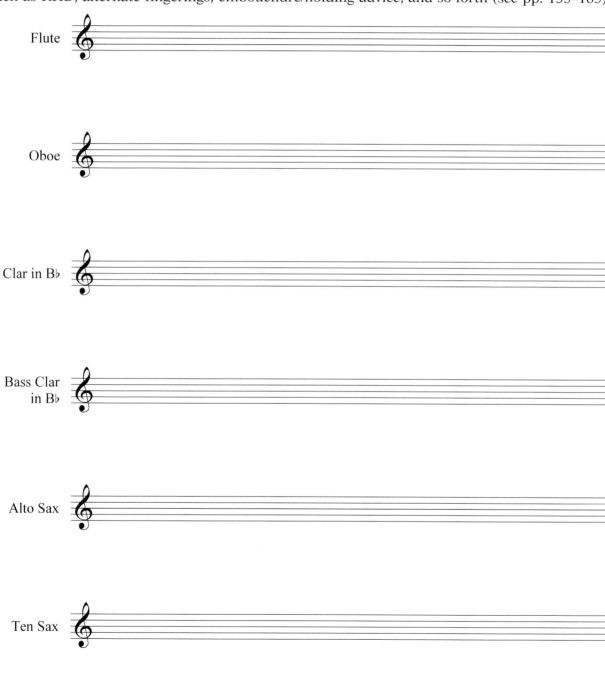

Teaching Scales—Junior High School

While student teaching, your supervisory teacher asks you to rehearse the woodwind section of a junior high school band in a performance of a one-octave C major scale. Write a transposed score of the scale with key signatures. Include a break crossing in each part and mark all break crossings with brackets. Using abbreviations, label all octave and register key mechanisms (RK, TOK, WK, etc.). Include pedagogical advice for performance problems your students might encounter such as RHD, alternate fingerings, embouchure/holding advice, and so forth (see pp. 135–185).

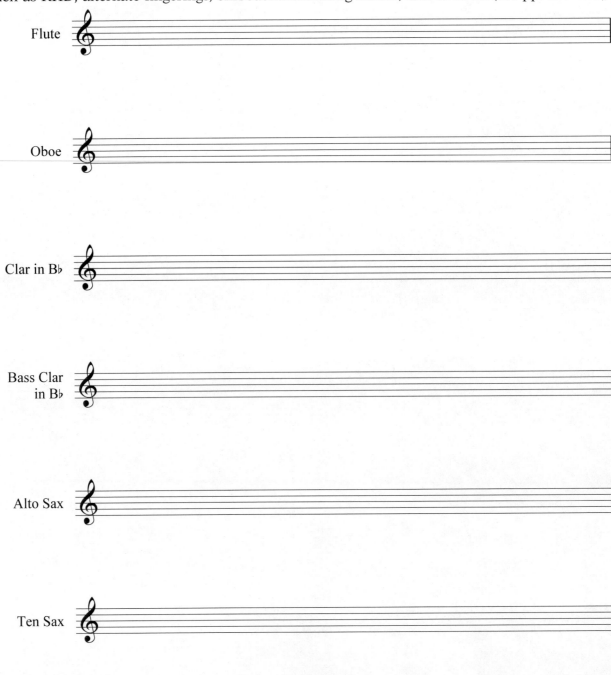

Teaching Tunes—Junior High School

Prepare this music for a junior high school band rehearsal by writing pedagogical notes below each staff. See pp. 135–185.

Row, Row, Row Your Boat—American Folk Song

Teaching Tunes—Junior High School

Prepare this music for a junior high school band rehearsal by writing pedagogical notes below each staff. See pp. 135–185.

Hey Ho, Anybody Home?—American Folk Round

Teaching Tunes—Junior High School

Prepare this music for a junior high school band rehearsal by writing pedagogical notes below each staff. See pp. 135–185.

Rakes of Mallow—Traditional Fiddle Tune

Teaching Scales—High School

While student teaching, your supervisory teacher asks you to rehearse the woodwind section of a high school band in a performance of a one-octave D melodic minor scale. Write a transposed score of the scale with key signatures. Include a break crossing in each part and mark all break crossings with brackets. Using abbreviations label all octave and register key mechanisms (RK, TOK, WK, etc.). Include pedagogical advice for performance problems your students might encounter such as RHD, alternate fingerings, embouchure/holding advice, and so forth. See pp. 53, 135–185.

Teaching Scales—High School

While student teaching, your supervisory teacher asks you to rehearse the woodwind section of a high school band in a performance of a one-octave F melodic minor scale. Write a transposed score of the scale with key signatures. Include a break crossing in each part and mark all break crossings with brackets. Using abbreviations label all octave and register key mechanisms (RK, TOK, WK, etc.). Include pedagogical advice for performance problems your students might encounter such as RHD, alternate fingerings, embouchure/holding advice, and so forth. See pp. 53, 135–185.

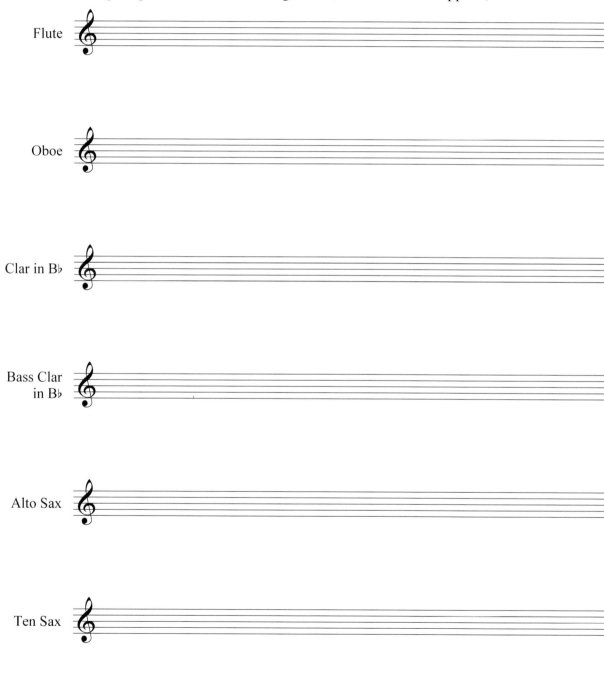

Teaching Scales—High School

While student teaching, your supervisory teacher asks you to rehearse the woodwind section of a high school band in a performance of a two-octave F major scale. Write a transposed score of the scale with key signatures. Include a break crossing in each part and mark all break crossings with brackets. Using abbreviations label all octave and register key mechanisms (RK, TOK, WK, etc.). Include pedagogical advice for performance problems your students might encounter such as RHD, alternate fingerings, embouchure/holding advice, and so forth. See pp. 53, 135–185.

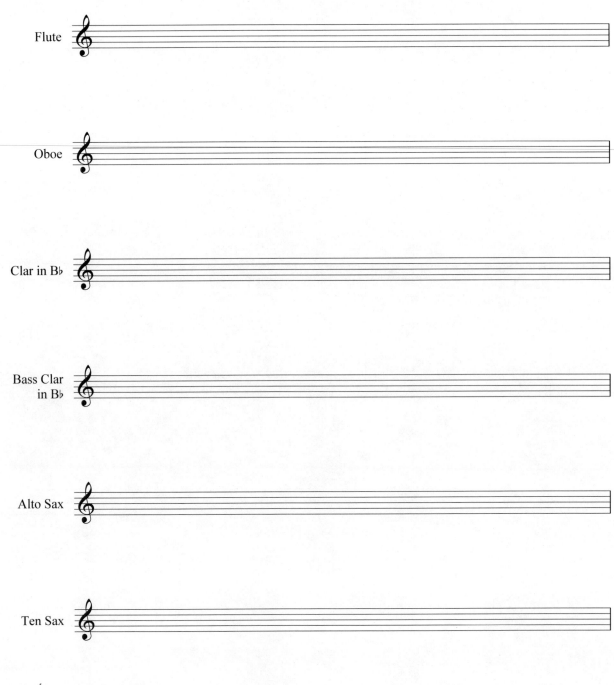

Teaching Scales—High School

While student teaching, your supervisory teacher asks you to rehearse the woodwind section of a high school band in a performance of a two-octave E♭ major scale. Write a transposed score of the scale with key signatures. Include a break crossing in each part and mark all break crossings with brackets. Using abbreviations label all octave and register key mechanisms (RK, TOK, WK, etc.). Include pedagogical advice for performance problems your students might encounter such as RHD, alternate fingerings, embouchure/holding advice, and so forth. See pp. 53, 135–185.

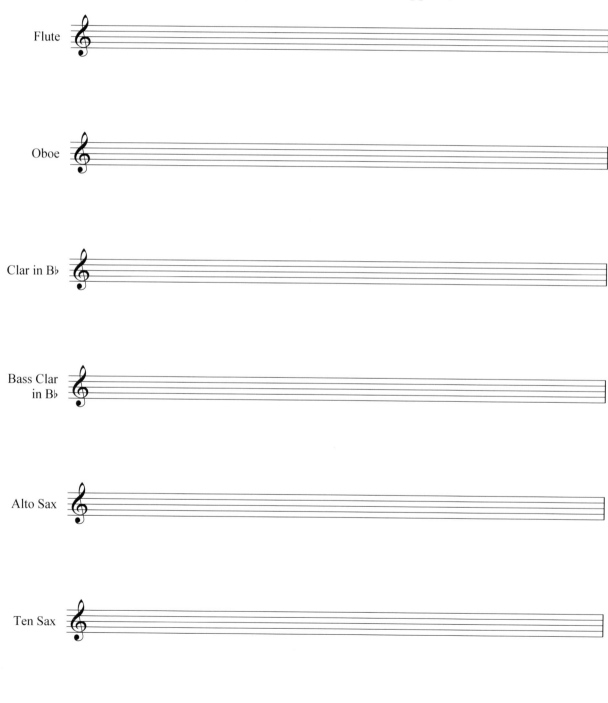

Teaching Scales—High School

While student teaching, your supervisory teacher asks you to rehearse the woodwind section of a high school band in a performance of a two-octave D♭ major scale. Write a transposed score of the scale with key signatures. Include a break crossing in each part and mark all break crossings with brackets. Using abbreviations label all octave and register key mechanisms (RK, TOK, WK, etc.). Include pedagogical advice for performance problems your students might encounter such as RHD, alternate fingerings, embouchure/holding advice, and so forth. See pp. 53, 135–185.

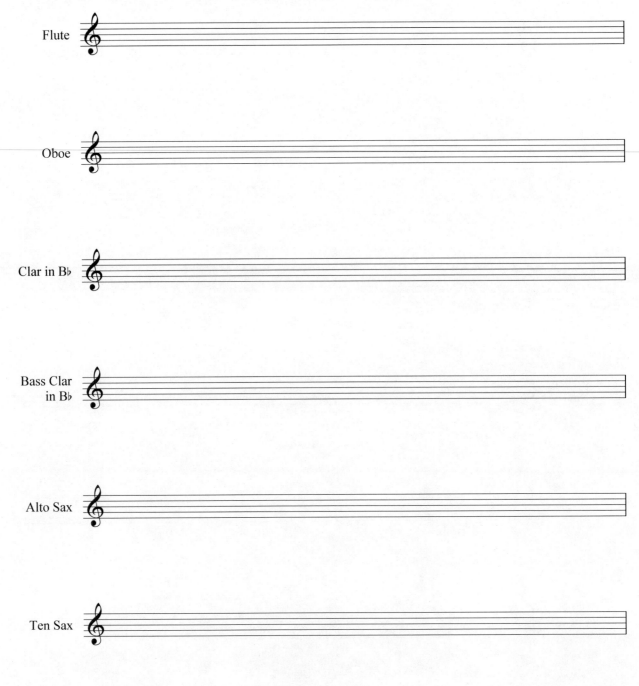

Teaching Tunes—High School

Prepare this music for a high school band rehearsal by writing pedagogical notes below each staff. See pp. 135–185.

Rondo alla Turca—W. A. Mozart (1756–1791)

Teaching Tunes—High School

Prepare this music for a high school band rehearsal by writing pedagogical notes below each staff. See pp. 135–185.

Austrian Folk Song—Anonymous

Teaching Tunes—High School

Prepare this music for a high school band rehearsal by writing pedagogical notes below each staff. See pp. 135–185.

Trumpet Voluntary—Jeremiah Clarke (1674–1707)

Teaching Tunes—High School

Prepare this music for a high school band rehearsal by writing pedagogical notes below each staff. See pp. 135–185.

American Patrol—F. W. Meacham

Teaching Tunes—High School

Teaching Tunes—High School

Prepare this music for a high school band rehearsal by writing pedagogical notes below each staff. See pp. 135–185.

Over the River and Through the Wood—American Folk Song

Teaching Tunes—High School

Prepare this music for a high school band rehearsal by writing pedagogical notes below each staff. See pp. 135–185.

Blow the Wind Southerly—English Folksong

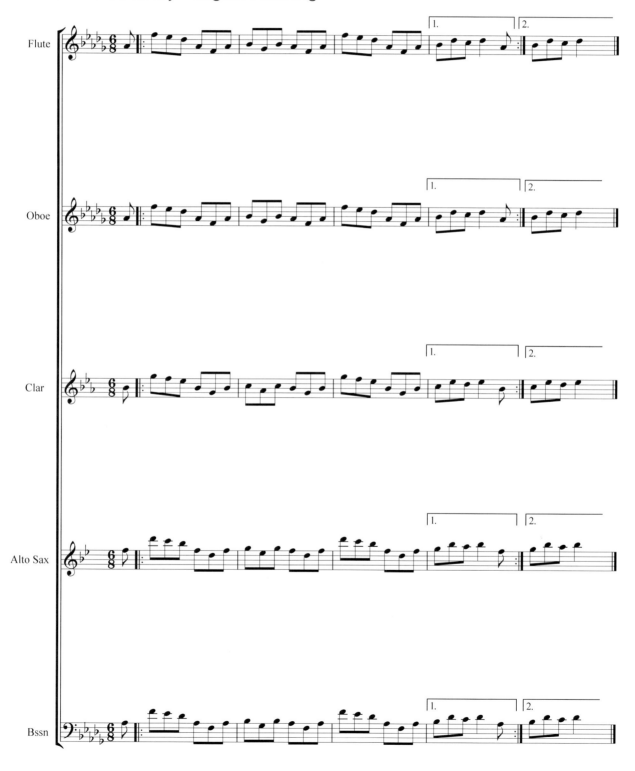

Alternate Fingering Review

Write a two-note passage illustrating the use of the given alternate fingerings. See pp. 217–221

Alternate Fingering Review

Write a two-note passage illustrating the use of the given alternate fingerings. See pp. 217–221.

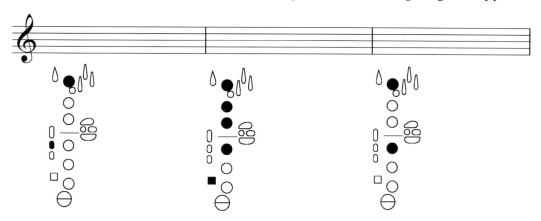

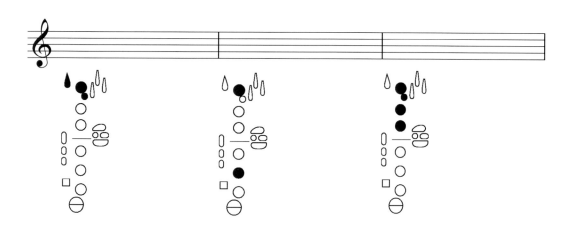

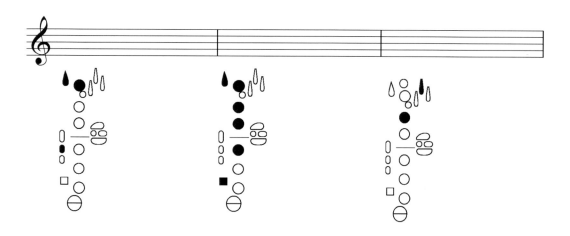

Alternate Fingering Review

Write a two-note passage illustrating the use of the given alternate fingerings. See pp. 217–221.

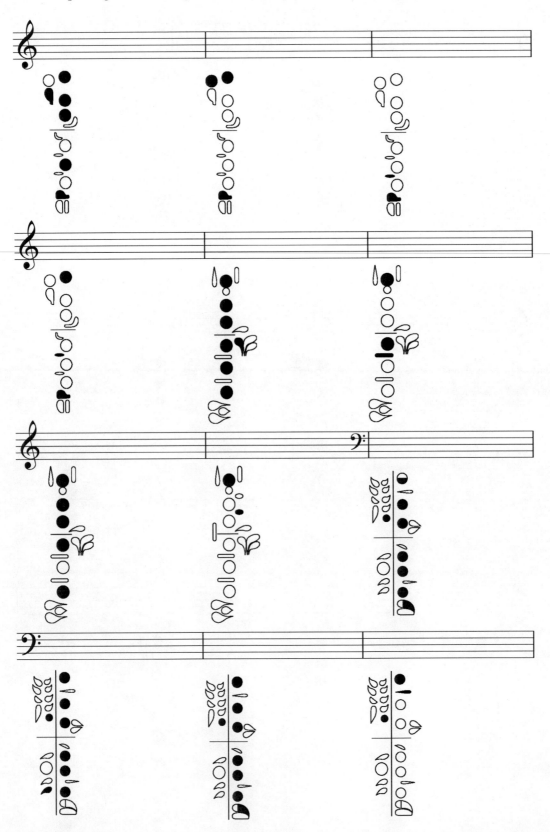

Review Questions—General

1. **T or F.** All woodwinds have three basic registers. (Refer to pp. 58–59.)

2. **T or F.** The third or highest register of any and all woodwind instruments has the simplest fingerings of all three registers. (Refer to p. 58.)

3. **T or F.** On most fingering charts the first fingering given for a note is the preferred and standard fingering. (Refer to p. 216.)

4. **T or F.** In finishing the ends of phrases followed by intervals of silence, the tongue should stop the flow of air. (Refer to p. 31.)

5. **T or F.** Jaw vibrato is recommended for the flute, oboe, and bassoon. (Refer to p. 34.)

6. **T or F.** Teaching involves communication between students and the teacher. The teacher must have the ability to recognize playing problems, analyze them, and suggest solutions. (Refer to p. 135.)

7. **T or F.** The clarinet requires a more constant air speed than the flute. (Refer to pp. 28–29.)

8. **T or F.** On all five woodwinds, students should be instructed to take breaths through the mouth. (Refer to p. 28.)

9. **T or F.** The middle register fingerings generally duplicate the fingerings of the lowest register. (Refer to p. 58.)

10. **T or F.** The flute requires less air than the oboe. (Refer to pp. 28–29.)

11. **T or F.** A wind instrument plays sharper when cold and flatter when warmer. (Refer to p. 33.)

12. Considering guide position of all ten fingers on all five woodwinds, which finger is the most curved? _____ (Refer to pp. 12, 14.)

13. The woodwind instrument having the most alternate fingerings between the two little fingers is: _____ (Refer to p. 87.)

14. What can be done if low notes do not speak on a woodwind instrument? (Refer to p. 84.)

Review Questions—Flute

1. **T or F.** In assembling the flute, make certain the key rods of the foot joint are aligned with the key rods on the body of the flute. (Refer to p. 4.)

2. **T or F.** Rolling the flute outward lowers the pitch. (Refer to p. 32.)

3. **T or F.** Raising the airstream raises the pitch. (Refer to p. 32.)

4. **T or F.** Extending the lower lip slightly outward lowers the pitch. (Refer to p. 32.)

5. **T or F.** Using a slower air speed raises the pitch. (Refer to p. 32.)

6. **T or F.** The flute should be parallel with the line of the lips while playing. (Refer to p. 18.)

7. **T or F.** Jaw vibrato is highly recommended for the flute. (Refer to p. 34.)

8. **T or F.** In order to ensure light hand pressure on the flute when assembling, vigorously rub the tarnish from the joints with a cotton cloth. (Refer to p. 4.)

9. **T or F.** The left thumb supports the flute while playing. (Refer to p. 66.)

10. **T or F.** Generally, for high notes on the flute, a larger amount of the embouchure hole is covered by the lower lip. (Refer to p. 18.)

11. **T or F.** The head may be slightly tilted while playing the flute. (Refer to p. 16.)

12. The three parts of the flute are the _____, _____, and _____. (Refer to p. 4.)

13. On the staff that follows, write the notes on which the right pinky E♭ key is NOT USED. (Refer to p. 115.)

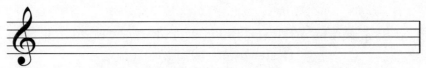

14. In general, higher tones require _____ (smaller or larger) air streams. (Refer to p. 18.)

15. What factors control the speed of the air stream? (Refer to p. 18.)

16. Discuss briefly the placement of the tongue for articulation on the flute. (Refer to p. 30.)

Review Questions—Flute

17. Explain in detail the problems involved on flute in "crossing the break." (Refer to p. 66.)

18. The lowest note in the highest register of the flute is ____. (Refer to p. 59.)

19. The lowest note in the middle register of the flute is ____. (Refer to p. 59.)

20. What is the highest note of the lowest register of the flute? ____. (Refer to p. 59.)

21. On the staff that follows, indicate two notes in the low and middle registers of the flute that have alternate fingerings. (Refer to p. 217.)

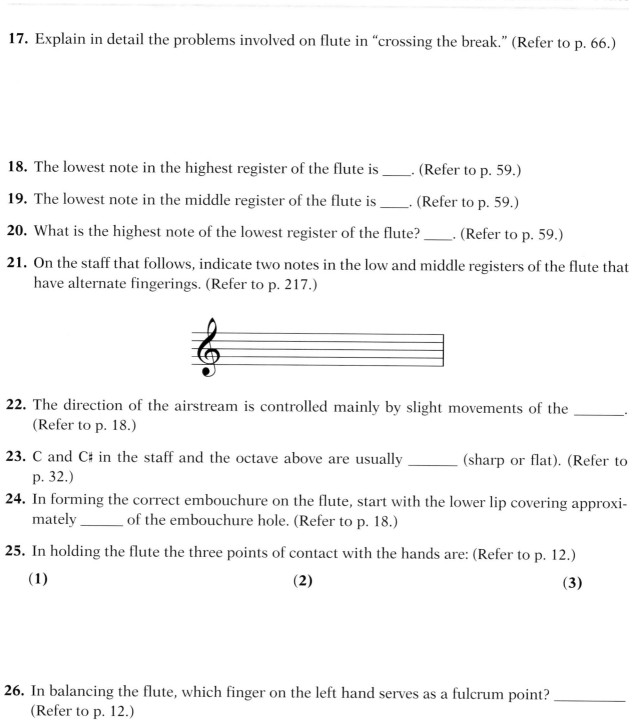

22. The direction of the airstream is controlled mainly by slight movements of the _____. (Refer to p. 18.)

23. C and C♯ in the staff and the octave above are usually _____ (sharp or flat). (Refer to p. 32.)

24. In forming the correct embouchure on the flute, start with the lower lip covering approximately _____ of the embouchure hole. (Refer to p. 18.)

25. In holding the flute the three points of contact with the hands are: (Refer to p. 12.)

   (1)   **(2)**   **(3)**

26. In balancing the flute, which finger on the left hand serves as a fulcrum point? _____ (Refer to p. 12.)

27. Comment briefly on the advantages and disadvantages of closed and open holes on the flute. (Refer to p. 42.)

28. If the aperture is too large the tone quality will be: (Refer to p. 19.)

Review Questions—Flute

29. Draw the desired shape and actual size of the flute aperture. (Refer to pp. 16, 19.)

30. A student plays consistently sharp throughout the range. Recommend three things he or she might try: (Refer to pp. 32, 189.)

31. If a flute student is expending his or her breath too rapidly and having to breathe too often, what remedial measures may be taken? (Refer to pp. 18–19, 28.)

32. Where and what are adjustment screws on the flute? (Refer to p. 51.)

33. What advice can you offer an advanced student whose high register is too harsh, loud, and breathy? (Refer to pp. 18–19, 189.)

34. What is the primary difference between a student-model flute and a professional flute? (Refer to p. 42.)

35. Why is the practicing of octaves on the flute so important? (Refer to p. 72.)

Review Questions—Flute

36. On the staff that follows, write the head joint exercise and describe its use. (Refer to pp. 18,26.)

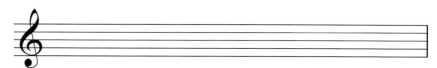

37. Recommend four things a student may try if he or she is consistently flat. (Refer to p. 32.)

38. Briefly discuss the use of size, direction, coverage, and speed in playing different ranges of the flute. (Refer to p. 18.)

39. Describe briefly the daily care and maintenance of the flute. (Refer to p. 4.)

40. What is a cupid's bow? (Refer to p. 38.)

41. Name three good books or articles that you could use for teaching the flute: (Refer to pp. 325–329.)

42. List a few pedagogical problems you may encounter in teaching the flute. (Refer to p. 40.)

Review Questions—Oboe

1. **T or F.** Of all the woodwinds the oboe is most susceptible to damage from poor assembly habits. (Refer to p. 5.)

2. **T or F.** Generally, oboists hold their instrument at a slightly higher angle than clarinetists. (Refer to p. 10.)

3. **T or F.** On double reeds the pitch can be raised by pulling the reed farther out of the mouth. (Refer to p. 22.)

4. **T or F.** With the double reed embouchure, there should be an equal amount of cushion all the way around the reed. (Refer to p. 16.)

5. **T or F.** If high notes do not respond, insert more reed into the mouth. (Refer to p. 22.)

6. **T or F.** Jaw vibrato is recommended for oboe students. (Refer to p. 34.)

7. **T or F.** Staples should be thrown away after the oboe reed has worn out. (Refer to p. 48.)

8. **T or F.** The finger span on oboe is larger than on clarinet. (Refer to pp. 12, 14.)

9. **T or F.** Half-hole fingerings are involved on the break crossing of the oboe. (Refer to p. 70.)

10. A very important factor in assembling the oboe is not to damage the _____ levers. How many of these levers do you find on student oboes? _____ (Refer to p. 5.)

11. Too much reed in the mouth will cause the oboe student to play _____ (pitch, volume, tone quality). (Refer to p. 22.)

12. Clipping the tip of a double reed _____ (raises or lowers) the pitch. (Refer to p. 49.)

13. The _____ is inserted between the blades of the reed whenever scraping is being done. (Refer to p. 49.)

14. The _____ is inserted into the tube of the reed while scraping. (Refer to p. 49.)

15. Briefly describe the steps for assembling the oboe. Of what must a student be most careful when assembling the oboe? (Refer to p. 5.)

16. Write a passage illustrating the use of the articulated G♯ key on the oboe. (Refer to p. 218.)

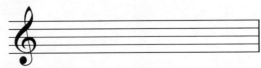

17. When inserting or removing the reed, where are the hands placed? Why? (Refer to p. 5.)

18. What type of reed case would you recommend for oboe students? (Refer to p. 3.)

Review Questions—Oboe

19. How can a stuck oboe reed usually be removed without ruining the reed or cork? (Refer to p. 5.)

20. List the three steps in forming the oboe embouchure. How much of the red part of the lower lip is visible? (Refer to p. 22.)

21. On the staff that follows, indicate the notes the require the $\frac{1}{2}$H, TOK, and SOK. (Refer to p. 59.)

22. Describe the two teaching approaches to using the TOK in conjunction with the SOK. (Refer to p. 68.)

23. Briefly describe the proper holding/hand position when playing the oboe. (Refer to p. 12, 14.)

24. How much reed should be inside the mouth? (Refer to p. 17.)

25. What sound is heard if too much reed is in the mouth? Too little reed? (Refer to p. 17.)

26. What three ways can be used to vary the pitch of the double reed? (Refer to p. 22.)

27. What pitch should be produced when crowing an oboe reed? (Refer to p. 24.)

28. What pitches should be produced when buzzing an oboe reed? (Refer to p. 24.)

29. How long should a reed be soaked before attempting to play it? (Refer to p. 25.)

30. If the reed is not soaked enough it will leak. How can one check his or her reed for leaks? (Refer to p. 25.)

31. How much of the reed should be moistened when soaking it? (Refer to p. 5.)

32. How open should the tip be when an oboe/reed is soaked and readied for playing? (Refer to p. 48.)

Review Questions—Oboe

33. How can the size of the tip opening be regulated? (Refer to p. 48.)

34. What sound is heard if the reed is too open? Too closed? (Refer to p. 48.)

35. Can an oboe player take in too much air? Explain. (Refer to p. 29.)

36. List the steps for teaching vibrato on the oboe. (Refer to p. 34.)

37. List ways in which an oboe can be checked for leaks. (Refer to p. 51.)

38. How can water be removed from beneath the pads? (Refer to pp. 3, 5.)

39. List a few pedagogical problems you may encounter in teaching oboe. (Refer to p. 40.)

Review Questions—Clarinet

1. **T or F.** The thumb rest lies midway between the tip of the thumb and the first knuckle. (Refer to p. 13.)

2. **T or F.** On the clarinet the left thumb assumes an approximate 45-degree (2 o'clock) angle with the body of the instrument. (Refer to p. 12.)

3. **T or F.** Tone quality can be affected by experimenting with the angle with which the clarinet is held. (Refer to p. 10.)

4. **T or F.** The corners of the lips should be firm when forming the clarinet embouchure. (Refer to p. 21.)

5. **T or F.** The proper amount of lower lip flex on the reed can be checked by achieving F♯ with the mouthpiece and barrel. (Refer to p. 20.)

6. **T or F.** One should push the mouthpiece against the upper teeth with firm upward pressure from the right thumb. (Refer to p. 21.)

7. **T or F.** Too much reed in mouth may cause squeaking. (Refer to p. 21.)

8. **T or F.** The register key is opened by sliding the left thumb upwards. (Refer to p. 64.)

9. **T or F.** Only the tip of the reed needs be soaked before playing. (Refer to p. 6.)

10. **T or F.** The ligature screws should be tightened as much as possible. (Refer to p. 6.)

11. **T or F.** In finishing the ends of phrases followed by intervals of silence, the tongue should stop the flow of air. (Refer to p. 31.)

12. **T or F.** Too much mouthpiece in the mouth creates a small, thin, and weak tone. (Refer to p. 20.)

13. **T or F.** The weight of the clarinet is supported by the left hand. (Refer to p. 12.)

14. **T or F.** The weight of the clarinet is on the right thumb under the thumb rest and balanced between this point and the upper teeth with no other fingers involved. (Refer to p. 12.)

15. **T or F.** The chin should be flat and pointed down when playing the clarinet. (Refer to pp. 20–21.)

16. **T or F.** A cold clarinet will play sharper than a warm one. (Refer to p. 33.)

17. **T or F.** About one-half of the "red" of the lower lip covers the teeth. (Refer to p. 21.)

18. **T or F.** Students should be instructed to place the reed on the mouthpiece before the ligature. (Refer to p. 6.)

19. **T or F.** For longer lasting reeds, be certain to instruct students to store their reeds in airtight cases. (Refer to p. 3.)

20. **T or F.** In general, the air flow used on the clarinet is more constant than the air flow used on flute and double reeds. (Refer to pp. 26–27, 29.)

Review Questions—Clarinet

21. T or F. In teaching good tone quality the two main factors involved are embouchure and air. (Refer to p. 21.)

22. T or F. In teaching legato tonguing on the clarinet, use "duh-duh-duh" tonguing with a continuous flow of breath as if playing a long tone without moving the lower jaw. (Refer to p. 31.)

23. T or F. Half-hole fingerings are never used on the clarinet. (Refer to pp. 103, 108.)

24. T or F. The shorter the mouthpiece facing, the more reed should be in the mouth. (Refer to pp. 20, 24.)

25. Name two recommended brands of ligatures. (Refer to p. 44.)

26. List five causes for squeaks occurring on the clarinet. (Refer to p. 21.)

27. Throat tones have a tendency to be _____ (intonation). (Refer to pp. 32–33.)

28. Write the lowest SOUNDING NOTE on the B♭ clarinet. (Refer to pp. 53–59.)

29. On the staff that follows, write the "throat tones" that exist between the chalumeau and clarion registers of the clarinet. (Refer to p. 59.)

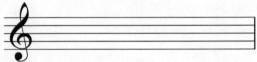

30. Two desirable characteristics visible with the "light test" on selecting a single reed are: (Refer to p. 46.)

31. Describe the thumbnail test used in selecting reeds. (Refer to p. 46.)

32. Discuss the relationship between mouthpieces and reed strengths. (Refer to pp. 44–45.)

33. Draw an outline of a clarinet mouthpiece. Label the tip opening, facing, and rails. (Refer to p. 45.)

Review Questions—Clarinet

34. How is the contact point for the lower lip on the single reed instruments determined? (Refer to p. 20.)

35. For preliminary tone production, write the pitch to be achieved on the alto clarinet with the mouthpiece, reed, and neck. (Refer to p. 20.)

36. On the bass clarinet the mouthpiece and neck combination should produce the following pitch: (Refer to p. 20.)

37. In forming the clarinet embouchure, how much lower lip is turned in over the lower teeth? (Refer to p. 21.)

38. Describe the pitch, articulation, and tone quality to be achieved with the mouthpiece + barrel exercise. (Refer to pp. 20, 24.)

39. Name the parts of the clarinet in order of assembly and specify those parts that have connecting levers. (Refer to p. 6.)

40. Describe the positioning of the left thumb. (Refer to p. 64.)

41. Approximately how far into the mouthpiece are the upper teeth placed? (Refer to p. 21.)

42. Name a "step-up" mouthpiece recommended for more advanced students. (Refer to p. 44.)

43. Describe the procedures used to select and purchase mouthpieces for your students. (Refer to p. 44.)

Review Questions—Clarinet

44. Describe briefly how and when you would teach a student to play the clarion register on the clarinet. On the staff, write a brief exercise associated with teaching this register. (Refer to p. 27.)

45. Describe a sequence of steps for introducing the highest register on the clarinet. On the staff, write a brief exercise associated with teaching this register. (Refer to pp. 102–103.)

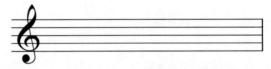

46. Describe two adjustments you can make on single reeds too stiff for the mouthpiece, which creates a tone quality that is too dark and breathy. (Refer to p. 47.)

47. Describe two adjustments you can make on single reeds too soft for the mouthpiece, which creates a tone quality that is too bright and sounds too thin. (Refer to p. 47.)

48. A student plays consistently sharp in all ranges. Recommend three solutions he or she might try. (Refer to pp. 32, 189.)

49. A student plays consistently flat in all ranges. Recommend three solutions he or she might try. (Refer to pp. 32, 189.)

50. A student tends to play flat as he or she progresses into the higher register. Recommend solutions he or she might try. (Refer to pp. 68, 102, 108.)

51. Define "pop test." When and why is it used? (Refer to p. 25.)

52. Besides tone quality, the most effective instrument angle should be determined by what physical factor of the student? (Refer to p. 10.)

Review Questions—Clarinet

53. List the three "air steps" used in taking a breath and starting a tone on the clarinet in order to ensure a good attack. (Refer to p. 28.)

54. The alto clarinet is in the key of _____. (Refer to p. 53.)

55. The bass clarinet is in the key of _____. (Refer to p. 53.)

56. **T or F**. Clarinetists occasionally use half-hole fingerings for high notes and always use half-hole fingerings for high notes on the bass clarinet. (Refer to pp. 103, 108.)

57. Describe the left-hand guide position when playing throat tones. (Refer to pp. 13, 80–81.)

58. What does RHD mean? When is it used? (Refer to pp. 66–67, 71, 82–83.)

59. Write the highest note of the *chalumeau* register of the clarinet. (Refer to pp. 58–59.)

60. Write the highest note of the *clarion* register of the clarinet. (Refer to pp. 58–59.)

61. Discuss briefly how you would teach the technique involved in "crossing the break." On the staff that follows, write a brief exercise illustrating steps for teaching break crossings. (Refer to pp. 66–67, 70–71, 82–83.)

62. List a few pedagogical problems you may encounter in teaching the clarinet. (Refer to p. 40.)

63. In working with a student's embouchure always encourage the use of a _____. (Refer to p. 57.)

64. On the staff that follows, indicate the notes that have alternate fingerings for chromatic passages. (Refer to p. 222.)

65. Use numbers to indicate the proper general sequence of steps in teaching articulation. (Refer to p. 30.)

_____ legato tonguing

_____ staccato tonguing

_____ slurring

Review Questions—Saxophone

1. **T or F.** If a student is sharp, it is best to advise pulling out the neck in order to lower the pitch. (Refer to p. 33.)

2. **T or F.** A softer reed will usually play higher notes more easily. (Refer to pp. 68, 102, 104.)

3. **T or F.** Jaw vibrato is recommended for saxophone students. (Refer to p. 34.)

4. **T or F.** Slightly more mouthpiece into the mouth enables the student to control high tones more easily. (Refer to p. 102.)

5. **T or F.** The chin should look "bunched" when playing saxophone. (Refer to pp. 20–21.)

6. **T or F.** Too much mouthpiece in the mouth creates a small, thin, choked tone. (Refer to p. 20.)

7. **T or F.** The right thumb pushes the saxophone forward in order to achieve a fulcrum for correct holding position. (Refer to p. 13, 15, 21.)

8. **T or F.** All the weight of the saxophone is suspended by the neck strap. (Refer to p. 13.)

9. **T or F.** Pressure from the left thumb pushes the instrument out of the mouth. (Refer to pp. 13, 21.)

10. **T or F.** Pressure from the right thumb pushes the instrument into the mouth. (Refer to pp. 13, 21.)

11. **T or F.** The neck strap ring acts as a fulcrum. (Refer to p. 13.)

12. **T or F.** A softer reed tends to play sharp while a stronger reed tends to play flat. (Refer to p. 33.)

13. **T or F.** As with the other woodwind instruments the motion of the tongue should be back and forth rather than up and down. (Refer to p. 31.)

14. **T or F.** One should depress the key pearls with the tips of the fingers. (Refer to p. 12.)

15. **T or F.** Alto and tenor saxes are best for starting students. (Refer to p. 39.)

16. **T or F.** Soprano, baritone, and bass saxes should be left to advanced students. (Refer to p. 39.)

17. **T or F.** Saxophone is one of the more accessible woodwind instruments to start. (Refer to p. 38.)

18. **T or F.** The major difference in sax and clarinet embouchures is the angle of the entrance of the mouthpiece into the mouth. (Refer to p. 21.)

19. **T or F.** The left thumb must be anchored on the pearl thumb rest below the octave key. (Refer to p. 13.)

20. **T or F.** The left-hand middle finger operates the high F palm key. (Refer to p. 93.)

21. **T or F.** In introducing high notes on the saxophone, the student should be instructed to play the high D key with the base of the left index finger. (Refer to p. 93.)

22. **T or F.** Always leave the mouthpiece on the neck when the instrument is not in use. (Refer to p. 7.)

23. The lowest written note for all saxophones is: (Refer to p. 59.)

24. The highest written note of the lowest register on the saxophone is: (Refer to p. 59.)

Review Questions—Saxophone

25. Write the highest note of the middle register of the saxophone. (Refer to p. 59.)

26. Name two brands of saxophones that you would recommend to your students. (Refer to p. 43.)

27. Name a recommended "step-up" mouthpiece for students to use in concert band. (Refer to p. 44.)

28. Name a recommended mouthpiece for students to use in jazz playing. (Refer to p. 44.)

29. The fingerings of the saxophone are similar to those of the _____ (chalumeau, clarion) register of the clarinet. (Refer to p. 69.)

30. Which fingering should be taught first for B♭ in the staff? (Refer to p. 118.)

31. On fingering diagram above, circle the palm keys found on the saxophone. (Refer to p. 93.)

32. Write the notes on which palm keys are used. (Refer to p. 59.)

33. Write a short passage showing the use of the Bis key. (Refer to p. 162, 220.)

34. Describe how you would check the seating of large pads on the sax with a piece of paper. (Refer to p. 51.)

35. For high E instruct the student to add the top right-hand key with the right index finger to the high ____ fingering. (Refer to p. 93.)

36. Write the pitch to be achieved on alto sax with the mouthpiece and neck alone. (Refer to p. 24.)

37. How does the teacher train the student to adjust the mouthpiece on the neck in order to achieve good intonation? (Refer to pp. 7, 33.)

Review Questions—Saxophone

38. If the clarinets parts (in B♭) are written in the key of A major, what key will the alto saxophones be in? _____ (Refer to p. 53.)

39. Write a note for each of the saxes that will sound D above middle C on the piano. (Refer to p. 53.)

Alto saxophone in E♭   Tenor saxophone in B♭   Baritone saxophone in E♭

40. There are _____ (number) connecting lever(s) on the saxophone. Where are they found? (Refer to p. 7.)

41. Describe the placement of the tongue on the reed for articulation. (Refer to p. 31.)

42. List a few pedagogical problems often encountered in teaching saxophone. (Refer to p. 41.)

43. How much of the saxophone reed should be moistened when soaking it? (Refer to p. 7.)

44. On the staff that follows, write the notes for which there are frequently used alternate fingerings. (Refer to p. 220.)

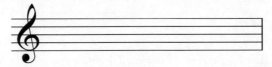

45. On alto sax the teeth will touch approximately _____ (distance) from the mouthpiece tip. Larger saxophones will be inserted farther into the mouth. (Refer to p. 20.)

46. What do you recommend to a student who produces a small, narrow tone? (Refer to pp. 21, 189.)

Review Questions—Saxophone

47. Discuss briefly the problems of matching the tone quality across the break. (Refer to pp. 16, 66, 82.)

48. What do you recommend to a student whose tone is too loud and sounds overblown? (Refer to pp. 21, 189.)

49. What do you recommend to a student who tends to play sharp in the high register of the saxophone? (Refer to p. 33.)

50. The vibrato on saxophone is produced by movement of the lower jaw while playing. This movement is the result of the player pronouncing the syllable _____. (Refer to p. 34.)

51. The written range of the saxophone is identical to that of which other woodwind instrument? (Refer to p. 59.)

52. Write a short passage illustrating the use of the articulated G♯ key on the saxophone. (Refer to p. 220.)

Review Questions—Bassoon

1. **T or F.** A #1 bocal will play flatter than a #2 bocal. (Refer to p. 33.)

2. **T or F.** The neck strap is more widely used than a seat strap to support the weight of the bassoon. (Refer to p. 11.)

3. **T or F.** One uses a more constant air stream on the clarinet than on the bassoon. (Refer to p. 29.)

4. **T or F.** Compared to clarinet, saxophone, and oboe, the bassoon embouchure is probably the most unrestrained. (Refer to p. 23.)

5. **T or F.** The bassoon reed should be soaked in the mouth for at least three minutes before playing. (Refer to p. 8.)

6. **T or F.** The finger span on the bassoon is larger than on any other woodwind. (Refer to p. 39.)

7. **T or F.** Bassoon reeds should be kept in airtight containers. (Refer to pp. 3, 9.)

8. **T or F.** On double reeds the pitch can be raised by pulling the reed farther out of the mouth. (Refer to pp. 22, 33.)

9. **T or F.** In order to play louder the bassoonist should tighten the embouchure. (Refer to p. 22.)

10. **T or F.** With the double-reed embouchure there should be an equal amount of cushion all the way around the reed. (Refer to pp. 16, 22.)

11. **T or F.** If high notes do not respond, insert more reed into the mouth. (Refer to p. 22.)

12. **T or F.** Jaw vibrato is recommended for bassoon students. (Refer to p. 34.)

13. Discuss lip flex and breath support for the bassoon as compared to other instruments. (Refer to p. 23.)

14. How much of the reed should be moistened when soaking it? (Refer to p. 8.)

15. Circle the desirable physical attributes of a bassoon student: even front teeth, large hands, protruding jaw, agile thumbs, and short upper lip. (Refer to p. 39.)

16. **T or F.** Other attributes to look for in a bassoon student include: good pitch discrimination, perseverance, and an ability to work with the hands (reed making). (Refer to p. 39.)

17. A good reliable bassoon recommended for school use is the _____ bassoon. (Refer to p. 43.)

18. Students should remove the _____ from the case first. Then assemble the _____ joint followed by the _____ joint. The _____ is then added followed by the _____. (Refer to pp. 8–9)

19. In addition to the reed, the most fragile part of the bassoon is the _____. What special care must be taken when assembling this part of the bassoon? (Refer to p. 9.)

Review Questions—Bassoon

20. An important factor in assembling the bassoon is not to damage the _____ levers. How many of these levers do you find on a student bassoon? _____ Where are they found? (Refer to pp. 8–9.)

21. What two joints must be swabbed after playing? In what way does swabbing the bassoon differ from swabbing other woodwind instruments? (Refer to p. 9.)

22. List the different ways in which a bassoon can be checked for leaks. (Refer to p. 51.)

23. How can the boot of the bassoon be checked for leaks? (Refer to p. 51.)

24. What type of reed case would you recommend to beginning bassoonists? (Refer to p. 3, 9.)

25. Describe the two points of contact with the hands in balancing the bassoon when a hand rest is used. (Refer to p. 13.)

26. For proper holding position the student should look at the music stand over the _____ (right or left) side of the bassoon. (Refer to p. 11.)

27. List the three steps in forming the bassoon embouchure. (Refer to pp. 22–33.)

28. How much reed should be inside the mouth? (Refer to pp. 17, 22–23.)

29. What kind of sound is heard if too much reed is in the mouth? Too little reed? (Refer to pp. 17, 22–23.)

30. What three factors control the pitch of the bassoon reed while playing? (Refer to p. 22.)

31. What pitch should be produced with the lips near the first wire when crowing a reed? (Refer to p. 24.)

32. What pitch should be achieved with the reed and bocal? (Refer to p. 23.)

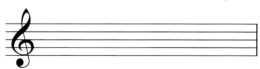

33. What fingering problems are most common to beginning bassoonists? (Refer to p. 41.)

34. In order to check air speeds and lip cushion, it is recommended that the bassoon student play the following pitches on the reed alone: (Refer to p. 23–24.)

Review Questions—Bassoon

35. List the steps for teaching diaphragm vibrato. (Refer to pp. 34–35.)

36. For players with short fingers, which finger is most prone to being pulled off a hole while playing? (Refer to pp. 13, 15.)

37. Should the angle and arch of each finger be equal? Explain. (Refer to p. 15.)

38. A stiff reed tends to play _____ (sharp or flat). A soft reed tends to play _____ (sharp or flat). (Refer to p. 49.)

39. If the reed is not soaked enough it will leak. How should a student check his or her reed for leaks? (Refer to p. 25.)

40. What sound is heard if the tip of the reed is too open? Too closed? (Refer to p. 48.)

41. How can the size of the tip opening be regulated? (Refer to p. 48–49.)

42. Clipping the tip of a double reed _____ (raises or lowers) the pitch. (Refer to p. 49.)

43. The _____ is inserted between the blades of the reed whenever scraping is being done. (Refer to p. 49.)

44. The _____ fits into the tube of the reed while scraping. (Refer to p. 49.)

45. List a few pedagogical problems you may encounter in teaching bassoon. (Refer to p. 41.)

46. There are _____ thumb keys on the bassoon. (Refer to p. 96.)

47. Why are "hovering" thumbs so important on the bassoon? Which thumb is most prone to "anchoring" rather than "hovering"? (Refer to p. 13.)

48. On the staff that follows, write the notes that use the whisper key (WK), the half hole ($\frac{1}{2}$H), and the flick (FLK) keys. (Refer to pp. 58–59.)

Review Questions—Bassoon

49. The whisper key is operated by the _____ thumb. (Refer to p. 13.)

50. T or F. The whisper key is involved in the break crossing. (Refer to pp. 59, 67.)

51. T or F. Half-hole fingerings are involved in the break crossing. (Refer to pp. 59, 67.)

52. Write the notes that use half holes. Explain the execution of the half-hole fingerings. (Refer to p. 59, 64.)

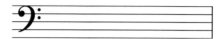

53. What and where is the E♭ resonance key on the bassoon? On which notes is it used? (Refer to pp. 90-91.)

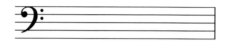

11 Terminology

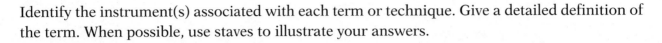

Terminology

Identify the instrument(s) associated with each term or technique. Give a detailed definition of the term. When possible, use staves to illustrate your answers.

Adjustment screws (refer to p. 51):

Air attack (refer to pp. 30–31):

Alternate fingerings (list general categories) (refer to p. 216):

Altissimo register (refer to pp. 58, 102):

Apertures (refer to pp. 16–17):

Articulated G♯ (refer to p. 220):

Barrel (refer to pp. 6, 32):

Basic Scale (refer to pp. 60–61):

Bis key (refer to pp. 162, 220):

Terminology

Bocal (#1) (refer to p. 33):

Bocal buzz (refer to pp. 23, 142, 158, 164, 168, 182):

Boot (refer to pp. 8–9):

Break crossings (refer to pp. 66–67, 82–83, 104–105):

Bridge keys (refer to pp. 5–9):

Buffet (refer to p. 43):

Chalumeau (refer to pp. 29, 58):

Chromatic C fingering (refer to pp. 92, 220):

Chromatic F♯ fingering (refer to pp. 92, 220):

Terminology

Circular cushion (refer to pp. 16, 22):

Clarion (refer to pp. 58, 88):

Condensation shape (refer to p. 19):

Coverage (refer to p. 18):

Cross fingering (refer to pp. 76, 78, 164, 216):

Crow (refer to pp. 22–23, 24):

F hole (refer to pp. 13, 60, 64, 138):

Facing (refer to pp. 44, 45, 46):

Flick keys (refer to pp. 72–73, 148–149):

Foot joint (refer to p. 4):

Terminology

Forked F (refer to pp. 138, 150, 318):

Fox (refer to pp. 9, 43):

Fulcrum (refer to pp. 12–13):

Hairline (refer to p. 6):

Half-hole fingerings (refer to pp. 58–59, 64–65, 68, 72, 103, 108):

Hand rest (refer to pp. 9, 13):

Harmonics (refer to pp. 19, 217):

Head joint exercise (refer to pp. 18, 24, 26):

High-note exercises (introductory) (refer to pp. 102–103):

Terminology

Hite premiere (refer to p. 44):

Jaw vibrato (refer to p. 34):

Key clusters (refer to pp. 84–93):

Lorée (refer to p. 42):

Mandrel (refer to p. 49):

Meyer (refer to p. 44):

Mouthpiece/reed exercises (refer to p. 24):

Neck (refer to p. 7):

Octave exercise (refer to pp. 22–23, 72–73, 102):

OK (refer to pp. 27, 58–59):

Terminology

Open C# (refer to pp. 13, 62–63, 82–83):

Open-hole key system (refer to p. 42):

PK (refer to pp. 58–59, 93):

Pop tests (refer to p. 25):

Practice (refer to p. 57):

Reed buzz (refer to pp. 22–24):

Reed trimmer (refer to p. 47):

Resonator E♭ key (refer to p. 90):

RHD (refer to pp. 66, 71, 82–83, 152–154, 156–158, 160–162, 166):

RK (refer to pp. 13, 27, 58–59, 72–73, 97):

Terminology

Roscoe reed supplies (refer to p. 50):

Rovner (refer to p. 44):

Selmer C* (refer to p. 44):

Side B♭ key (refer to p. 217):

Soda straw exercise (refer to p. 19):

SOK (refer to pp. 26, 58–59, 68–69):

Staple (refer to pp. 48, 50):

Tenon (refer to p. 3):

Three-step breath procedure (refer to p. 28):

Three-step embouchure formation (refer to p. 22):

Terminology

Throat tones (refer to pp. 59, 70, 80–81):

Thumb B♭ key (refer to pp. 162–163, 217):

Thumb F♯ key (refer to pp. 99, 221):

Thumb rest (refer to pp. 12, 13):

Tip opening (refer to pp. 48, 50):

TOK (refer to pp. 26, 58, 68):

Touch-tone-teaching (refer to pp. 26–27):

Transposition (refer to p. 53):

Tuning (cleaning) rod (refer to p. 32):

Tuning stopper (refer to p. 32):

Terminology

Twig keys (refer to pp. 94–95):

Vandoren (refer to pp. 44–45):

Whistle tones (refer to p. 19):

Wire (1st) (refer to p. 50):

Wire (2nd) (refer to p. 50):

WK (refer to pp. 58–59, 98):

12 Blank Fingering Charts

Blank Fingering Charts for Reviewing and Testing of Fingerings

Flute: Regular Normal Fingerings—Teach First

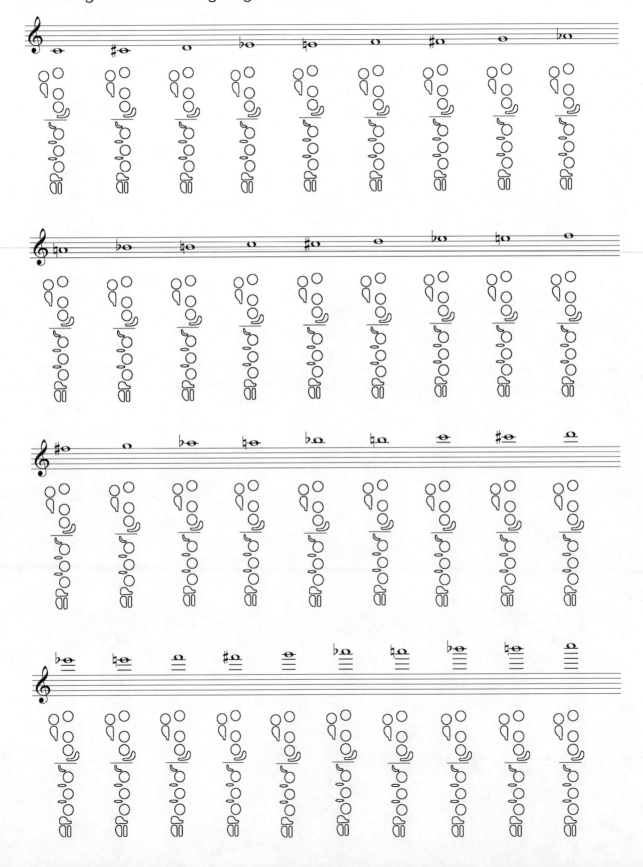

Blank Fingering Charts for Reviewing and Testing of Fingerings

Oboe: Regular Normal Fingerings—Teach First

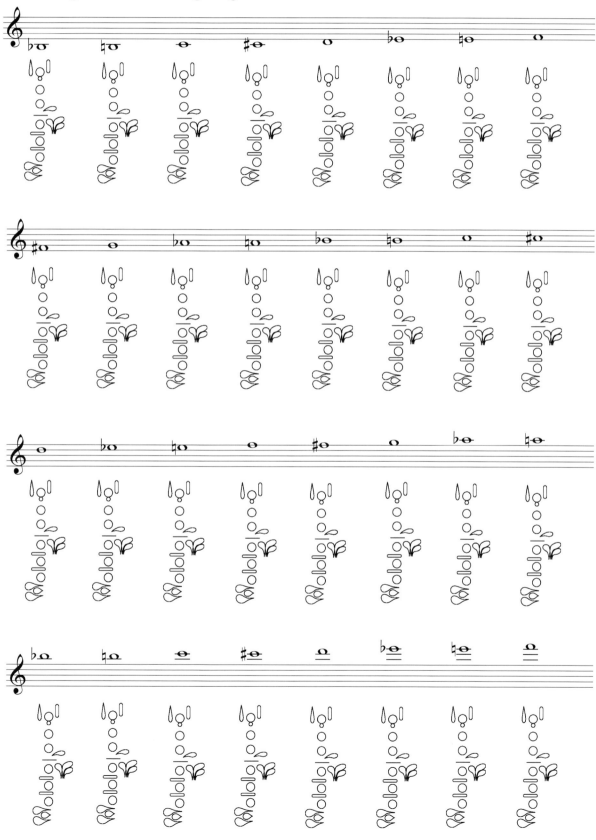

Blank Fingering Charts for Reviewing and Testing of Fingerings

Clarinet: Regular Normal Fingerings—Teach First

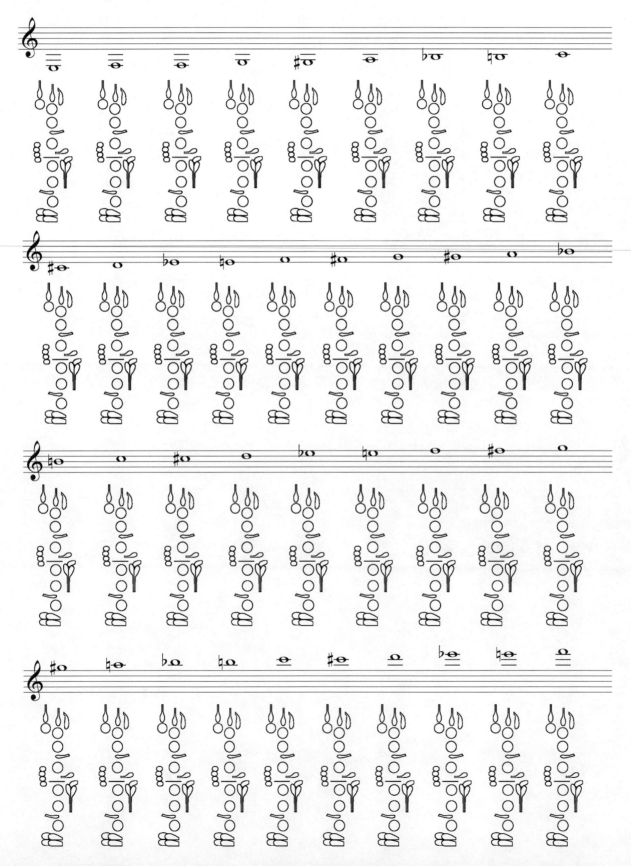

Blank Fingering Charts for Reviewing and Testing of Fingerings

Saxophone: Regular Normal Fingerings—Teach First

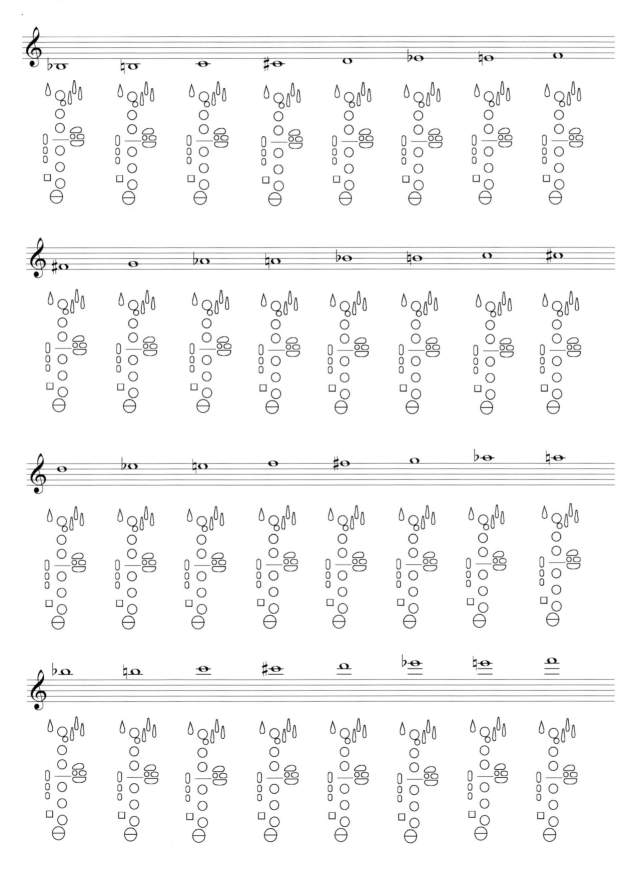

Blank Fingering Charts for Reviewing and Testing of Fingerings

Bassoon: Regular Normal Fingerings—Teach First

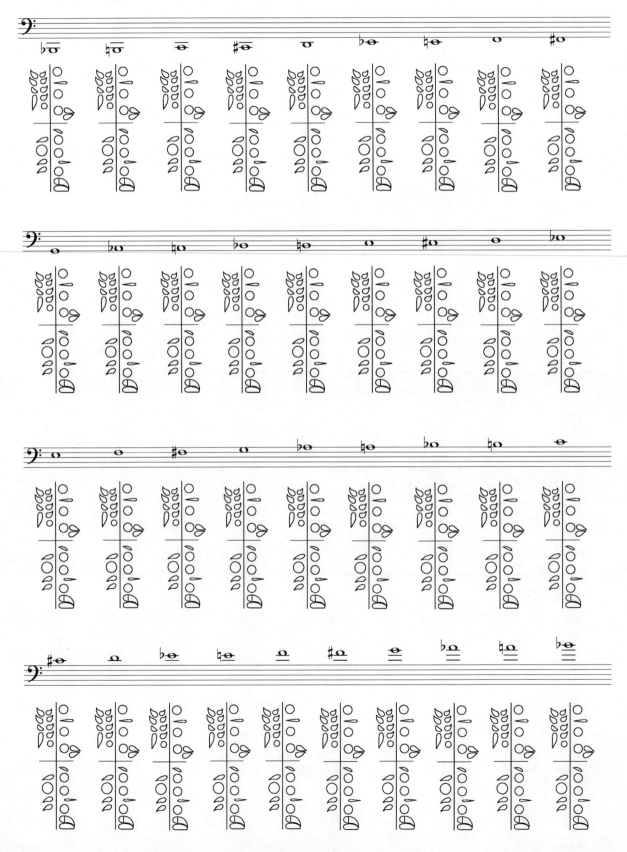

Blank Fingering Charts for Reviewing and Testing of Fingerings

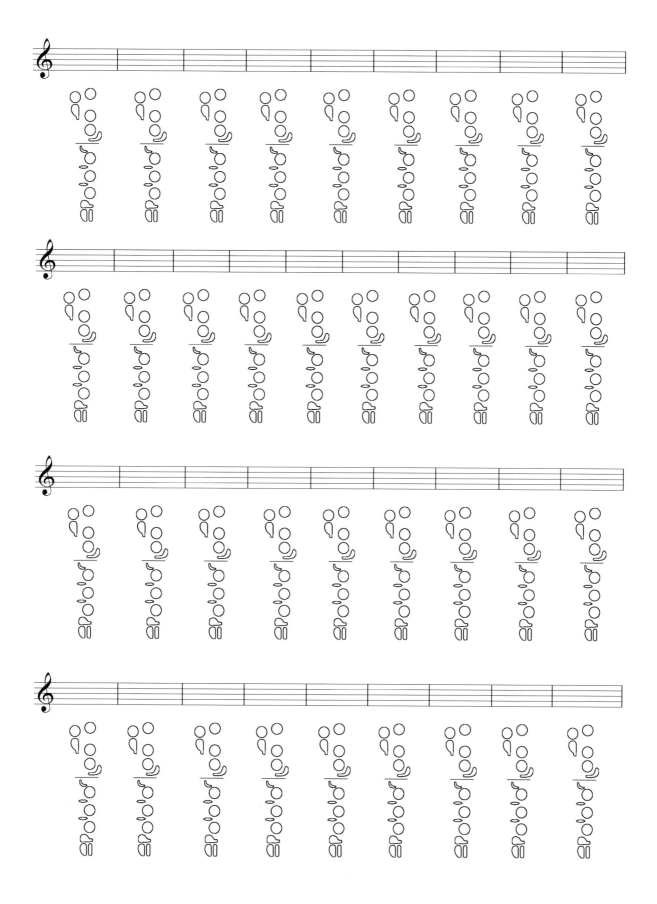

Blank Fingering Charts for Reviewing and Testing of Fingerings

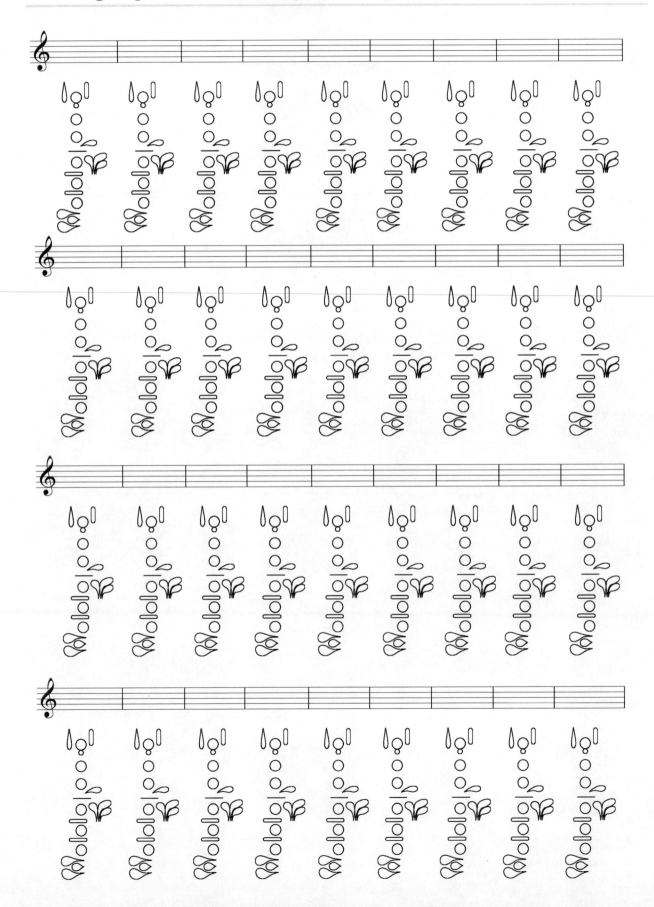

Blank Fingering Charts for Reviewing and Testing of Fingerings

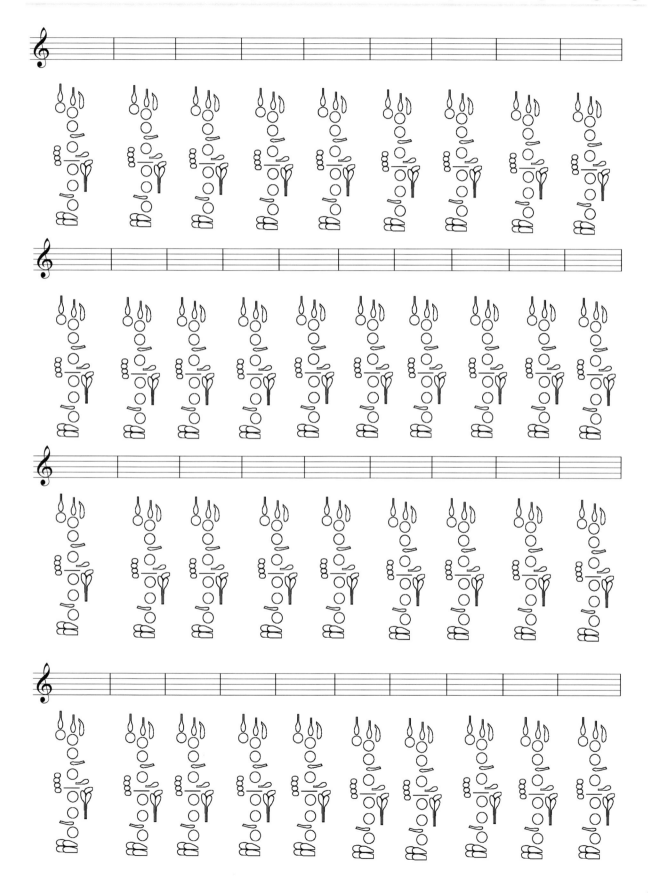

Blank Fingering Charts for Reviewing and Testing of Fingerings

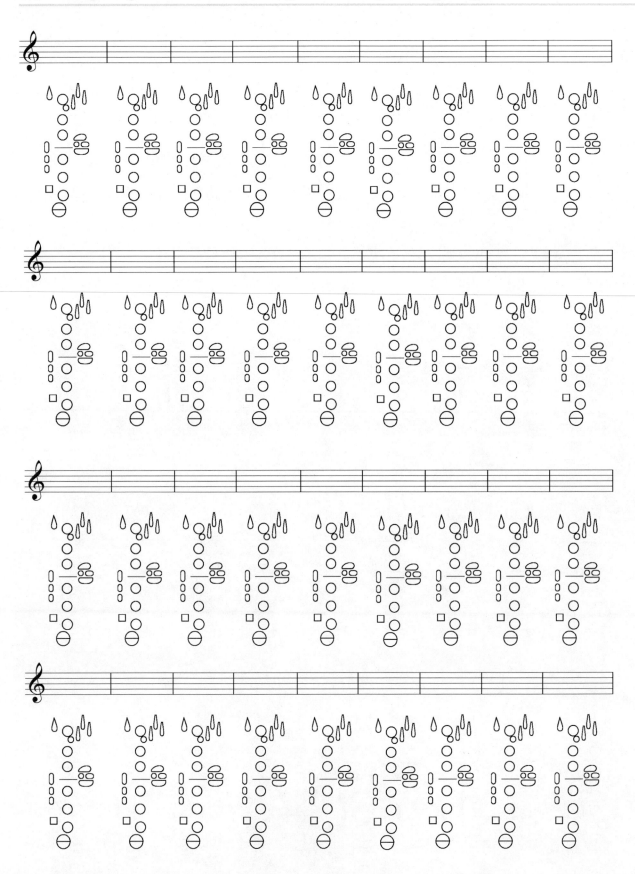

Blank Fingering Charts for Reviewing and Testing of Fingerings

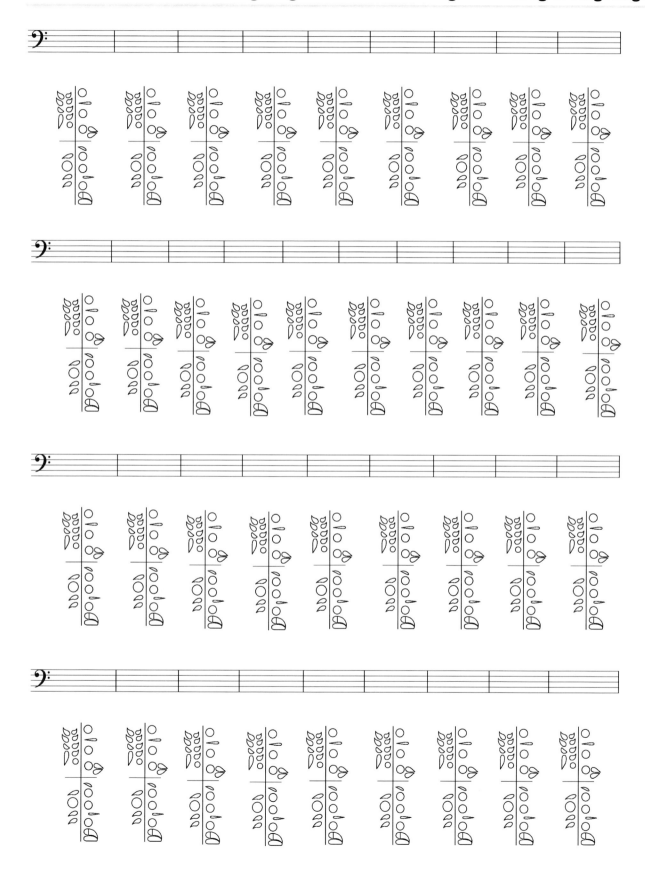

Bibliography

Books

Brand, Erick. *Band Instrument Repairing Manual*. Battle Creek, MI: Ferree's Tools, Inc., 1993.

Burton, Stanley. *Instrument Repair for the Music Teacher*. 7th ed. Van Nuys, CA: Alfred Music Publishing, 1976.

Colwell, Richard. *The Teaching of Instrumental Music*. Upper Saddle River, NJ: Prentice Hall, 2002.

Dietz, William, ed. *Teaching Woodwinds, A Method and Resource for Music Educators*. New York: Schirmer Books, 1998.

Fox, Hugo. *Let's Play Bassoon*. South Whitley, IN: Fox Products Corp., 2000.

———. *Let's Play Oboe*. South Whitley, IN: Fox Products Corp., 2000.

Galway, James. Flute. London: Khan & Averill, 1990.

Gingras, Michèle. *Clarinet Secrets*. Lanham, MD: Scarecrow Press, 2004.

Hewitt, Stevens. *Method for Oboe*. Philadelphia: Stevens Hewitt, 614 65th Ave., Philadelphia, PA 19126, 1966.

Krell, John. *Kincaidiana*. Culver City, CA: Trio Associates, 1973.

Palmer, Harold G. *Teaching Techniques of the Woodwinds*. San Antonio, TX: Southern Music Co., 1963.

———. *Teaching Techniques of the Woodwinds*. Rockville Centre, NY: Belwin, 1952.

Phelan, James. *Complete Guide to the Flute*. 3rd ed. Shirley, MA: Burkart-Phelan, Inc., 2006.

Putnik, Edwin. *The Art of Flute Playing*. Evanston, IL: Summy-Birchard Co., 1970.

Rehfeldt, Phillip. *Playing Woodwind Instruments, A Guide for Teachers, Performers, and Composers*. Prospect Heights, IL: Waveland Press, Inc., 1998.

Saska, Ronald. *A Guide to Repairing Woodwinds*, Glenmoore, PA: Northeastern Music Publications, Inc., 1987.

Saucier, Gene. *Woodwinds, Fundamental Performance Techniques*. New York: Schirmer Books; London: Collier Macmillan, 1981.

Sawhill, Clarence and Bertram McGarrity. *Playing and Teaching Woodwind Instruments*. Englewood Cliffs, NJ: Prentice-Hall, 1962.

Schmidt, Robert, *A Clarinetist's Notebook*, Vol 1. Ithaca, NY: published by author, Ithaca College, School of Music, 1971.

Spencer, William. *The Art of Bassoon Playing*. Evanston, IL: Summy-Birchard, 1969.

Sprenkle, Robert and David Ledet. *The Art of Oboe Playing*. Evanston, IL: Summy-Birchard Pub. Co., 1961.

Springer, George H. *Maintenance and Repair of Wind and Percussion Instruments*. Boston: Allyn and Bacon, 1976.

Stein, Keith, *The Art of Clarinet Playing*. Evanston, IL: Summy-Birchard, 1958.

Stubbins, William. *The Art of Clarinetistry*. Ann Arbor MI: Ann Arbor Publishers, 1965.

Teal, Larry. *The Art of Saxophone Playing*. Secaucus, NJ: Summy-Birchard, 1963.

Tiede, Clayton H. *Practical Band Instrument Repair Manual*. Dubuque, IA: W. C. Brown, 1976.

Westphal, Frederick. *Guide to Teaching Woodwinds*. 5th ed. Dubuque, IA: W. C. Brown Publishers, 1990.

Web Sources

Double Reed Information
http://www.2reed.net/

Flute Links and Hand Position
http://www.jennifercluff.com/lineup.htm

International Clarinet Society
http://www.clarinet.org/home.asp

International Double Reed Society
http://idrs2.colorado.edu/home/

International Saxophone Home Page
http://www.saxophone.org/

National Flute Association
http://www.nfaonline.org/

North American Saxophone Alliance
http://www.saxalliance.org/

Sound Samples of the American Saxophone Quartet
http://www.sonsofsound.com/artists/asq/biography.html

Sound Samples of Well-known Bassoonists and Contrabassoonists
http://www.crystalrecords.com/bassoon.html

Sound Samples of Well-known Clarinetists and Bass Clarinetists
http://www.crystalrecords.com/clarinet.html

Sound Samples of Well-known Oboists and English Hornists
http://www.crystalrecords.com/oboe.html

Sound Samples of Well-known Woodwind Trios, Quintets, and other ensembles
http://www.crystalrecords.com/woodwind_ensemble.html

The Journal of the International Double Reed Society
http://idrs.colorado.edu/Publications/Journal/Journal.Index

Woodwind Anthology

A compendium of articles from *The Instrumentalist*, Northfield, IL: Instrumentalist Co., 1976.

General

Cheyette, Irving	"Basic Techniques for Wind Players"
Waln, George	"Is Individual Study Necessary?"
Waln, George	"It's Tone Quality That Counts"
Waln, George	"Repair of the Woodwinds"
Waln, George	"Teacher, Start Right!"
Waln, George	"Teaching Emphasis - Where?"

Flute

Ambs, Robert	"Approaching the Upper Register"
Ambs, Robert	"Teaching Vibrato"
Pellerite, James	"Improving Tone Production in Flute Performance"
Riley, James	"Toward a Better Flute Tone"
Taylor, Laurence	"Difficulty with Upper Notes"
Taylor, Laurence	"Weak Points in Flute Teaching"
Taylor, Laurence	"Which Fingering for B-Flat?"
Waln, George	"First Flute Lesson"
Willoughby, Robert	"Flute Tone and Intonation"

Oboe

Fitch, William	"An Outline for the Teaching of Oboe and Bassoon"
Fitch, William	"Transfer to Oboe"
Hilton, Lewis	"Oboe Playing and Breath Support"
Northrup, Jean	"Three Often Neglected Aspects of Oboe Technique"
Reimer, Bennett	"The High School Oboist Can be Taught by the Regular Band Teacher"
Revelli, William	"Practical Guidance for Student Oboists"
Seltenrich, Charles	"Is Your Oboe a Hobo?"
Wilson, Clayton	"The Oboe"

Clarinet

Hovik, Karl	"Use of the Right Hand in Clarinet Playing"
Langenus, Gustave	"Playing the Clarinet"
Mark, Michael	"The Band Director and the Bass Clarinet"
Norton, Donald	"Hints on Playing the Bass Clarinet"
Rithie, Ralph	"The Clarinet Mouthpiece"
Stickler, Steve	"Clarinet Throat Tone Problems"
Warnick, Edward	"The Clarinet and the Student"
Weerts, Richard	"Developing a Good Clarinet Staccato"

Saxophone

Douse, Kenneth	"The Saxophone"
Lang, Rosemary	"Teaching Vibrato"
Rascher, Sigurd	"The Saxophone"
Ross, Edgar	"The Saxophone—A Popular but Slighted Instrument"
Rousseau, Eugene	"Saxophone Tone Quality"
Teal, Larry	"Preparing to Start the Saxophone Tone"
Teal, Larry	"Saxophone FUN-damentals"
Waln, George	"Saxophone Playing"

Bassoon

Jones, Edwin	"Those Bubbling, Blurting, Beautiful Bassoons"
Palmer, Harold	"Bassoon Fundamentals"
Simpson, Wilbur	"Bassoon Reeds—How to Adjust and Trim Them"
Spencer, William G.	"Bassoon Vibrato "
Waln, George	"Starting the School Bassoonist"
Waln, George	"The Bassoon"
Waln, Ronald	"From ? to Bassoon"
Wilson, George	"The Beginning Bassoonist"

The Instrumentalist

"The Magazine for School Band and Orchestra Directors," Northfield, IL.

General

Oct 2003, p. 18	Petersen, Elizabeth	"Work Harder to Survive as a Student Teacher"
Oct 2002, p. 58	Wenz, J.	"Develop Ensembles in Small-School Programs"
Sept 2000, p. 38	Jones, Brian	"Basic Woodwind Maintenance"

Flute

Sept 2000, p. 68	Garner, Lisa	"Troubleshooting Flute Problems"
Apr 1999, p. 46	Bonner, Joseph	"Flute Section Intonation"
Jan 1997, p. 12	Debost, Michel	"Basics for Beginning Flutists"
Aug 1995, p. 112	Debost, Michel	"Flute: Finding the Paths to Tone and Technique"
Sept 1993, p. 81	Delzell, Judith K	"Flute Embouchure Problems"
Aug 1992, p. 30	Wilson, Kathleen	"Erratic Intonation in Flute Sections"
Jan 1990, p. 20	Galway, James	"Thoughts on Playing the Flute"
Aug 1989, p. 42	Knight, John W.	"Flute Intonation"

Oboe

Jan 1998, p. 58	Frost, Kathryn	"Of Oboes and Reeds"
Oct 1997, p. 28	Katz & Grover	"The Basics of Playing Oboe"
Aug 1995, p. 122	Guregian, Elaine	"Oboe: Conquering the Tiny Aperture"
Sept 1994, p. 50	Niblock, Howard	"Troublesome Oboe Fingerings"
June 1989, p. 34	Niblock, Howard	"Developing and Improving Oboe Vibrato"
Feb 1979, p. 42	Wilson, Margaret	"In Tune with Oboe Intonation"
Feb 1977, p. 60	Probasco, R.	"Selecting, Soaking, and Adjusting Oboe Reeds"
Feb 1971, p. 41	Adelstein, Stephen	"Basics for Oboe Performance"

Clarinet

Feb 2003, p. 71	Jessup, Carol	"Developing a Clarinet Sound"
Apr 2003, p. 70	Maxey, Larry	"Clarinet Section Intonation"

Sept 2002, p. 54	Rhodes, Ruth	"Posture, Exercise, and Relaxation for Intonation"
Dec 2000, p. 50	Kerstetter, Tod	"Crossing the Clarinet Break"
Dec 1999, p. 44	Jones, Brian	"Eliminating the Clarinet Break"
July 1998, p. 46	Winkle, Carola	"Woodwind Clinic: Clarinet Hand Technique"
Sept 1990, p. 64	Holton, Arthur J.	"Guiding Beginners on Clarinet and Saxophone"
Mar 1990, p. 34	Hinson, James	"Breaking in Clarinet Reeds"
Mar 1987, p. 50	Hornsby, Richard	"Achieving Success on Bass Clarinet"

Saxophone

Apr 2003, p. 46	Smiley, Richard	"Alternate Saxophone Fingerings"
Nov 2002, p. 42	Jones, J. Derek	"Jazz Band Experience for Young Saxophonists"
Nov 2000, p. 49	Brown, Jeremy	"Improved Intonation Through Altissimo Exercises"
Apr 1998, p. 40	Stewart, J. Terry	"Common Adjustments for Better Sax Sections"
Apr 1997, p. 24	Hemke, Frederick	"Basics of Teaching New Saxophone Students"
Aug 1995, p. 168	Hemke, Frederick	"Embouchure and Reeds to Saxophone Artistry"
Sept 1990, p. 64	Holton, Arthur J.	"Guiding Beginners on Clarinet and Saxophone"
Mar 1988, p. 36	Holton, Arthur J.	"A Reed Awakening for Clarinet and Saxophone "
Oct 1984, p. 98	Reilly, Allyn D.	"Improving Saxophone Intonation"

Bassoon

Mar 1999, p. 28	Ewell, Terry	"Basic Bassoon Articulations"
Aug 1998, p. 56	Jensen, Kristin W.	"Bassoon Embouchure and Fingering Adjustments"
Apr 1995, p. 93	Dietz, William	"Bassoon Tonguing Techniques"
Feb 1994, p. 28	Ramey, Richard	"Adjusting Bassoon Reeds"
Nov 1993, p. 38	Barris, Robert	"Holding a Bassoon Correctly"
Aug 1993, p. 36	Ramey, Richard	"Subtle Differences in Bassoon Bocals"
May 1990, p. 50	Dietz, William	"Supporting the Bassoon"
Aug 1985, p. 52	Cook, Cathy	"Bassoon Care and Maintenance"

Index

Photo Credits

Cover Photos: H. Gene Griswold.

Chapter 1: p. 04 Denis Karp; **p. 5a** H. Gene Griswold; **p. 5b-d** Sabrina McLaughlin; **p. 6a&d** H. Gene Griswold; **p. 6b-c** Allison Bridges Yacoub; **p. 7a-b** Jane Marsilio; **p. 7c** H. Gene Griswold; **p. 8a-b,d,f-g** H. Gene Griswold; **p. 8c,e** Eddie Sanders; **p. 9** Eddie Sanders; **p. 10a** Denis Karp; **p. 10b** Sabrina McLaughlin; **p. 10c** Allison Bridges Yacoub; **p. 11a** Jane Marsilio; **p. 11b** Eddie Sanders; **p. 14 top/left-right** Denis Karp; **p. 14 middle/left-right** Sabrina McLaughlin; **p. 14 bottom/ left-right** Allison Bridges Yacoub; **p. 15 top/left-right** Jane Marsilio; **p. 15 middle-bottom/left-right** Eddie Sanders; **p. 18** Denis Karp; **p. 19** Denis Karp; **p. 20 top** H. Gene Griswold; **p. 20 bottom-left** Jane Marsilio; **p. 20 bottom-right** Allison Bridges Yacoub; **p. 22** Sabrina McLaughlin; **p. 23 top a-b** Eddie Sanders; **p. 23 bottom a-b** Andrew Barrett Delclos; **p. 25 top** Denis Karp; **p. 25 middle a-b, bottom a** Sabrina McLaughlin; **p. 25 bottom b** H. Gene Griswold; **p. 29** Jane Marsilio/Sabrina McLaughlin;

Chapter 2: p. 47a Sabrina McLaughlin; **p. 47** b-e Jane Marsilio; **p. 48** H. Gene Griswold; **p. 49** H. Gene Griswold; **p. 50** H. Gene Griswold; **p. 51** H. Gene Griswold;